Diverse Communities

Diverse Communities is a critique of Robert Putnam's social capital thesis, re-examined from the perspective of women and cultural minorities in America over the last century. Barbara Arneil argues that the idyllic communities of the past were less positive than Putnam envisages and that the current 'collapse' in participation is better understood as change rather than decline. Arneil suggests that the changes in American civil society in the last half-century are the result not so much of generational change or television as of the unleasing of powerful economic, social and cultural forces that, despite leading to division and distrust within American society, also contributed to greater justice for women and cultural minorities. She concludes by proposing that the lessons learned from this fuller history of American civil society provide the normative foundation to enumerate the principles of justice by which diverse communities might be governed in the twenty-first century.

BARBARA ARNEIL is Associate Professor in the Department of Political Science at the University of British Columbia. She won the Harrison Prize for the best article published in *Political Studies* in 1996 and is the author of *Feminism and Politics* (1999) and *John Locke and America: A Defense of English Colonialism* (1996).

Diverse Communities

The problem with social capital

Barbara Arneil

University of British Columbia, Vancouver

CAMBRIDGE
UNIVERSITY PRESS

CAMBRIDGE UNIVERSITY PRESS
Cambridge, New York, Melbourne, Madrid, Cape Town, Singapore, São Paulo

Cambridge University Press
The Edinburgh Building, Cambridge CB2 2RU, UK

Published in the United States of America by Cambridge University Press, New York

www.cambridge.org
Information on this title: www.cambridge.org/9780521673907

First published 2006

Printed in the United Kingdom at the University Press, Cambridge

A catalogue record for this publication is available from the British Library

ISBN-13 978-0-521-85719-2 hardback
ISBN-10 0-521-85719-8 hardback

ISBN-13 978-0-521-67390-7 paperback
ISBN-10 0-521-67390-9 paperback

This book is dedicated to Doug and Katie Anne,
with whom I share my life,
and to the memory of my cousin and friend,
Alastair Boyd of Dumbarton, Scotland,
who left us all far too soon

Contents

Abbreviations

AAU	American Athletic Union
AAUW	American Association of University Women
AAWB	American Association of Workers for the Blind
ABA	American Bar Association
ABA	American Breeders Association – now AGA
ABPHEGIA	American Blind People's Higher Education and General Improvement Association
ABWA	American Business Women's Association
ACLU	American Civil Liberties Union
ADA	Americans with Disabilities Act
BPW	Business and Professional Women
CBC	Canadian Broadcasting Corporation
CWA	Committee on Women's Athletics
ESPN	Entertainment and Sports Programming Network
GFWC	General Federation of Women's Clubs
GSS	General Social Survey
KKK	Ku Klux Klan
LLDEF	Lambda Legal Defense and Education Fund
LWV	League of Women Voters
NAFE	National Association for Female Executives
NCAA	National Collegiate Athletic Association
NCC	National Council for Churches
NCCPT	National Congress of Colored Parents and Teachers
NES	National Election Survey
NFSHSA	National Federation of State High School Associations
OES	Order of the Eastern Star
PAL	Police Athletics League
PCO	Privy Council Office
PPS	Parents for Public Schools
PTA	Parent–Teachers Association
PTO	Parent–Teacher Organization
RSPT	Roper Social and Political Trends

SGMA	Sporting Goods Manufacturing Association
TIPS	Terrorist Information and Prevention System
USOC	United States Olympic Committee
VIPS	Volunteers in Police Service
WBC	Women's Bowling Congress
WCTU	Women's Christian Temperance Union
WUSA	Women's United Soccer Association

Acknowledgements

Writing a book about anything requires considerable 'social capital', most particularly a network of people from whom one can draw support and seek scholarly advice. I would like to begin by thanking the Social Sciences and Humanities Research Council of Canada for providing me with a grant to support this research project. Out of that grant I was able to hire several research assistants, who have contributed in various ways to the development of the research, including Rita Dhamoon, Fiona MacDonald and Sarah Pemberton. This book might never have happened if I had not been invited to a workshop at the annual Canadian Political Science Association meetings in Toronto, in 2002, by Brenda O'Neill and Elizabeth Gidengil, and I thank them for including me in that initial meeting. I also want to thank Lisa Young, who suggested to me, after I submitted a sixty-page paper to this workshop, that what I really had was a book rather than an article. I am grateful to all the participants in that original workshop on gender and social capital, as well as those at a second conference at the University of Manitoba on the same theme, who provided me with important feedback, encouragement and criticism. At a critical point, when I was still wondering if there was a book to be written, my friends Pauline and Bernie Hadley-Beauregard and Boris and Tess Tyzuk gave me the final push towards that end over a memorable dinner party. I want to thank Kate Jalbert, who delivered countless cups of coffee and other kinds of nourishment to keep my body and soul together as I was rewriting various drafts of chapters at the Sage Bistro at the University of British Columbia. With respect to particular chapters and arguments within the book itself, I want to thank Peter Hall, Mark Warren, Tannis Macbeth, David Green, John Helliwell, John Torpey, Matt James, Eric Uslaner and a variety of other individual scholars and students, who all provided me, through email, meetings or presentations at various forums, with useful interjections and feedback that have made the book better than it otherwise would have been. Needless to say, any flaws that remain in the argument are entirely my own. Finally,

I want to thank John Haslam at CUP for his support as editor on this book, and the two reviewers for their comments.

This book is dedicated to three very important people. The richness of our lives is largely constituted by those individuals whose paths we cross or share in the past and present. My own life has been immeasurably enriched by the presence of family, both near and far. It is three particular members of my family (so close to my heart as I write: Doug Reimer, Katie Anne Reimer and Alastair Boyd) to whom I dedicate the work represented in the pages that follow.

1   Social capital, justice and diversity: an introduction

'Social capital' is a term used by Robert Putnam in his best-selling book *Bowling Alone: The Collapse and Revival of American Community* (2000). It is a clarion call for a renewed civic engagement in the Western industrialized world, most particularly the United States of America. The social capital thesis has proven to be extraordinarily powerful, spawning a veritable industry of research that analyses every facet of social capital in America and beyond. Its impact has been felt from the highest of political offices through academic circles and local community organizations to average American citizens.

Social capital, as a concept, has had such a profound impact in such a short time for several reasons. First, it represents an important shift in focus, within Western political theory, away from either the state or citizen to the civic space in between. In this regard, the social capital thesis parallels two influential schools of thought within contemporary liberal democratic theory, namely communitarianism and 'third way' theory. In both cases, civic space or community is the starting point of analysis, rather than either the rights-bearing citizen of liberalism or the equality-bearing state of socialism or social democracy. This theoretical shift is relatively young, but the potential significance is profound. In essence, a new theoretical paradigm that seeks to transcend the left/right divide through an emphasis on the space in between the individual and the state is challenging the two great ideologies of the modern era, liberalism and socialism.

But social capital, in the hands of Robert Putnam, is also powerful because it goes beyond a normative theory of civic space, to bring a hard, quantitative edge to the analysis of community, through the evaluation of an extraordinarily large amount of collected data of individual behaviour and opinion. Social capital, unlike the philosophical versions of 'community', is thus 'quantifiable', according to Putnam. He is attempting to ensure that his analysis of community is based not simply on a normative or prescriptive vision of the past or future, but on a theory of civic society

1

rooted in empirical science.[1] By measuring participation in civic associations and social activities, changing attitudes of trust and reciprocity in the general public through longitudinal surveys, and declining rates of voter turnout and involvement in political parties and organizations, Putnam provides data to buttress his theories empirically. As such, his thesis potentially represents an equally important development in the broader world of social sciences, namely a bridge between the 'scientifically' oriented discipline of economics, with its emphasis on quantifiable results and individual aggregate analysis, and the more culturally or normatively focused study of politics, society and community. It has been argued, by some, that this conduit will work both ways, by bringing a tough, quantitative edge to the study of society, while simultaneously opening up economic research to 'social' variables that had previously been considered extraneous.

Important as these theoretical shifts are in both economic and political theory (and they will be examined in more detail shortly), neither of them provides the full explanation for the powerful appeal of *Bowling Alone*. Ultimately, it will be necessary to go beyond the realms of academic literature to the current state of US society, and liberal democracies more broadly, in order to get to the heart of this phenomenon. The popular power of *Bowling Alone* lies not in its theoretical innovations in the academic world, important though these changes may be, but rather in the emotive central appeal, particularly in the United States of America, of the fundamentally Christian narrative (paradise, the fall, the promise of redemption) that lies at the heart of Putnam's thesis: an idyllic and unified 'American community' of the past has, over the last thirty years, 'fallen' apart, and can be redeemed in the future only through a renewed commitment to civic participation and unity.

As I develop my argument in the pages that follow, I shall challenge this 'meta-narrative' underlying Putnam's analysis by examining its three stages – the past, present and future of social capital – in light of the gendered and cultural dimensions, which are often hidden, of this story of 'collapse' and 'revival'. For, appealing as Putnam's story might be to a large number of American citizens and scholars, I will argue that the changes that have occurred within American society over the course of the twentieth century have very different meanings when viewed from the vantage point of either women or cultural minorities.[2] The paradise of

---

[1] As Partha Dasgupta said of Putnam's work: 'Empirical study gave Putnam's contention force – empirics made it something more than a tract on civic friendship' (Skinner et al., 2002, p. 17).

[2] The term 'cultural minorities' is not an altogether satisfactory one. It refers to those groups of Americans who have suffered, based upon a particular cultural marker (ethnicity,

the Progressive Era suddenly becomes much less idyllic than imagined; the 'pulling apart' of American communities is no longer as negative as suggested by Putnam, to the degree that it serves to correct past injustices. And the current divisive nature of civic society may even be positive if it represents the continuing struggle for equality, recognition and the inclusion of women and cultural minorities in contemporary America. Put simply, the central theme in the narrative of twentieth-century America as seen from the perspective of historically subordinated groups may not be one of 'collapse' or 'pulling apart' at all but the, as yet, unfinished and, at times, profoundly divisive story of realizing justice in an increasingly diverse society. Recognizing these multiple and conflicting narratives in American civic history, as well as analysing the degree to which the search for justice in diverse communities is either complementary or counter to the search for civic connectedness, unity and solidarity, are particularly important as one moves beyond the past and present of American community into the future.

Social capital: definitions

Social capital was defined in a number of different ways over the course of the twentieth century. L. Judson Hanifan, an American Christian educator of the Progressive Era, was the first to use the term 'social capital', in 1916. His definition began an American tradition in the social capital literature: one that tends to emphasize the functional nature of social

---

race, disability or sexual orientation), from discrimination (in various forms, as I shall demonstrate) within US society and community. Much of multicultural political theory tends to reduce 'cultural minority' to mean ethno or national cultural minority. I include other aspects of cultural identity, such as sexual orientation and disability, within this general term, because each of these categories sheds new and different light on the nature of American community in the past, present and future (as I shall discuss at different points in the analysis). It remains, nevertheless, a problematic term, for two important reasons: the danger of essentialism and the loss of agency. The first (essentialism) is the problem of identifying any 'group' as culturally bounded and internally homogeneous with respect to a particular identity. The second problem is that, by identifying groups as cultural minorities because they lack power, one tends to construct them simply as 'victims' of larger processes rather than as agents in their own history. Theorists such as Gaytari Spivak and Chandra Mohanty are significant in this tradition of arguing both for the recognition of agency and against essentialism. I deploy the term 'cultural minorities' as shorthand to identify those Americans who have been defined *as groups* by the state or wider society and either *excluded* from civic space because of particular cultural characteristics or targeted for assimilation; thus, the categories deployed are political rather than ontological. At the same time, I am cognizant throughout the analysis of the need to document the importance of the agency of these historically subordinated groups, and the impact these actions have had on the changing nature of the civic sphere in terms of both participation and trust.

capital, as an investment in the present that will reap larger public and private benefits at some point in the future.

> In the use of the phrase social capital . . . [I refer to] good will, fellowship, sympathy, and social intercourse among the individuals and families who make up a social unit . . . The community as a whole will benefit by the cooperation of all its parts, while the individual will find in his associations the advantages of the help, sympathy, and the fellowship of his neighbours. (Putnam and Goss, 2002, p. 4)

As Putnam concludes: 'Hanifan's account of social capital anticipated virtually all of the crucial elements of later interpretations of this concept' (Putnam and Goss, 2002, p. 5).

Canadians provided the next account of social capital, through both academic and official channels. In 1957 the Royal Commission on Canada's Economic Prospects published a report entitled *Housing and Social Capital*. Unlike the American view of social capital, this report sees the building of community as an end in itself rather than an instrumental tool to serve other, presumably larger, goals. 'Social capital and its associated institutions . . . [are] what is meant by civilization in the highest sense; they are worth having in themselves; they justify industry even as they facilitate it' (Dube et al., 1957, p. 3).

The American school of social capital: Tocqueville, Coleman and Putnam

Putnam follows in Hanifan's functionalist tradition, defining social capital as the 'connections among individuals – social networks and the norms of reciprocity and trustworthiness that arise from them' (2000, p. 19) that ultimately 'enable participants to act together more effectively to pursue shared objectives' (1996, p. 56). Putnam's thesis also builds upon the work of American sociologist James Coleman, who uses an economic model to define social capital as the set of resources that inhere in family relations and in community organizations that are useful for the development of children (Coleman, 1988). Putnam is also explicitly part of a peculiarly American school of civic thought, stretching from Alexis de Tocqueville to Gabriel Almond and Sidney Verba, who see civic society as the critical component of a robust American democracy (Putnam, 1993). Community is thus the repository of a common 'civic culture', which unites citizens in a sphere distinct from, and often antagonistic to, the liberal state. This academic context is critical to understanding the meaning of social capital in the American context. Tocqueville, Almond and Verba all saw voluntary associations of individuals as *the* critical *means* by which the *end* of a strong American democracy is ensured. This view of civic society is imported into both Coleman's and, especially, Putnam's versions of social capital.

Putnam's and Coleman's theories of social capital, however, are different from the perspective of either Tocqueville or Almond and Verba on three grounds. The first is the centrally held belief of Putnam and Coleman that civic life in the United States, once robust and leading to good outcomes for individuals, has declined or collapsed. This decline has led to negative effects, from bad government, poor neighbourhoods and economic ills (Putnam) to increased levels of high school drop-outs and poor educational outcomes (Coleman). Thus, America needs to consider, it is argued, the ways in which social capital may be rebuilt in the future. Due in part to the functional aspect of community in Coleman's and Putnam's theories of social capital, the focus is largely on the *amount* of social connectedness rather than a detailed analysis of the *nature* of any past or present connections.[3] Thus, *future* prescriptions need only increase the *amount* of connectedness in American society with little reference to the *nature* of these connections. As shall be demonstrated throughout this book, *how* communities are formed, as well as the *kinds* of connections by which they are constituted, are absolutely critical to the meaning of community and the changes to it, from the perspective of both women and cultural minorities. Given the historical forces of exclusion and assimilation in civic society in the past, the nature of the connections (namely the kinds of organizations and relations that are either fostered or discouraged) will ultimately decide whether the needs of historically subordinated groups are served within any future community. Thus, the *nature* of the connections in any given community is what ultimately determines its capacity for justice.

The second important difference between Putnam's and Coleman's thesis and either the historic civic culture tradition of American letters *or* the contemporary communitarian and third way theories is the centrality of the term 'capital' in their theories. The use of 'capital' as a term (as opposed to employing alternatives such as community or civil society) allows Putnam and Coleman to deploy all the connotative, normative

---

[3] Putnam does make a distinction between 'bridging' and 'bonding' capital in attempting to address this problem of the nature of connections within the community, but, as shall be discussed, his analysis really addresses the issue of 'bad' social capital, namely the Ku Klux Klan problem, as opposed to the wider sweep of historical exclusion and assimilation to which I refer. Secondly, his 'bridging capital' does not address the different historical experiences of cultural minorities such as homosexuals or Native Americans (who faced assimilation), for whom 'bridging capital', therefore, would be singularly ill-suited to rectifying the specific injustices of American communities in the past with regard to these particular groups of Americans.

and methodological underpinnings of other forms of capital. Thus social capital, like other forms of capital, is an asset that accrues through hard work and commitment. It is an investment now, for greater dividends in the future; and is available to anybody who works hard to get it and who makes the right choices in terms of their own time and resources. In other words, for Coleman and Putnam, social *capital* is a largely unproblematic, instrumental concept; the functional means by which greater ends are achieved. Capital building, needless to say, is perceived to be almost entirely positive in terms of its outcomes. As such, community is seen as an entity that ultimately allows its members to 'more effectively pursue shared objectives' – that is, to solve the problem of social cooperation amongst self-interested individuals.

It should be noted that the 'capital' of social capital, for Putnam and Coleman, is different from other forms of human or physical capital, because, while the proceeds for investment in either human, physical or financial capital return largely to the individual, any investment in social capital will often benefit others rather than the individual making the investment of time or energy (Putnam, 2000, p. 20; Coleman, 1988, p. S116). Thus, while somebody might work hard to accrue human, physical or economic capital, and reap the resulting profits, an individual making investments in social capital will probably see other members of the community reap the rewards. This unique aspect of social capital is critically important, particularly in relation to the gendered dimensions of social capital formation in Coleman's and Putnam's analyses. While they both see this element of social capital as largely unproblematic, their analyses tend to brush over the unequal role played by women in past and present forms of other-oriented social capital building; perhaps most worrying, however, is their tendency to provide future prescriptions of social capital building that continue to incorporate an unequal burden on women. Thus, the extent to which women are expected to invest in social capital formation in order that their children, husbands and communities may benefit is, as will be shown, an underlying and sometimes hidden assumption in the American social capital literature, beginning with James Coleman, but adopted in a more sophisticated version in Robert Putnam's thesis.

The third and final way in which Putnam differs from Tocqueville is with regard to the meaning he gives to 'social' in social capital. The 'social' sphere has from its inception within liberal theory been a separate sphere from that of the political, the former being associated with the diversity of voluntary relations between individuals, the latter ultimately with the coercive and unifying power of law. But the 'social' aspect of social capital goes beyond a liberal or Tocquevillean notion of civic participation to an appeal for civic virtue and unity. Thus, implicit within the call for the 'revival' of American community is the transcendence of difference: a 'coming together' of disparate parts under one unified set of shared civic values. This is not a new thesis. As Sheldon Wolin argues, the notion of 'social' in the liberal thought of the late nineteenth and early twentieth centuries 'largely centered on the attempt to restate the value of community, that is, the need for human beings to dwell in more intimate relationships with each other, to enjoy more affective ties, *to experience some closer solidarity* than the nature of urbanized and industrialized society seemed willing to grant' (Wolin, 1960, pp. 363–4, emphasis added). To the extent that Putnam ultimately seeks a civic community in which citizens transcend difference in order to 'come together' to form a common 'civic culture', his particular version of 'social capital' goes beyond the economists' model of cooperative self-interest or Tocqueville's 'nation of joiners' to reflect a *neo-republican vision* of civic society. As shall be shown, however, through an analysis of both historical and present articulations of social capital theory, such unity can represent an enormously threatening force for those groups that have historically been excluded from or assimilated to American society based on the values or attributes of the dominant cultural group, or that even today contest certain ostensibly 'universal' norms in the name of cultural diversity or justice. There is, in a seemingly innocent word such as 'social', a potentially very dark side to American community.

The European school of social capital: a critical perspective

My analysis will begin with a different definition of social capital as its starting point: what I describe as a critical perspective on social capital and civic society most famously associated with French critical cultural theorist Pierre Bourdieu, but with roots in the thought of Karl Marx and Antonio Gramsci as well as the analysis of civil society by Jean Cohen and Andrew Arato (1992).[4] Bourdieu describes his theory of social capital in a famous article published in 1986.[5] He begins by breaking down capital into three forms: economic, cultural and social. The use of the term 'capital' 'signals the intention of addressing differential resources of

---

[4] I am grateful to Matt James for bringing Bourdieu's thesis to my attention, and, more broadly, for his insights into the 'capitalist' nature of social capital.

[5] This article builds on theories of cultural capital in Bourdieu's earlier work (1970, 1984), in which he makes the case that it is through cultural reproduction that the existing power relations between groups and classes are reproduced. The important catch here is that the dominant group's culture is seen as universal to all, thus legitimizing its dominance in a similar way to Karl Marx's 'false consciousness' or Jean Paul Sartre's 'bad faith'.

power, and of linking an analysis of the cultural to the economic' (Baron et al., 2000, p. 3). Like Marx's analysis of economic capital, Bourdieu believes that social (and cultural) capital are largely *accumulated* in specific ways as a result of historical relations of power. Bourdieu takes aim at the functionalist, ahistorical and methodologically individualist account of social capital found in economic versions of this theory:

> The social world is accumulated history, and if it is not to be reduced to a discontinuous series of instantaneous mechanical equilibrium between agents who are treated as interchangeable particles, one must reintroduce into it the notion of capital and with it accumulation and all its effects. (Bourdieu, 1986, p. 241)

Thus, at the heart of Bourdieu's analysis is the central role that history and power play in the particular constitution of civil society in America or elsewhere. Bourdieu's point is critical, for capital, from his perspective, does not simply work in an instrumental way, as a free-flowing and functional means of exchange either in the past or the present; it is built up or accumulated over time in particular ways. Moreover, the opportunities for social capital accumulation are not equally open to all, as some might suggest. The past accumulation of social capital weighs heavily on the types of groups and social activity that currently exist (including the degree to which they are seen or measured), as well as shaping the nature of future opportunities for further development.

Social capital is not, therefore, a benign force working equally in the interests of each and all, but, by virtue of past accumulation, draws boundaries around and between people, reconstructing the same power differentials between those who belong and those who do not in more formal institutions. Thus, Bourdieu concludes that social capitalism as much as economic capitalism is an ideology of inclusion and exclusion: a means by which the powerful may protect and further their interests against the less powerful.

> Exchange transforms the things exchanged into signs of recognition and, through the mutual recognition and the recognition of group membership which it implies, re-produces the group. By the same token, it reaffirms the limits of the group. (p. 250)

Bourdieu's definition of social capital is intimately connected with the power that accrues to particular group members as a result of a given network.

> The aggregate of the actual or potential resources which are linked to possession of a durable network of more or less institutionalized relationships of mutual acquaintance and recognition . . . which provides each of its members with the backing of collectively-owned capital. (p. 250)

Thus, what distinguishes Bourdieu from the American school of social capital is both a critical perspective and a preference for networks and resources rather than the functional theory of social capital, which depends on the transformation of connectedness into trust and, with that, the lubrication and glue that make societies function better.

In addition to Bourdieu's theory of social capital, Cohen and Arato provide an alternative view of civil society, rooted in Gramsci's notion of hegemony. Thus, from a Gramscian perspective, civil society is not a space within which individuals cooperate in various associations and come together but a locus of contestation and division where the hegemony of one culture fights to dominate others. As Jean Cohen summarizes:

> [Gramsci's] most important category hegemony . . . is meaningless without its corollary concept civil society . . . the cultural dimension of civil society is not given or natural. Rather it is a state of social contestation: its associations and networks are a terrain to be struggled over and an arena wherein collective identities, ethic values and alliances are forged. Indeed, competing conceptions of civil society are deployed in a continual struggle either to maintain cultural hegemony by dominant groups or to attain counter-hegemony on the part of subordinate collective actors. (Cohen, 1999, p. 214)

Applying Bourdieu's, Cohen's and Arato's theories to the more recent (and more famous) iterations of social capital allows us to consider the extent to which the 'genesis' for Putnam's thesis (the early twentieth-century flourishing of civic groups), serving both as a point of origin from which to measure the decline of 'social capital', as well as the model for a future promised land, is shaped by both culture and power. It will become clear that this historical vision of a mythical comparison point from which the present 'decline' is measured reflects both historical accumulation and exclusionary cultural boundaries. We shall also examine the extent to which civil society, particularly in the last thirty years, has become a site of social contestation and division as previously dominant groups and norms are contested by women and cultural minorities in the name of justice. Bourdieu's emphasis on networks and resources rather than trust and shared norms may also make his theory of social capital much easier to reconcile with a multicultural and diverse society.[6]

My analysis departs from Pierre Bourdieu's theory of social capital on two counts. First, I will argue that there are important non-economic

---

[6] It may also be that Bourdieu's definition makes it easier for those wishing to measure social capital to distinguish cause from effect more effectively. To this end, it is interesting to note that the Privy Council Office in the Canadian government has chosen to use Bourdieu's theory of social capital (as networks and resources) over the Coleman/Putnam functional version of social capital. Thus, a PCO discussion paper in October 2003 argues: 'In contrast to functional conceptualizations, network-based approaches to social capital may offer a much cleaner definition. To this end, many scholars have come to "rediscover" the work of Pierre Bourdieu on social capital' (PCO, 2003, p. 13).

factors involved in the accumulation of social capital that Bourdieu did not address fully; to this end I will go beyond class relations to examine both the gendered and cultural dimensions of social capital. Secondly, I will also incorporate the idea of resistance or agency by historically subordinated groups, which Bourdieu – strangely – overlooks in his analysis, as a central explanatory factor in the changing nature of communities and their norms.[7] Thus, as Bourdieu ultimately argues, all forms of capital, including social capital, must be analysed in terms of the effect that accumulated power relations have on different groups of people, particularly those who were, and are, negatively affected by such boundaries. But, equally, the shape of social capital accumulation in the past, present and future must also be examined in light of the growing resistance by the marginalized during the course of the twentieth century to just such boundaries and norms.[8]

The past, present and future: the challenge of justice and diversity

Putnam's thesis is daunting in its scope and the sheer weight of evidence amassed. As one critic commented: '[It's like] taking a sip from a fire hydrant.'[9] In order to maintain a sharp focus on the questions at hand, this book concerns itself with the issues of civic participation and trust in the past, present and future of the United States. Throughout, I subject the social capital thesis to analysis from both a cultural and a gendered perspective. It is important, given the very different histories of particular groups in America during the twentieth century, not to assume that there is one 'universal' story of community to be told; such meta-narratives would obscure the specific (and unique) histories of women and cultural minorities during the same time period. Women's specific civic experience in both the historical 'paradise' of the Progressive Era as well as

[7] As Baron et al. (2000, p. 2) comment: '[Bourdieu's theory] strangely lacks a sense of struggle: the various forms of dominant capital are presented as simply dominant without account of the subordinated forms of capital, how they resist dominant capitals and how they come actively to be subordinated.'

[8] Michel Foucault is perhaps most closely associated with this theory of resistance as integral to a full understanding of the way power works in society: 'There are no relations of power without resistance' (1980, p. 142). Robert Wuthnow (2002a), in a more recent iteration of this idea of marginalization, sees the central normative question in social capital today as this: 'Can social capital in the US be developed in ways that do a better job of bridging the privileged and the marginalized than appears to be the case at present?' (p. 60). Wuthnow tends to be more concerned with race and class than other forms of marginalization, such as disability, sexual orientation or ethnicity, but the question still holds.

[9] 'Lonely in America': interview with Robert Putnam, www.theatlantic.com/unbound/interviews, 21 September 2000.

during the current 'decline' is one central focus. Similarly, the specific and diverse experiences of cultural minorities in both the past and present of social capital building provide a second lens through which the story of community may be observed. The purpose of this analysis is not simply to correct some perceived 'politically incorrect' wrong. Rather, it is to serve the most traditional of academic goals: to give the most thorough and comprehensive explanation of the particular phenomenon under investigation, in this case social capital, by analysing it from a variety of key perspectives. The critique corresponds roughly to the three stages of Putnam's narrative – past glory, present malaise or collapse, and future revival – with the bulk of the analysis (like Putnam's) focused on the current state of 'collapse'.

We begin in the past. The first general question to be addressed (in chapter 2) is whether the 'past' ideal of an American society used by Putnam (and by Richard Rorty in *Achieving Our Country*; 1999) as a model for the future of American communities, namely the Progressive Era, is as idyllic when seen from the perspective of either women or cultural minorities. In this chapter we look at many of the Progressive Era's key civic associations, as well as the projects in which they were involved, in order to ascertain fully the nature of social capital accumulation during this time period. We examine the distinct histories of 'fraternal' versus 'maternal' organizations, as well as the role that their educational and social reform projects played (or failed to play) in the lives of new immigrants, African-Americans and Native Americans.

Chapters 3 to 5 address the empirical and normative dimensions of the social capital 'decline' over the last forty years. Putnam uses many different kinds of data to prove, empirically, that social capital is in decline while simultaneously making the normative argument that this pattern of decline is a bad thing. Using the eleven women's civic associations identified by Putnam in appendix III as his chosen barometer of women's civic participation, I begin by re-examining the *empirical* evidence for decline in women's civic activity in each of these specific associations. Simultaneously, we examine the *normative* question of whether such a 'decline' is necessarily a bad thing, seen from the perspective of women and cultural minorities at the close of the twentieth century. The normative and empirical aspects of decline then come together as we go beyond these eleven associations to consider the empirical reality of *newer* forms of civic participation as well as the extent to which they represent a more positive normative dimension to contemporary civic society, and ask whether their existence is the direct result of the increasingly successful push by women and cultural minorities for inclusion, equality and recognition over the last forty years.

Chapter 4 examines the causal explanations for decline by exploring the specific reasons that Putnam gives for its onset (television, the Second World War, dual-career families). Chapter 5 considers the issue of civic trust, its decline and the extent to which it should be linked to civic participation, either as a correlate, cause or effect. It also introduces a second empirical dimension to trust, namely the *gap* between the privileged and marginalized with respect to generalized trust. The link between 'trust' and civic unity is examined, along with the role that 'shared norms' play in functional social capital theory. At the end of the chapter I provide an alternative causal explanation for the patterns of both the decline and the gap in trust within American society based on an understanding of the broad historical context within which these changes occurred.

Chapter 6 addresses the contemporary implications of Putnam's analysis in light of additional research carried out by his Saguaro Seminar on cultural diversity and religious involvement in civic engagement, as well as the concrete manifestations of 'social capital' in the domestic initiatives proposed by the Bush administration in response to 9/11. The final chapter (7) looks to the future, and asks what lessons are to be learnt from the past and present. This chapter shifts the analysis from a critical examination of Putnam and social capital to an explicitly normative one, setting out a blueprint for just communities within diverse societies based on the preceding analysis.

Underpinning my exploration of social capital are the normative issues raised by 'justice' on the one hand and 'diversity' on the other, and it is worth making explicit at the outset what I mean by 'justice' and 'diversity'. First, since the publication of John Rawls' *A Theory of Justice* in 1971, Western political theory has returned to the very old question of 'justice', first introduced by the ancient Greeks, as a central focus of scholarly research. Rawls, along with subsequent commentators such as Ronald Dworkin, Jeremy Waldron and Raymond Geuss, have attempted to define and defend a contemporary version of liberal justice, one that protects and preserves individual liberties from the potential abuse of either the state or public opinion while defending the equality of citizens and the interests of the least well-off. The liberal state, in Rawls' view, must both protect and preserve the rights of the individual (in keeping with the classical liberal theories of J. S. Mill and John Locke) while addressing the inequality of the poor (in keeping with the reform liberal theories of T. H. Green and T. H. Marshall). Liberal justice, in Rawls' theory, thus involves both *negative* and *positive* rights or freedoms, as famously delineated by Isaiah Berlin.

Liberal justice in America therefore requires, for example, from a *negative* rights perspective, that atheists, communists, gay men, lesbian women and people following a minority faith are to be protected from overt discrimination and/or societal pressure to conform to a dominant set of values at the hands of either the state or civil society. Such negative rights, rooted in Lockean ideas of toleration and the limited power of the state, have traditionally required that a sharp line be drawn between religion and the state on the one hand and the political and social spheres on the other. Both J. S. Mill and Alexis de Tocqueville warn of the threat represented by the 'majority will' in a liberal society in relationship to both individual freedom and minority rights, and make the case that safeguards should be in place to provide some protection. From the perspective of *positive* rights, liberal justice has, more recently, required the state to meet basic social needs while addressing the question of equality of opportunity for the less well-off. At various points in this book I deploy these precepts of contemporary 'liberal' justice to examine both the theory and practice of social capital. As we shall see, the emphasis on shared norms, civic unity, the marriage of church, state and community in reviving civic society are in considerable tension with the negative rights aspects of liberal theory, and the emphasis on civic society alone (as opposed to the state) leaves social capital theory nearly mute on the question of positive rights.

Also underlying my analysis is a 'multicultural theory' of justice that takes us beyond the principles of individual liberty or equality, described above, to the emerging questions posed by diversity and difference in contemporary society through multicultural political theory. Where the liberal view of justice is concerned largely with equal treatment and protecting individuals' rights or liberties against either the state or the majority, the multicultural perspective is concerned with protecting and preserving cultural differences against the homogenizing power of a dominant set of group norms (Taylor, 1994; Kymlicka, 1995; Young, 1990). Thus, multicultural justice seeks to create the conditions for historically subordinated groups not only to exist as individuals but also to flourish, as groups, free from the forces of discrimination or assimilation. For liberal multiculturalist Will Kymlicka the protection of ethno-national culture, where it is threatened, is crucial to the exercise of liberal citizenship. For communitarian Charles Taylor the fundamental problem is one of 'misrecognition' – that is, the failure by the dominant community to recognize and protect cultural differences because of the overarching need in liberal theory to view everybody as the 'same'. Even American liberal theorists such as Amy Gutmann have accepted the need to recognize cultural group difference within democratic states such as the United States of America:

> Recognizing and treating members of some groups as equals now seems to require public institutions to acknowledge rather than ignore cultural particularities, at least for those people whose self-understanding depends on the vitality of their culture. This requirement of political recognition of cultural particularity – extended to all individuals – is compatible with a form of universalism that counts the culture and cultural context valued by individuals as among their basic interests. (Gutmann, 1994, p. 5)

Thus, the emphasis on shared norms, trust and unity within a functional theory of social capital may prove to be in tension not only with liberal notions of individual rights but simultaneously with multicultural commitments to diversity and difference.

Finally, my analysis is also rooted in contemporary feminist theory and the examination of the gendered dimension of justice within communities both past and present. Recent third wave feminist analysis (Arneil, 1999) has emphasized the need to recognize diversity and difference amongst women, while simultaneously interrogating the exclusion of women as well as the disproportionate burden often placed on women to do the work that is least valued in society. As we shall see, both Coleman's and Putnam's social capital theories, to the extent that they place a disproportionate burden on women to generate social capital, are inconsistent with gender equality. At the same time, like the multicultural dimensions of justice described above, the emphasis on unity and shared norms have particular implications for women who belong to specific cultural minorities.[10] Ultimately, the challenges posed by liberal, multicultural and feminist visions of justice will be used to analyse whether social capital is the best conceptual vehicle for creating diverse communities that seek to be not only connected but just.

---

[10] I would like to thank the anonymous reviewer who pointed out the need to articulate what I mean by 'justice' at the outset of this book. Having laid out, in the brief overview above, three key dimensions of 'justice' from recent political theory (liberal, multicultural and feminist) I am under no illusion that these three normative threads are easily reconciled to each other (indeed, the question of how to bring together such conflicting normative claims has been the subject of numerous recent studies). For the purposes of this book, however, each of these aspects of political theory is pertinent both in critiquing the 'collapse' of society in the functional model of social capital and in thinking about the 'revival' of community – that is, what kind of civic society we wish to build in the future. Thus, as I outline in chapter 7 of this book, it is precisely because there are important and conflicting claims with respect to justice that our understanding of the 'social' must continue to be a process rather than an entity; a process marked more by contestation than unity at this particular juncture in history.

2   The Progressive Era: past paradise?

In the penultimate chapter of *Bowling Alone*, Robert Putnam makes the
case that the Progressive Era,[1] a society he considers to be replete with
social capital, provides a largely positive model of social connectedness.
This chapter is important, therefore, not only for a historical account of
the origins of social capital in twentieth-century America, but as a proto-
type for the future. As Putnam comments when asked why he expanded
his original article to a full-length book: 'The deep parallels between our
current predicament and the problems facing America at the end of the
Gilded Age had not occurred to me when I wrote the article, and I had
not begun to think about how to "fix" the problem.'[2] If the transition
from the Gilded Age[3] to the Progressive Era is to be used as a model for
'fixing' current problems, one must be extremely careful to understand
the nature of the 'community' of this historical era, including both its
negative and positive features.

The first three sections of this chapter are an analysis of the civic associations that emerged during this period and the projects in which they were
engaged. Both are critical to analysing how social capital was accumulated
in the Progressive Era, as well as the impact on those defined as 'outside'
the American community and its mainstream organizations. Putnam's

---

[1] The Progressive Era in the United States dated from the end of the nineteenth century
to around 1920 and was marked by a movement for social reform, particularly in urban
centres, whereby community provision was made for the less well-off and immigrants
(through settlement houses and kindergartens, for instance), as well as by the larger
political reforms of the Suffragette movement (resulting in the Nineteenth Amendment).
'Progress', as we shall see, also has its dark side for those seen to be 'drags' on the progress
of society, including certain ethnic groups and the disabled.

[2] 'Lonely in America': interview with Robert Putnam, www.theatlantic.com/unbound/
interviews, 21 September 2000.

[3] The Gilded Age is the period of American history that directly preceded the Progressive
Era and is often associated with an age of unregulated capitalism. During this period
many families made their fortunes through the industrialization of America but many
others were left in poverty. Mark Twain and Charles Dudley Warner coined the term in
their book *The Gilded Age: A Tale of Today* (1873).

focus on the positive side of these projects, in relationship to economic amelioration, will be countered in this chapter by a different, more negative, side to the story.[4] As associations turn from simply providing forums for interaction with each other within a self-defined community to social reform *projects*, the goal of 'progress' is made manifest: to 'improve' those defined as 'others' (largely in terms of class, race, ethnicity or religion) who can be improved through education or social reform and to limit the numbers of those who cannot (through limitations on immigration or sexual sterilization). Through the social and educational projects of the Progressive Era in the larger context of 'progress', we will examine the impact on different cultural minorities of the forces of exclusion (African-Americans), assimilation (immigrants and Native Americans) and repression (the disabled and certain kinds of immigrants). Thus, the Progressive Era may have been the era of the Social Gospel, but it was also the age, as Desmond King (1999, 2000) has detailed, of 'eugenics', wherein the repression of population through immigration controls and/or sterilization was seen by many 'progressive' thinkers as central to the evolution or 'progress' of both the human species and the American nation.

In the final section, I explore the associations and projects that were managed by historically subordinated groups by and for *themselves*, including specific associations and projects that were constituted, during the Progressive Era, by individuals with disabilities and African-American women. The agendas, not surprisingly, will prove to be different from other kinds of organizations during this era, as they tended to be focused more on empowerment than charity. These associations and their agendas are important not only in terms of a recognition of historical agency amongst subordinated minorities but also because these groups represent the embryonic roots of the divisive politics that came to dominate the second half of the twentieth century and shifted the emphasis in civil society from service to advocacy, charity to empowerment and unity to division as they challenged the existing norms of a 'progressive' American community, along with the forces of exclusion, assimilation and eradication that have, historically, arisen within them.

---

[4] This is not to say that there are not positive aspects of the Progressive Era, particularly, as Putnam argues, if it is compared to the more individualistic and self-interested Gilded Era, but this should not be the only point of comparison when seen from the beginning of the twenty-first century. What I am attempting to do in this chapter is examine a period of history from the vantage point of both women and cultural minorities. Seen from this 'other' perspective, there is an equally important negative side of these associations and their projects that needs to be told before using them as models for social capital building in the future.

The Progressive Era's civic associations: the politics of exclusion and assimilation

Gender exclusion: maternalism versus fraternalism

Gender is an important organizing principle for the organizations that Putnam discusses in this era. As he points out, almost all civic associations were segregated by sex and the most prominent groups during this era were 'fraternal'. He concludes that fraternalism is a positive development that sprang up in the Progressive Era and represented 'a reaction against the individualism and anomie of this era of rapid social change, asylum from a disordered and uncertain world' of the Gilded Age (2000, p. 389). However, as Carole Pateman and other feminists have shown, fraternalism is not something that emerged in the early twentieth century but can be traced back to the founding of the modern state in the seventeenth century (Pateman, 1988, 1989). Fraternalism underpinned the seventeenth- and eighteenth-century social contract theories of Thomas Hobbes, John Locke and Jean Jacques Rousseau, as a direct challenge to the premodern paradigm of patriarchalism as the basis of authority in society. Authority, according to the social contract theorists, was rooted *not* in the hierarchical relation of father to son, king to subject, or God to Adam, but on an equal relationship of brother to brother. As Pateman points out, this transition, while changing the nature of power within the group of men classified as citizens, does nothing to change the power relations between men and women. Moreover, the positive aspect of fraternalism (to include more, although not *all*, men in civic life and to counter materialism or individualism) must be juxtaposed against its simultaneous power to exclude *all* women. Fraternalism, from its inception, is not simply about building social connections between men, but is also about excluding women, and some racially defined men, from the 'brotherhood'.[5] Thus, as fraternalism emerges in twentieth-century men's organizations, it is not simply a *positive* non-political means to build social capital amongst men (particularly through the service groups mentioned by Putnam) but, *equally*, it is a *negative* and political tool to exclude women (and racially defined men) from all the exchanges, networking and business contacts that developed through such organizations.

Women's civic engagement in the Progressive Era must be viewed in light of fraternalism, for the birth of women's associations is not simply

---

[5] Charles Mills has shown, in an analysis similar to Pateman's gendered critique of social contract theory, that fraternalism is also shaped by race (Mills, 1997). This exclusion is true both theoretically and historically, as groups of racially defined men were excluded from full citizenship.

the result of a meaningless kind of sex segregation, as Putnam implies, but rooted in women's reaction to the forces of exclusion, from fraternal civic associations as well as politics more generally. Thus, in this description of gender differentiation in the golden age of social capital, Putnam fails to analyse how the *power* differential between men and women profoundly impacts the nature and goals of women's organizations specifically and social capital more generally. Social capital, when you are in a position of power, is largely a positive thing aimed at solidifying trust and cooperation and reinforcing the shared norms of members of the already powerful group and community at large. If, on the other hand, you lack power, social capital, as Bourdieu argues, can be used for very different purposes. Those excluded from power, consequently, often do not see their goal as *solidifying* the existing status quo, but *challenging* the very foundations upon which the 'community', including its boundaries, membership and norms, is constituted. Such challenges are *political* by definition, for they question the very power relations that exist and have accumulated through the type of connections that are allowed, and not allowed, to exist in society. Ultimately, Putnam's definition of social capital as a largely *positive* and *non-political* force that will inevitably lead to better political and economic outcomes is problematic when put into this historical perspective. Seen from the perspective of middle-class white men in fraternal organizations, such a view of the purpose and nature of civic associations is valid, but, for women of this era, civic associations took on a more *political* and *divisive* character arising from conditions of exclusion and social distrust. Thus, the idea that communities in the past were united compared to today's divisive politics is in some sense a myth. While it is true that subordinated groups had less power than they do today to agitate for change, there existed within the Progressive Era serious political divisions, for example over women's right to vote. It was the divisiveness over shared norms within civic society, however, that led to the suffrage for women and a more just society.

As Elisabeth Clemens has shown, the main reason why many women's groups formed in the first place is exactly because they were denied power in a more formal way (Clemens, 1999, p. 86). Social capital was exclusive *to men* through formal political parties as well as the organizations described above, and created the singular option of organizing under the rubric of 'women's clubs'. Theda Skocpol and Morris Fiorina argue that Putnam's emphasis on women's associations in the Progressive Era as non-political and builders of social trust sidesteps the political nature of these groups as vehicles for breaking down the accepted boundaries, membership and exclusive nature of the community and society within which they lived (Skocpol and Fiorina, 1999, pp. 14–17). What is striking is how these groups sought to change public policy almost from the beginning. The three major women's groups formed at the end of the nineteenth century were the Women's Christian Temperance Union, in 1874, the General Federation of Women's Clubs, in 1890, and the National Congress of Mothers (later the PTA), in 1897. These women's associations, if seen through a gendered lens, were not so much build-ing social trust as providing forums within which women could channel their misgivings about the way politics were being run, particularly in the area of social policy. Thus, women's associations were the products of 'organized conflict and *distrust*' (Skocpol and Fiorina, 1999, p. 14). As such, they need to be understood not just as instrumental 'facilitators of individual participation and generalized social trust' but as 'sources of popular [or political] leverage' (pp. 14 & 15). It is no coincidence that these women's organizations spearheaded the fight for women's right to vote: a goal that was both divisive and political, destabilizing to families, communities and American society as a whole.

Such divisive gender politics required some cultural camouflage to make women's political objectives more palatable, as much to them-selves as others. Thus, appeals to traditional feminine roles were made to justify the radical platforms adopted. Women's organizations often couched their political aims in the language of 'mothering' (Skocpol, 1992; Clemens, 1999). Clemens comments:

When the Civil War amendments failed to provide for their enfranchisement, women gradually regrouped . . . women's organizations and causes were estab-lished alongside, but largely apart from, the nations' formal political institu-tions . . . As a key element of the era's social reform constituency, these groups contributed to the founding of America's distinctively 'maternalist' welfare state. (Clemens, 1999, p. 86)

While men could appeal to 'fraternity' as the underpinning of their organi-zations, a parallel reference to 'sisterhood', with its implications of equal-ity and empowerment, was impossible for women of this era. Maternal-ism, implying a motherly concern for others' needs, was at the heart of these organizations' objectives, rather than self-interest or empowerment. Women's social capital building, from the beginning of the twentieth cen-tury through to James Coleman's analysis of educational outcomes, car-ried with it the gendered idea that the investment of a woman's own time and energy was done in order to benefit others (Coleman, 1988, p. S116). At the same time, this appeal to a more feminine instinct often softened the bluntly *political* nature of their objectives and allowed women to introduce new ideas such as the right to vote and welfare reforms. This basic gender difference, between maternal and fraternal social capital, during the Progressive Era is worthy of further analysis. The distinction is telling in terms of gender differences, particularly given that the second wave of feminism in the latter part of the twentieth century eventually did appeal to an idea of sisterhood (and with it direct reference to the need for women's empowerment). In summary, social capital was created and accumulated by women in very gendered and non-threatening terms (not as women but as mothers) in response to their exclusion from other groups in society. It was often wielded, however, for very political and divisive purposes that were destabilizing in the short term to the existing community and its exclusionary norms.

Cultural exclusion and assimilation

If the link between gender and exclusion in social capital building of the Progressive Era is touched on only lightly by Putnam, then the cultural (including religion, ethnicity, race and disability) dimensions are almost entirely ignored. As we shall see, the fraternal and maternal groups were exclusionary in relation to cultural identities. In the words of Pierre Bourdieu, they reinforced the boundaries of accumulated social capital by excluding those who did not have the 'right' characteristics and/or making them into charitable projects. As we shall see, within these civic associations was the tendency towards the assimilation or 'Americanization' of non-Protestant Christian 'others' (immigrants, Native Americans and religious minorities) through educational and social welfare projects by 'progressive' proponents of social capitalism. Indeed, the very name of this era, 'progressive', carries with it implications of a movement away from a 'backward' or unenlightened state to a more improved one. This transformation had profound religious and cultural connotations.

In order to analyse the negative side of social capital accumulation during the Progressive Era, it is first necessary to recognize the historical differences between ethnic and racial cultural groups in America. We examine three broad groups in our analysis: the new non-Protestant immigrants arriving from eastern and southern Europe in the first two decades of the twentieth century, Native Americans, and African-Americans.[6] Each of these groups has a unique relationship to the dominant model of white, middle-class, Protestant America. Indeed, one of the problems of considering the role of ethnicity in American history and politics is the tendency to see all groups through the filter of black/white racial conflict. Important as the exclusion or segregation of African-Americans

---

[6] The Asian-American community would provide another example of broad social exclusion based on race, largely on the west coast, during this period. Chinese immigrants were subject to the Chinese Exclusion Act, and there were broader pieces of anti-Asian laws at the start of the twentieth century (Min and Kim, 2002, p. 21; Hing, 1993). Other ethnic groups were also denied citizenship, including Sikhs and Japanese immigrants (King, 2000).

is to American culture and history, one must be careful not to apply the same lens to understand the experience of other historically subordinated groups. Thus, while exclusion or segregation may be seen as the central concern of the African-American community during the twentieth century, the opposite force – assimilation and acculturation – is more often than not the threat for the other two groups. Exclusion and assimilation are two sides of the same story of social capital accumulation during the Progressive Era.

Robert Putnam views the ethnic/cultural dimension of civic associations in the Progressive Era as largely unproblematic. In the same way that he sees men's and women's organizations as simply groups differentiated by sex, Putnam brushes off the 'white', middle-class, Protestant nature of civic association building in this era by stating: 'Fraternal organization was definitely not limited to middle-class white males. As illustrated by the Knights of Columbus, B'nai B'rith and Prince Hall Freemasonry (an organization for black Masons), various ethnic groups tended to spawn their own fraternal organizations' (Putnam, 2000, p. 389). It is worth noting that the first two of these organizations do not fall outside the 'middle-class white male' designation that Putnam uses. Strangely, Putnam chooses not to refer to the characteristic that *does* distinguish these two groups from the other fraternal organizations he considers – Protestant Christianity. This specific religious dimension is critical, not only as a source of exclusion but, as we shall see, as a force for assimilation.

The exclusionary and assimilationist tendencies of the Progressive Era can only be understood in light of the historical context within which they grew. Specifically, they were fuelled by deep cultural anxieties in Protestant America about relations with 'other' groups of people, exacerbated by increases in immigration from eastern and southern – as opposed to northern – Europe and the impact of the First World War. The change in immigration patterns between the end of the nineteenth century and the beginning of the twentieth is summarized by Louis Gerson in an article that otherwise slams the 'revival of ethnicity' at the expense of 'Americanization':

In the decade 1861–1870 the percentage of immigrants from Southeastern Europe was 1.5, that from Northwestern Europe 87.8. In the decade preceding the First World War the percentages were almost reversed: 70.8 and 21.7 . . . Few of the newcomers were Protestant, most were unskilled and even illiterate in their own language . . . Their fear mirrored the anxieties, as well as the ignorance of their contemporaries. (Gerson, 1976, p. 338)

Moreover, this growing tension between the 'American way' of life and 'other ethnicities' was compounded by the First World War, which had the effect of heightening ethnic tensions, as some immigrant minorities in America supported their Slavic compatriots in Europe; what Gerson describes as 'the hyphenated roar' in the United States (p. 339) (Koven and Michel, 1990, p. 1080). Simultaneously, the First World War increased the sense of American global power amongst middle-class, white, Protestant Americans, particularly progressives, reinforcing their sense of strength and commitment to 'American' values (Leuchtenburg, 1952, p. 503).

The response to these intersecting historical forces was a policy of 'Americanization', which influenced not only state initiatives but also the nature and growth of civic associations:

> The xenophobia of the 1910s and 1920s encompassed all immigrant groups. The resulting hysteria led to an environment in which the assertion of ethnic pride and practice of ethnic rituals aroused great suspicion. Americanization . . . often meant the desire to eliminate or, minimally, to subdue all previous ethnic ties. (Reich, 2002, p. 24)

While Putnam recognizes the enormous changes happening in industry, technology and society more widely, he fails to acknowledge how the profound anxiety over immigration and nationalism shaped the accumulation of social capital in specifically Protestant Christian civic associations and the types of projects upon which they embarked during the Progressive Era. Putnam implies that any tendency towards a defensive assimilationist policy is more closely associated with the earlier Gilded Age. Using one organization as his barometer for what he calls 'nativism', Putnam concludes that while the 'American Protective Association' had 2.5 million members in 1887, it 'declined rapidly thereafter', as the Progressive Era unfolded (2000, p. 375). By focusing on just one association, Putnam fails to recognize that such 'nativism' may not have dwindled at all in the twentieth century but instead expanded and filtered into other associations and unions taking up the same anti-immigrant crusade under many different banners:

> From the late nineteenth century on, in a movement that gathered momentum *after* the turn of the century, teachers, settlement house workers, and professional patriots aimed to 'Americanize' these immigrants, to guide and hasten the process of acculturation by which they might embrace the values and behavior of mainstream America. During and immediately after World War I, the movement became a kind of crusade as employers, nationalist groups, as various state and federal agencies sought to remold the values and behaviour of immigrant workers and their families. (Barrett, 1992, p. 997,[7] emphasis added)

---

[7] On the Americanization of immigrant workers during this period, see Higham, 1971; McClymer, 1982, 1980; and Crocker, 1992.

Moreover, Putnam's view that 'nativism' declined at the start of the twentieth century does not square with the changes in immigration described above. The figures would suggest that the anxiety of a Protestant Christian America would be more threatened in the Progressive Era (when southern non-Protestant Europeans arrived) than in the nineteenth century (when immigration was dominated by northern Protestant Europeans).

Putnam's recognition of organized labour during this period as a story of *positive* community building, where unions empowered the working class and gave it a sense of security (2000, p. 393), again glosses over the role that unions played in either excluding or 'Americanizing' waves of immigrant labour.

Through their craft unions, churches, fraternal organizations and other institutions, they created their own cultural worlds, ones that often left little room for newcomers . . . the demand for restriction revealed an exclusionary quality of workers' thinking, and it sometimes betrayed a narrow, nativist conception of 'labour' shared not only by the American Federation of Labour craft unionists but also by Knights of Labour activists. (Barrett, 1992, pp. 1000–1)

The problems of exclusion and assimilation are the same if one looks at the women's organizations of the Progressive Era. Almost all the 'women's' organizations listed by Putnam engaged in the same racial and religious exclusion. Linda Gordon, in her article on women's welfare activities, describes them as the 'usual *white* women's network civic organizations – YWCA, League of Women Voters, Women's Trade Union League, American Association of University Women [and] the Federation of Business and Professional Women' (Gordon, 1991, p. 576, emphasis added). Anne Firor Scott argues that white women's organizations were deliberately and fundamentally exclusive during the Progressive Era, resisting any move towards inclusion.

'Progressive' white women behaved in quite irrational ways when even the most tentative step toward integration was proposed. The General Federation of Women's Clubs, for example, was thrown into turmoil when one highly educated black woman attempted to represent her club at a national convention. The Chicago Women's Club, which prided itself upon its forward looking progressivism, argued for a year before admitting one black member – the exceedingly respectable Fannie Barrier Williams. (Scott, 1990, p. 21)

Assimilation was also on the agenda of women's groups. As Putnam himself suggests, the women's temperance movement 'appealed to native-born Protestants fighting against "vices" [which] they saw most clearly in immigrant cultural traditions' (2000, p. 375). This notion of cultural superiority is motivated by racial and racist politics. Putnam's description, therefore, a few pages later of the temperance movement as 'an early example' of an organization dedicated to the 'nonpolitical purposes' of 'reciprocal responsibility' is to lose sight of these powerful (and political) forces of racism and assimilation being unleashed by the WCTU on non-Protestant immigrant populations (p. 396). Similar assimilationist sentiments were expressed in relation to the Native American and native Hawaiian populations by members of the WCTU in Hawaii (Grimshaw, 2000). For native Hawaiian women, the WCTU's fight for the vote was particularly ironic since they had enjoyed more power than simply the right to vote in the nineteenth-century Hawaiian kingdom, including the right to seats in the upper house (Gething, 1997). As Grimshaw concludes: 'Through American influence, they lost their political status, only to be graciously given it back by Americans decades later in 1920' (Grimshaw, 1989, p. 9).

If, as Putnam argues, progress in the Progressive Era was the critical factor in the projects of these civic associations,[8] the idea of progress almost always carried with it a particular Protestant Christian religious character. From the Masons, to the Women's Christian Temperance Union to the Order of the Eastern Star, associations were defined by their connection to the Protestant Church. During the Progressive Era a particular version of the Protestant Church, namely the 'Social Gospel', developed, and with it religion was increasingly seen as not just a forum for individual faith, prayer and self-reflection but a platform for changing the lives of others. The Social Gospel targeted the poor and marginalized. There is a powerful positive story to be told in this period regarding the Church's role in alleviating poverty and helping those who were down on their luck to better their situation; but the marginalized also often happened to be cultural minorities, and this side of the story provides another dimension to the Social Gospel story. Putnam's framing of the historical shift between the Gilded Age and the Progressive Era solely in terms of economic amelioration allows him to see this religious awakening as a largely positive force for economic equality – 'The Social Gospel represented a reaction against individualism, laissez-faire and inequality' (2000, p. 391) – without acknowledging the negative impacts on either ethnic or religious minorities of these associations or their projects.

Putnam and other champions of this period of American history reply that there were ethnic and non-Protestant religious associations that coexisted with the white Protestant ones, suggesting a kind of pluralistic civic

---

[8] Putnam comments: 'Religion played a substantial role in the civic revitalization of the period' (2000, p. 391).

society unfolding in an embryonic and developing form. But, while it is important to recognize the agency of marginalized groups in forming their own collective associations, the critical point here is that these groups had much less power in relation to the enormously powerful white Protestant organizations (both male and female). Moreover, the commitment of many of the white Protestant Christian organizations to the Social Gospel, as described above, meant that the goal was not only to alleviate economic suffering but to convert immigrants and others to a particular religion seen as synonymous with an *'American'* way of thinking and being. Thus, as will become apparent in our analysis, in the next section, of the projects undertaken by Churches and other Protestant associations, is that the 'American' citizen used as the model for 'Americanization' had a decidedly 'Protestant Christian' character, and the underlying assimilationist aspect of many of these groups' projects had an enormous negative impact on those defined as a religious or ethnic 'other'.

Projects: Americanization through social welfare and education

To understand more fully how the forces of assimilation and exclusion worked in relation to different groups of people, it is necessary to look beyond the associations themselves to the projects they promoted. As stated earlier, the Social Gospel is key. Largely through this particular version of Protestant Christianity, the idea of associations becoming 'active' in the community grew. The emphasis was twofold: social welfare and education. Two fundamental projects undertaken under this dual rubric were settlement houses and kindergartens, respectively. Through these tools, certain groups within America were to be 'helped' and 'improved'. Putnam endorses both these concrete manifestations of social capital accumulation during this period as largely positive, with little reference to the differential impact such projects might have had on specific groups of people who fell outside the accepted definition of 'American'. If one stops to consider how those who were actually subject *to* these morally 'uplifting' projects for 'improvement' were impacted – namely non-Protestant immigrants, American natives and, to a certain but more complicated extent, African-Americans – a different story emerges.

One important goal of projects such as kindergartens, religious schools and settlement houses was to separate individuals from their own cultural identity in favour of an 'American' Protestant Christian one. Putnam's focus is clearly on those who 'give' service rather than those who receive it, and he states without any indication of an analysis of the impact on the latter that 'the most significant long-term effect of the settlement house was *not on the recipients of the service*, but on the service givers' (2000, p. 394, emphasis added). Analysing the various impacts on the recipients is especially important if these projects are to provide appropriate lessons for the future. Thus, Putnam suggests, in his closing remarks of *Bowling Alone*: 'Some of the innovations of the Gilded Age and Progressive Era, like the settlement house and the Chautauqua movement, though not narrowly religious, could inspire twenty-first-century equivalents' (p. 410). Before using these projects as models for the future, we must fully consider their role and impact in the past.

The settlement house: social welfare project

Putnam describes 'settlement houses' as 'one of the most notable social inventions of the Progressive Era' (p. 393). Settlement houses, growing out of both the English Social Gospel of Toynbee Hall and the Northern American missions to free men in the South after the civil war, were spiritually rooted urban centres that brought well-meaning middle-class progressives to help 'improve' the lot of the largely immigrant poor (Crocker, 1992, p. 212). Seen through the lens of 'class' inequality, it can be argued that such projects, which showed concern by the middle class for the poor, were an improvement on the laissez-faire attitude of the Gilded Age. Certainly, Putnam sees them in exactly this light: 'Fraternalism represented a reaction against the individualism and anomie of this era of rapid social change' (p. 389). The questions that arise with respect to the settlement house are: who was helped and why?

Allen F. Davis estimates that 283 out of 307 settlement houses listed in the *Handbook of Settlements* served immigrants (Davis, 1967, pp. 84–94; Crocker, 1992, p. 243). While historians have some disagreement over the degree to which the settlement house was a successful vehicle for the assimilation of new immigrants (Crocker, 1992, p. 42), most agree that that was a key objective. Moreover, recent scholarship suggests that even those settlement houses considered models for cultural pluralism, such as Hull House, were also Americanizing agencies (Lissak, 1989, 1983; Crocker, 1992). Lissak has demonstrated that 'Americanization' was also the goal of Hull House, but that the methods were more liberal in flavour (1989). As Jane Addams, the force behind Hull House, once wrote: 'Americanism was then regarded as a great cultural task and we eagerly sought to invent new instruments and methods with which to undertake it' (Addams, 1919, p. 210). For Addams as much as for supporters of the more vulgar forms of Americanization, 'pluralism was merely a sociocultural fact, a description of the present situation, *not a norm* of their future vision of America' (Lissak, 1989, p. 173).

At the heart of this norm was the belief in a unified American culture, '*e pluribus unum*',[9] in which immigrants would eschew their previous cultural traditions, beliefs and values in favour of 'American' society. Crocker summarizes the overall assimilationist goal of the settlement house movement:

> We will look in vain in the settlement literature for the idea that immigrant culture had anything of permanent value to contribute to American society; instead, the settlement workers saw American culture as something fixed, to which immigrants would soon conform. The goal was 'adjusting their life to ours'. (Crocker, 1992, p. 213)

The settlement house movement was motivated by a religious as well as a political message. As Crocker comments: 'The two great parent movements of the settlements [are] the Social Gospel of Toynbee Hall with its Anglican affiliation and the missions to freedmen in the post-Civil War South' (p. 212). Ralph Luker has made the case for this second root of settlement houses, arguing that histories that take seriously the black American's experience of this movement well recognize this link:

> Although the literature on settlement houses almost invariably identifies them as institutions inspired by the English example and adapted for use in American urban immigrant communities . . . the black experience with settlements points to an American root – planted in the rural South. (Luker, 1984, p. 102)

In both cases, there was an underlying Christian as well as Americanizing agenda to this movement. As Eleanor Stebner comments: 'Rather than embodying a so-called secular or modern movement, the social settlement movement was ultimately religious and spiritual in its underpinnings' (Stebner, 1997, p. 27). It was a new kind of Christianity, however.

The Social Gospel of both Toynbee Hall and Southern missions saw Christianity as 'social' rather than 'private': that is, religion should focus on changing not just individuals through prayer and worship but also communities through education and social welfare. The ultimate purpose was to create a more socially cohesive and unified whole. While some of its adherents tried to draw distinctions between proselytizing 'missions' and 'settlements' (Stebner, 1997, pp. 37–9), most saw their task as morally uplifting their clients by providing an environment and education couched in largely Christian values. Putnam absorbs some of the proselytizing language of the era when he states, without irony, that

---

[9] 'From many comes one' – the original motto for the United States until it was replaced in 1957 by 'in God we trust'.

the immigrant population was 'uplifted' by such projects: 'Settlement houses hosted idealistic young middle class men and women who lived for several years in urban slums seeking *to bring education and "moral uplift" to the immigrant poor*' (Putnam, 2000, p. 393, emphasis added).

The impact of the settlement house on the urban African-American population was different from that of the immigrant community. As Davis (1967) has argued, the vast majority of these houses were directed at immigrants. Elisabeth Lasch-Quinn concludes that, while newly landed immigrants were seen as clients for settlement houses (to be assimilated), African-Americans who lived in the same neighbourhood were not. Thus the story was one of exclusion rather than assimilation:

> The settlement house movement grew out of an awareness of the severe conditions facing newcomers to the city. While it attempted to address the needs of white immigrants, it largely ignored the parallel situation of African Americans when they began to replace whites in settlement neighbourhoods. (Lasch-Quinn, 1993, p. 1)

The one assimilationist aspect of these settlements in relation to black Americans was found amongst northerners who came to 'settle' in the South, after the civil war, and teach the new 'freed coloured man' the northern, Protestant, Christian way of life. As Luker comments:

> The task was to make the south 'American' by making it Christian and that process required the building of institutions that could extend Northern Christian influence, education, and relief throughout the region. Thus the mission stations planted in the South were to be reproductive units of the redeeming community, serving the multiple functions of church, school and social settlement. (Luker, 1977, p. 86)

The complicating factor for African-Americans' experience of the settlement house is their relationship to Christianity and the extent to which it is seen as an empowering, indigenous force or (for some of the early African-American supporters of Islam) a 'colonizing' religion. Unlike many of the new immigrants, the African-American community had a long historical attachment to American forms of Christianity. Indeed, as Luker argues, because of racism, poverty and the 'hard social environment' encountered, 'the church had long been the central social institution in the black community, serving a wide variety of functions' (Luker, 1984, p. 105). Moreover, in some cases African-Americans were the workers as well as the clientele, again creating a different and more complex kind of relationship than that of the immigrant community in settlement houses.[10]

---

[10] This strong connection between black America and Christianity has lived alongside a very strong link to the Islamic faith, however, as is discussed in more detail in chapter 6, when we look at the role of religion and multiculturalism in social capital building.

The kindergarten: educational project

The second kind of project mentioned by Putnam and discussed in this chapter is the kindergarten. Once again, he sees kindergartens as wholly positive in their aims and methods:

Kindergartens were inspired by an innovative educational philosophy that encouraged childhood creativity. Their volunteer organizers sought both to provide a *wholesome educational environment for immigrant children* and to influence the child-rearing techniques of their parents. (2000, p. 395, emphasis added)

Again, when set against the backdrop of an American society deeply anxious about immigration and dedicated to the Americanization of immigrant workers, one dimension of the kindergarten story is the need to assimilate parents, through their children, into a Protestant Christian 'America'. As one Presbyterian missionary stated of her task:

In the kindergarten, the wee ones are easily led into the English tongue; American ways and Christian influences. As a wedge into the homes and an avenue to the parents' hearts, the kindergarten is indispensable. (Ross, 1976, p. 46)

It should be noted that there were many within the kindergarten movement who saw it as a tool for building cross-cultural understanding and diversity, but this viewpoint tended to be the exception rather than the rule (Ross, 1976, pp. 40–1). The American kindergarten movement grew out of the writings of Frederich Froebel, a German educational philosopher who saw unity as the central principle of his education (Ross, 1976, p. 4). The God of Froebel's pedagogical vision was not that of organized Christianity but a 'pantheistic font of life and growth of Romantic philosophy' (Brosterman, 1997, p. 32). Those who followed Froebel were often more supportive of a culturally pluralistic vision of education, but American progressive educational thinkers such as John Dewey transformed 'unity' to mean a 'melting pot' in education. 'The unity of the public-school system is the best guarantee we possess of a unifying agency to deal successfully with the diversified heterogeneity of our population' (Dewey, 1915, pp. 283–4; see also Lissak, 1989, p. 49).

The issue of kindergarten, or education more broadly, has a particular resonance within the Native American community. While immigrant populations were subject to the forces of northern American Protestant acculturation, there is no more vivid example of the cultural damage incurred through 'education' than the schooling of Native (or aboriginal) Americans by Church and state in both Canada and the United States in the first half of the twentieth century. What Putnam describes, in uniformly positive terms, as the Progressive Era's 'impulse to educate and assimilate' from 'kindergarten to high school' needs to be examined in light of the experience of the residential or boarding school system for 'Indians' (Putnam, 2000, pp. 393 & 395). The education of indigenous Americans shared the same driving force as much of the social capital literature: to foster 'civic virtue', to 'morally uplift' and to build 'civilization' through the progressive vehicle of education. But, as Cole Harris (see also Barman, 1995; Dyck, 1997; Grant, 1996) describes this history of assimilation in North America, it might be seen more accurately as cultural warfare:

Either they would disappear or be remade into Europeans. Virtually everyone assumed so . . . the missionaries who worked to turn natives into one or other European vision of Christian perfection. Reserves, the Indian Act, the Indian residential schools all were bent to the same end: if Natives did not die out, they would be assimilated. (Harris, 1991, p. 680)

David Wallace Adams has made a similar case in the United States in his book entitled *Education for Extinction: American Indians and the Boarding School Experience (1875–1928)* (Adams, 1997). Adams argues that, by 1880, there was a reorientation of Indian policy away from conquest and displacement and towards 'reform' and 'improvement'. Indians became the subject of a reform movement and 'philanthropic' efforts that drew together a number of civic organizations, including the Indians Rights Association (the goal of which was 'to secure the civilization of the . . . Indians of the United States . . . and to prepare the way of their absorption into the common life of our own people') (Adams, 1997, p. 9), the Board of Indian Commissioners, the Boston Indian Citizenship Association and the Women's National Indian Association, 'devoted to the cause of Indian uplift and assimilation' (p. 10). In conjunction with government, these organizations, through the language of reform and uplift, were ultimately focused on assimilation, and education was central to that plan.

As with many of the settlement houses and kindergartens, it was the Churches that were deeply involved in the residential or boarding schools for Indians. What appeared to be well-intentioned social capital building premised on the idea of creating civil communities with educated citizens instead caused profound cultural damage and pain in its wake, and left the Churches in a very fragile moral and financial state.[11] This history has come home to roost north of the US border, where the Catholic, United and Anglican Churches in Canada have faced potential bankruptcy or

[11] There is an enormous literature on the residential school system in Canada and its link to the Christian Church. A succinct summary can be found in Royal Commission on Aboriginal Peoples, 1996.

financial ruin as a result of the lawsuits filed by aboriginal people seeking redress and compensation for the damages inflicted (Harvey, 1999; Foot, 1999; *The Christian Century*, 1999).

The resistance by Native Americans to such 'improvement' can be seen in America as early as 1744, when six chiefs in Virginia responded to an offer of education for their children in the following terms, as recorded by Benjamin Franklin:

Several of our young people were formerly brought up at the colleges of the Northern Provinces. They were instructed in all of your sciences but when they came back to us they were bad runners, ignorant of every means of living in the woods; unable to bear either cold or hunger; know neither how to build a cabin, take a deer or kill an enemy; spoke our language imperfectly; were therefore neither fit for hunters, warriors or counselors; they were totally good for nothing. We are however, none the less obligated by your kind offer, though we must decline it. (Huff, 1997, p. 2)

During the Progressive Era, a determined effort was made by the US government to assimilate the Native Americans in the same kind of residential schooling system that had been introduced in Canada (Diner, 1998, p. 117).

Throughout the Progressive Era, US officials attempted to assimilate the Indians by . . . establishing schools to educate young Indians as Americans, . . . by forcibly suppressing Indian culture. The schools prohibited Indian dress, songs, dances, rituals and the use of Indian languages. (Diner, 1998, p. 116)

As Diner concludes, the forced assimilation was ultimately a failure:

A minority of Native Americans achieved substantial security by accepting the concept of private property, Christianity and the majority culture. Most however, although largely dependent on the government economically, resisted forced assimilation. (p. 119)

Women's associations provided moral support for the education of Native Americans. Patricia Grimshaw, in a detailed cross-national analysis of the role the WCTU played in relation to indigenous peoples, refers to the fact that Jessie Ackerman of the Australian WCTU dedicated her book *The World through a Woman's Eyes* to Richard Pratt, the superintendent of the Indian Industrial School in Carlisle, Pennsylvania, 'whom she called the founder of the "Greatest Educational and Individualizing Enterprise in the World"', and through his work 'the great possibilities of the Red Man may become better known'. As Grimshaw concludes: 'As Christian evangelicals with a heritage of humanitarianism . . . [the WCTU] assessed indigenous women and men on the steps they had made in "progress" toward Western educational, religious and cultural norms' (Grimshaw, 2000, p. 7). In Hawaii the situation was the same in relationship to the native Hawaii population: 'The local WCTU women, nearly all of them descendants of or married to descendants of the first missionaries, similarly declared American progress and liberty good for Hawaiians' (Grimshaw, 2000, p. 8).

'Progress' and the control of populations: civil society, eugenics and immigration controls

Perhaps the most damaging aspect of the emphasis on 'progress' through the associations and projects of the Progressive Era was the impact on those who were seen to be beyond the reach of 'improvement' by education or social welfare. The answer became population control. Central to 'progress' during this period were two important underlying factors. The first was Charles Darwin's theory of evolution. Biological progress, it was argued, occurred through the natural selection of superior genetic material. This was both an empirical reality, and – for eugenicists – a normative good. This theory, when applied to the social and cultural spheres, became known as negative eugenics: a philosophy of removing from the national gene pool those people whose genetic make-up was 'weakening' or 'dragging down' the majority of the population. The second important aspect of 'progress' at the start of the twentieth century in America was the discovery of the use of the data survey to describe the 'norm' of society, famously represented in the bell curve. Lennard Davis has explored the connection between eugenics and the birth of official statistics in his book *Enforcing Normalcy: Disability, Deafness and the Body*.

The use of statistics began an important movement, and there is a telling connection . . . between the founders of statistics and their larger intentions. The rather amazing fact is that almost all the early statisticians had one thing in common: they were eugenicists . . . While this coincidence seems almost too striking to be true, we must remember that there is a real connection between figuring the statistical measure of humans and then hoping to improve humans so that deviations from the norm diminish. (Davis, 1995, pp. 13–14)[12]

Davis's argument is that, prior to the end of the nineteenth century, the generally held view in the West was that of an idealized human (drawn largely from religious thought or moral philosophy). Everybody was seen as being relatively weak or strong, as nobody (other than Christ or a prophet) could be thought to live up to the ideal. With the advent of

---

[12] Davis is referring to individuals such as Sir Francis Galton and Karl Pearson in Britain, who created the first department of applied statistics at University College, London, in 1911, which had as its foundational chair the chair of eugenics: both saw their statistical work as inextricably bound up with their eugenics agenda.

statistics, there was an important cultural and intellectual shift at the end of the nineteenth century towards a focus on the 'norm' rather than the 'ideal'. Scientists and statisticians sought to distinguish between people who were 'normal', as represented by the norm of the bell curve, and those who could be designated as 'abnormal', existing at the margins of the statistical chart as well as society (but generally encompassing the poor, mentally ill, disabled, criminals, prostitutes).[13] Unlike some of the other groups we have been speaking of, who could be 'improved' by education and welfare, these groups were seen as beyond redemption, and – perhaps most importantly, for the eugenicists – as a 'drag' on the rest of the population. Thus, the emerging view in the Progressive Era towards those who fell outside the 'norms' of American community, and could not 'evolve' towards them or be improved through education, was a policy of separation (into state institutions), sterilization and/or population control.

Civic associations were key to the development of the eugenics agenda in the United States during this period with respect to both people with disabilities and immigrants. The American Eugenics Society, in a book called *Tomorrow's Children*, estimated that there were 2.5 million people in the United States ('enfeebled', epileptics and mentally disabled) who deserved to be sterilized, and 'another five million people [who] should be segregated from society, based on their poor educational achievements' (Huntington, 1935; Mehler, 1987). The American Breeders Association, established in 1903, was an organization of farmers and academics that grew very rapidly in its first few years of existence and gradually adopted a policy of support for genetic engineering amongst humans. By 1906 it had forty-three committees, including one on eugenics chaired by the president of Stanford University (Reilly, 1991, p. 58). In 1913 the ABA published a report which concluded that approximately '10% of our population, primarily through inherent defect and weakness, are an economic and moral burden on the 90%' (Reilly, 1991, p. 60). As Davis has suggested, those who organized themselves around statistical norms by definition created 'outliers'; the focus immediately turned to

---

[13] 'Without making too simplistic a division in the historical chronotype, one can nevertheless imagine a world in which the hegemony of normalcy does not exist. Rather, what we have is the ideal body . . . not attainable by a human . . . the concept of the norm, unlike that of an ideal, implies that the majority of the population must or should somehow be part of the norm. The norm pins down that majority of the population that fall under the arch of the standard bell-shaped curve . . . any bell curve will always have at its extremities those characteristics that deviate from the norm. So, with the concept of the norm comes the concept of deviations or extremes. When we think of bodies, in a society where the concept of the norm is operative, then people with disabilities will be thought of as deviants. This . . . is in contrast to societies with the concept of an ideal, in which all people have a non-ideal status' (Davis, 1997, p. 14).

how these 'marginal' members of society were dragging down the major-ity norm. The report goes on to conclude: 'It is impossible to measure the industrial and social handicap caused by these individuals. But just as the leaders of successful human endeavor exert an influence altogether incommensurate with their number, so this class, doubtless, constitute a drag on society of similar magnitude' (Reilly, 1991, p. 60). The solution ultimately proposed was the sterilization of the 'feebly minded, epileptics, insane, congenitally deformed and those having defective sense organs, such as the deaf-mutes, the deaf and the blind' (p. 60).

A strong connection was also made between the disabled and new immigrants to American society. The general anxiety in the Progressive Era was the pulling apart or watering down of what was viewed as the norms of 'American' community. Harry Laughlin, who penned the ABA report, went on to do further research on the link between ethnicity and disability/mental illness by analysing census data in relation to the pro-portion of ethnic groups in institutional populations. The survey found that, 'making all logical allowances for environmental conditions, which may be unfavorable to the immigrant, the recent immigrants (largely from Southern and Eastern Europe), as a whole, present a higher percentage of inborn social inadequate qualities than do the older stocks' (Reilly, 1991, p. 64). Jonathan Young describes the connection between the views held during this era toward ethnic minorities and those with disabilities in the following terms:

Racism, ethnic imperialism and xenophobia plagued early twentieth-century America . . . Many believed it was in the best interest of humanity to eliminate or at least curtail populations considered inferior, as witnessed in the treatment of African Americans and Jews. These ideas adversely affected persons with dis-abilities. (Young, 1997, pp. 13–14)

The 1924 Immigration Restriction Act, in response to the work done by Laughlin and others, was designed to stem the tide of immigrants deemed 'mentally deficient' from southern and eastern Europe (non-Protestant) by limiting the number of immigrants from that part of the world. This was only one of several pieces of legislation passed during this period that limited naturalization and immigration on the basis of ethnicity and race.[14]

Justice Olive Wendell Holmes gave ultimate expression to the eugenicist point of view in the 1927 case of *Buck v. Bell*, involving a challenge before the Supreme Court of the United States on the practice of state-imposed

[14] See King (1999, pp. 294–5). Legislation included the 1906 Naturalization Act, the 1907 Immigration Act, the 1917 Immigration Act, the 1917 Literacy Test, the 1921 Emergency Quota Act and the 1924 Immigration Restriction Act.

sterilization for mentally disabled Americans. Holmes ruled that sterilization was legitimate, for it was 'better for all the world, if instead of waiting
to execute degenerate offspring for crime, or to let them starve for their
imbecility, society can prevent those who are manifestly unfit from continuing their kind' (Young, 1997, p. 13). Like ethnic minorities, persons
with disabilities were seen as 'others' in relation to a particular model of
who belonged to the 'American' community. 'Although sterilization and
segregation practices targeted those classified as "feeble-minded" persons – or people with mental retardation, mental illness, and epilepsy –
it reflected a general intolerance for those who allegedly did not fit the
model for the rugged individualistic, capitalistic American'[15] (Young,
1997, p. 14). Thus, the strongest form of pushing an agenda of 'Americanization' and 'improvement through progress' during the Progressive
Era went beyond assimilation or exclusion to the most extreme policy
of restricting the population growth of the 'feeble-minded', through the
policies of sterilization, segregation and immigration restrictions.[16]

As a result, civic engagement, through associations and projects, in
the Progressive Era had the positive aspect noted by Putnam of reaching
across classes to create, within the burgeoning urban centres of early
twentieth-century America, a more economically equitable and inclusive
environment. At the same time, the specific 'American' contours of this
social capital accumulation also involved the negative aspects of exclusion,
assimilation and eradication based on both gender and cultural attributes.
As we shall see in the next section, the Progressive Era story would not be
complete without also examining the development of civic associations
and projects by cultural minorities by and for themselves. This aspect
of civic society is important not only because it recognizes the historical
agency of groups who faced the forces described above but also because
these groups and projects represent the seeds of the advocacy politics that
will emerge in the second half of the twentieth century.

Self-advocacy: cultural minorities, own associations and projects

While recognizing that the Progressive Era associations and their projects
often had negative impacts on various groups of people, it is important

---

[15] *Buck v. Bell*, US citation: 274 US 200 (1927), docket: 292.
[16] Mehler comments: 'A thorough eugenics program would combine sterilization, segregation, and the vigorous promotion of birth control among the lower classes. Nevertheless,
it is clear that the eugenicist advocated the sterilization of millions of Americans right
up until 1940' (http://about.ferris.edu/ISAR/archives/mehler/eliminating.htm, accessed
February 2005).

to recognize, as Putnam points out, that subordinated groups were not just *victims* but also active *agents* in creating their own organizations. Recent historical literature, particularly scholars working in the fields of women's history, African-American history and 'new disability histories', have emphasized the need to analyse the role of subordinated groups as *agents* as well as victims of any given period in history (Gordon, 1988, 1991; Koven and Michel, 1990; Scott, 1990; Longmore and Umansky, 2001). Most analysts have underestimated or ignored, for example, the breadth and strength of African-American women's associations. Perhaps most importantly, the goals of such organizations are often not the same as their culturally dominant counterparts. Historical agency must be analysed in the context of the power relations within which all associations operated and created their projects.

We begin with a consideration of African-American women's associations and projects: a group of Americans who were subject to discrimination on the basis of both gender and race during the Progressive Era (and beyond). While there has been some academic literature on African-American women and their associations, this historical agency and the differences in purpose and structure from those of white women have been largely ignored (Gordon, 1991; Davis, 1933; Giddings, 1984; Neverdon-Morton, 1989; Scott, 1990). Scott comments:

[M]ost historians of women . . . [have] concentrated on white women . . . the histories of black women and of their organizations are just now beginning to be reconstructed and the picture emerging . . . Wherever northern occupation brought freedom, black women had begun, with whatever meager resources they could gather, to create, first, welfare organizations and, then, schools, health centers, orphanages, and many other institutions. (Scott, 1990, pp. 4–5)

While both white and black women were agents of social capital, it is critical to recognize that their approaches to social problems were very different.

One major difference in the orientation of the two groups was that the whites, well into the Great Depression, more strongly saw themselves as helping others – people who were 'other' not only socially but also ethnically and religiously . . . the black women were more focused on their own kind . . . there was less distance between helper and helped than among white reformers . . . Concentrating their efforts more on education and health, and proportionally less on charity or relief, meant that they dealt more often with universal needs. (Gordon, 1991, p. 578)

As Gordon demonstrates, the key characteristic of projects by white reformers is the notion of *charity*. For black female reformers, the goal was more likely to be *empowerment*. It is not surprising, therefore, to find that black and white female reformers differed in their perspective on women's economic role and the projects required as a result. In essence, the further you are from power in society the increased likelihood that you will concentrate on your own group rather than others, that you will see your projects less as charity than empowerment, and that you will have a more radical view of the community and its existing norms.

One specific example is the difference between black and white reformers on gender norms as a result of different lived experience. While white female reformers tended to see marriage and women's dependence on their husbands as desirable, and employment by women as temporary and unfortunate, African-American women tended to see the long-term employment of women as inevitable (Gordon, 1991, pp. 582–4). This distinction has important implications for the nature and degree of support for projects such as kindergartens. White Protestant reformers saw kindergartens as tools to inculcate immigrants in American culture; they also regarded them as directly contrary to their interests as 'mothers' and 'wives'.[17]

Virtually no northern white welfare reformers endorsed [kindergarten] programs as long term or permanent services until the 1930's or 1940's . . . The white reformers in the first decades of the 20th century . . . feared that daytime child care would be used as an alternative, forcing mothers into poor jobs. (Gordon, 1991, p. 584)

Black female reformers, on the other hand, recognized the need for kindergartens and daycares for *their own community*. As Gordon suggests, black women were more likely to accept the notion of woman as worker than 'wife' because this was their reality. 'We see the greater black acknowledgement of single mothers in the high priority black women reformers gave to organizing kindergartens' (Gordon, 1991, p. 584; see also Harley, 1990). Kindergartens, in other words, were important not for creating unity or inculcating American values but for the grittier reason, amongst black women, that it was a necessity for working women, their economic independence and the well-being of their families.

A second example of the link between identity, power and agency can also be found amongst disability organizations in the Progressive Era, specifically within the blind community. In a fascinating article, Catherine Kudlick compares the objectives of two organizations within the blind community of this period: the American Blind People's Higher Education and General Improvement Association, the membership of which consisted largely of blind people, and the American Association of Workers for the Blind, made up largely of sighted professionals. She analyses the

---

[17] There are several notable exceptions to this point of view, particularly amongst the founders of the kindergarten movement (see Ross, 1976, and Snyder, 1972).

differences through the content of their magazines, *The Problem* and *The Outlook for the Blind*, respectively (Kudlick, 2001). In the same way that white reformers sought to 'help' immigrants, so too the AAWB consisted of sighted experts who saw their organization as philanthropic: 'helping' the blind '*other*'. Similarly, just as black female reformers saw themselves working to empower their own communities, the ABPHEGIA saw itself as a forum for blind people to *organize themselves*.

> In general, *The Problem* conveyed an optimistic, inclusive picture of blind Americans . . . blind and sighted had much to teach each other, and all of humanity would gain as a result . . . [While] *Outlook for the Blind* also presented a philosophy of helping Americans better understand the blindness world, it spoke *about* and *to* blind people more often than considering them as having voices in their own right. (p. 194)

What we see in the Progressive Era, amongst those groups that are run by what may be called in present-day parlance 'self-advocates' (associations run by black female reformers or blind people), represents the seeds of what will become a much broader shift in purpose in the second half of the twentieth century, from service to advocacy. By recognizing the roots of such a shift, in notions of empowerment for historically subordinated groups, the critique, articulated by both Putnam and other civic society advocates such as Theda Skocpol, of the growing membership in advocacy associations at the expense of more traditional service organizations might be mitigated in the present era by an understanding of both the profound historical experiences to which groups such as African-Americans and/or the disabled are responding.

Conclusions

In chapter 23 of *Bowling Alone*, entitled 'Lessons of history: the Gilded Age and the Progressive Era', Putnam lays out how America at the turn of the last century, under ostensibly similar conditions to today's, suffering from the same needs, amongst so much technological change and industrial/corporate development, revitalized its social capital. Putnam suggests that the one 'striking feature of the revitalization of civic life in America' at this time is the 'boom in association building' and their associated social welfare and educational projects (Putnam, 2000, p. 383). His underlying thesis is that the shift from the laissez-faire Gilded Age of individualism and the market to the socially concerned Progressive Era (as the title of the chapter implies) was a *positive* development, which brought about greater equality between the classes through 'non-political' civic associations. But, as we have examined these associations and their projects in this chapter from the perspective of both women and cultural minorities, it is clear that social capital accumulation has profound gendered and cultural dimensions that Putnam barely touches on. Recognizing these dimensions provides a different, in many cases more *negative*, version of the positive story of economic amelioration told by Putnam. Moreover, it is clear that these associations are indeed *political*, rooted in the very powerful forces of exclusion, assimilation and eradication that inscribed individual lives as 'deviant' in accordance with the norms of the day.[18] Thus, consistent with Bourdieu's notion of social capital, the Progressive Era's social capitalization was accumulated in particular ways that reinforced boundaries and sanctioned outsiders. By applying both a gendered and cultural lens, one gets a more complete picture of this era; one in which both the *political* and *negative* aspects of social capital come in to clearer focus with regard to specific groups of Americans.

Putnam concludes the chapter by arguing that the one lesson to be learned about the 'dark side' of the Progressive Era is that social capital should not 'exacerbate division' (p. 400).[19] The lesson we have learned from this analysis may be the exact opposite: it is not *division and diversity* but civic unity based upon a shared set of *norms* that posed the greatest threat to cultural minorities, particularly when it was combined with the idea of 'progress' or 'improvement'. The means used to serve the goal of progress were extreme. Moreover, it is clear from this chapter that civic society plays a critically important role (through both associations and projects) in defining the unifying norms of any given historical era. Thus, the central lesson we have learned is that, while civic culture may be critical, in a Tocquevillean sense, to the well-being of a democratic state, it can also represent a powerfully constraining, disciplining or exclusionary force for those groups of people who deviate from the given norms, along religious, ethnic, cultural or gendered lines. As such, a very robust civic society can be a very unjust one as well. At the same time, the specific examples of suffragette organizations, African-American civic associations, disability organizations constituted by self-advocates and Native

---

[18] 'Political' is defined not simply as that which relates to the government or state but, more broadly, as the exercise of power within society; see Arneil, 1999.

[19] 'Even more troubling is the fact that racial segregation and social exclusion were . . . so central to the public agenda . . . not all the "civic innovations" of the Progressive Era were beneficent and progressive. Those of us who seek inspiration for contemporary America in that earlier epoch of reform must attend to the risk that emphasizing community exacerbates division and exclusion' (p. 400). Putnam is correct in acknowledging the darker side of the Progressive Era, but the problem goes beyond the exclusion of particular organizations to involve the broad forces of acculturation, assimilation and even eradication that are embedded in the idea of progress as discussed. Thus, there is a much wider and broader 'dark side' of social capital than Putnam allows.

American bands resisting the offer of 'educational progress' all provide evidence of the persistence of the agency across time of a diverse set of cultural minorities and women. It is these twin forces of agency and empowerment that will grow and eventually challenge the norms of early periods of American history in the name of both cultural and gendered justice. As Cohen and Arato (1992) have argued, civic society is a site of ongoing contestation over the governing norms of society. The changing face of civic culture and civic society during the second half of twentieth-century America, understood as a set of diverse, conflicting, and divisive narratives, is what we now turn to examine in the next three chapters.

3   The present malaise in civic participation: empirical and normative dimensions

From this glorious period of an American society replete with social capital, Putnam's main focus in *Bowling Alone* is the current malaise, within which he postulates a general decline in social capital accumulation over the last forty years. Putnam measures the decline in the United States of public involvement from its zenith in the middle of the twentieth century in terms of political participation (through voter turnout, town hall attendance and service on committees, for example), trust in others, connections in the workplace, informal social connections (through survey data) and civic participation[1] (by size of membership in voluntary associations). The sheer volume of data Putnam collects is impressive and he is careful to provide both a rigorous account of, as well as his doubts about, sources and methodology, within the text itself, and through notes, appendices and afterthoughts. He exhibits, in this regard, a very high level of scholarly integrity when it comes to the transparency of his analysis. As most academics know, it is possible to present one's findings with a perfunctory acknowledgement of both the sources of information used and any counter-examples that one may come across. Putnam represents the opposite, providing his own questions and doubts. His reflections on his own choices and methods, while making him more vulnerable to attack, simultaneously set a very high standard of transparency and openness of debate for those who wish to challenge him.

As with the previous chapter, I will use both a gendered and cultural lens to shed new light on Putnam's thesis of decline in civic participation in the contemporary era. By explicitly focusing on *women's* participation in formal organizations in this chapter, I will demonstrate that it is a mistake to subsume men's and women's experiences into one overarching narrative of decline, as the history of *women* in America over the course of the twentieth century has an enormous and differential impact on

---

[1] I use the term 'civic participation', as Putnam does, to mean involvement in formal organizations, distinguishing it from both social participation (dinner with others, bowling, etc.) and membership in professional organizations (although I touch on this latter issue in the discussion to follow).

the nature and extent of their participation in civic life: a story largely overlooked by Putnam's theory of universal decline. In order to focus our analysis of the patterns of participation of women in formal organizations in America, I will use the eleven female associations (out of thirty-two in total) that Putnam lists in appendix 3 of *Bowling Alone* (pp. 440–4) and the charts in figure 8 (p. 54).[2] Through these eleven organizations, we can analyse, in detail, the empirical and normative dimensions of Putnam's 'theory of decline' with respect to women. I will also use them as windows into other, newer, forms of civic participation engaged in by women, and other historically marginalized groups – activity that may have been overlooked by Putnam by virtue of his choice of measurement tools. Finally, we will examine in detail the counter-examples to Putnam's generalized trend, namely those women's associations that have actually gained or held steady in membership over the last twenty years, and consider what factors may have led to this differing pattern from the rest.

The eleven female civic associations

To measure 'civic participation', Putnam chooses thirty-two national chapter-based organizations with a membership that he can record across time. Most of the organizations are gender-segregated. With the exception of two rural organizations (4-H and Grange) and the Red Cross, all the other associations used by Putnam to measure civic participation have either male or female membership (pp. 438–9). In order to understand women's specific story in the 'decline' of civic participation, we examine the female associations chosen by Putnam. They are: American Association of University Women; Business and Professional Women; General Federation of Women's Clubs; the Women's Christian Temperance Union; League of Women Voters; Order of the Eastern Star; Parent–Teachers Association;[3] Women's Bowling Congress; Hadassah; Moose (Women); and Girl Scouts. When one looks at this list, it seems at first glance an odd (and outdated) set of associations from which to deduct the 'whole' story of *women's* participation within American society over the last century. Putnam chooses these particular organizations because

---

[2] Putnam uses both the formal membership of organizations and survey data of individuals to measure the 'decline' in civic participation. This chapter focuses on the former dimension (through the eleven organizations that Putnam himself chooses as his benchmarks listed in appendix 3). The survey data will be examined in the following chapter in the section on generational change when I compare Putnam's findings to those of Peter Hall in the United Kingdom.

[3] The PTA grew out of the Congress of Mothers, and although it is no longer an exclusively female association I have included it here because its origins are the same as the other groups, the factors affecting its downturn are similar, and it has been studied more than any other organization listed.

they are large, national, chapter-based groups that exist over a long time period, enabling him to track longitudinal change (p. 450, fn. 15), and because they 'involve their members directly in community-based activity' (p. 53). As we shall see, however, it is exactly these criteria that limit a full understanding of women's *changing* civic participation in the twentieth century.[4]

This chapter addresses both the empirical and normative dimensions of decline. On the *empirical* side, there are three questions to address. First, is there a *decline* in overall civic activity or just certain kinds of civic associations? Secondly, is this decline real in relation to the specific populations against which it is measured, or have the populations themselves declined, and, moreover, how should the population against which one is measuring growth or decline be defined? Thirdly, are there new kinds of civic activity that Putnam does not account for which have particular relevance with respect to gender or culture? The *normative* dimensions of the decline story are twofold. The first is whether or not the story of decline is necessarily negative when seen in light of both the mandate of certain organizations and the changing status of women in American society. The second is whether the shift from chapter-based *service* organizations to either professional or *advocacy* associations, considered by Putnam (and Skocpol) to be such a negative development in civic society, has the same normative meaning when seen from a gendered or cultural perspective or if we take into consideration new notions of community. Thus, civic decline must be analysed from the specific point of view of women and cultural minorities if the different *meaning* such shifts have for different kinds of American citizens is to be fully incorporated into the analysis of the current malaise.

Putnam himself acknowledges, in his epilogue, one aspect of the empirical dimension of social capital, namely the need to account for new forms of civic participation, but suggests that he is limited by the existing data sets:

The most commonly cited weakness of 'Bowling Alone' had been clear to me from the start – by drawing membership in specific formal groups, I had ignored the possibility of offsetting increases in other groups or in informal types of connectedness . . . [While recognizing] the possibility that other overlooked forms of social capital were expanding [,] I simply could think of no source of systematic evidence of civic engagement in general. (2000, p. 508)

---

[4] It should be noted that Putnam measures the decrease in membership in relation to the size of the relevant population in order to ensure that he is not simply measuring the growth in the overall numbers of Americans, rather than the civic activity specifically (pp. 53–4; 450, fn. 15). The question of what the 'relevant' population is, however, an important and contested one, as I shall discuss.

Even within the sources used by Putnam, scholars interested in charting civic activity must consider new categories of civic participation. For example, the thirty-eighth edition of the *Encyclopedia of Associations* (2002) lists eighty-one feminist organizations, thirty-five gay and lesbian organizations and seventy-four disability groups – growing civic activity that Putnam largely overlooks.[5] While one must be careful regarding how representative such organizations are, the numbers simply indicate that there is available data on the changing nature of civic activity. A quantitative analysis that would shed some light on this question would move beyond organizations that have been around for a century (important as they might be from one perspective) to examine new *categories* of organizations and the membership represented. Relying on longitudinal data that spans the century will necessarily limit the data available for analysis. By analysing what *kinds* of categories and associations are either growing or declining in the *Encyclopedia* as a whole, *in addition* to looking at a handful that date from before the turn of the last century, one would get a much more representative picture of the changing, and – more specifically – newer, civic participation landscape: one that may not be in decline at all.

The first six: traditional women's associations

The first six of the eleven organizations (the AAUW, BPW, GFWC, WCTU, LWV and OES) are all traditional women's associations with certain characteristics. First, their structure, mandate and orientation were founded on (and continue, to a greater or lesser extent, to be shaped by) the concerns of older, more traditional, middle-class Protestant Christian homemakers. For example, the current WCTU has evolved, but it is still fundamentally shaped by its foundations. The resolutions passed at the 2001 annual convention reflect this history. The preamble to these resolutions states that the WCTU has assembled 'for the purpose of praising God . . . and for making strategic plans for the year ahead'.[6] These plans include recommendations to commend colleges for adopting alcohol-free status, to support a National Family Day, to participate in a Pray for the Children Weekend, to encourage everyone to read the Bible daily, and to protest to Campbell Soup Company for 'the use of wine in their

---

[5] *Encyclopedia of Associations* (2002), Vol. I, *National Organizations of the US*, part 2, entries 1–343–22486, pp. 1822–32, 1312–16 and 1281–90. It should be noted that these are the organizations listed within one sub-heading (i.e. public affairs or social welfare). Vol I, part 3, provides even longer lists of organizations across the different sub-headings.
[6] See www.wctu.org; accessed 6 June 2002.

products'.[7] The goals are consistent with the founding mandate of this organization but may be less relevant to a younger generation of American women than they would be to an older, more traditional, generation.

Secondly, many of these associations have, historically, been exclusionary in terms of race or ethnicity. Linda Gordon, as was discussed in the last chapter, referred to almost exactly the same list of six organizations as the 'usual white women's network civic organizations' (Gordon, 1991, p. 576). Throughout their history, such organizations were often resistant to including ethnic minorities amongst their membership (Scott, 1990, p. 21). Although efforts are being made to respond to this exclusionary history, it is clear that it may be necessary for these more traditional organizations to make alliances with other associations in order to meet the demands of multicultural diversity. For example, the AAUW's first African-American executive director, Jacqueline Woods, admitted in an interview: 'Many African-American, Hispanic and other women of color . . . fighting equity issues . . . have not seen themselves using this organization as a vehicle' (Brotherton, 2002, p. 36). As a result, she sees the need to form partnerships with *other* organizations if the AAUW is to be relevant to *all* women. 'We want to be seen as a good partnership organization . . . that is welcoming and living diversity, and actively seeking new voices' (p. 37). The extent to which the AAUW overcomes its exclusionary past remains to be seen, but the fact that this organization's membership is down may reflect a positive rather than a negative development – namely the demand, which the AAUW itself recognizes, to have inclusive associations for *all* women.

Thirdly, these traditional women's associations were born, as has been discussed, out of the exclusion of women from both fraternal organizations and the wider spheres of political and economic life (the public realm in general). In essence, these organizations represent at their inception an *indirect* path to political *influence* (through an appeal to maternalism) rather than a *direct* path to political *power* for women in their own right.[8] It is perhaps not surprising that women born during and after the second wave of feminism have chosen to take a direct rather than indirect route to political change. As Darcy et al. (1994) note, the increase in the number of women running for political office over the last four decades has been dramatic, and contradicts Putnam's conclusion that there is a universal decline in direct political participation over this same time period. For example, in local politics women office holders increased fourfold

[7] See www.wctu.org; accessed 6 June 2002.
[8] This is not to say that these organizations have refused to evolve in line with the changing views of women. For an interesting analysis of the important (and changing) role of the LWV in women's politics in the 1970s, see Chappell (2002).

between 1975 and 1988 (p. 31); in state legislatures the proportion of women members increased from 13.3 per cent in 1981 to 21.2 per cent in 1993 (p. 54), and rose further to 22.3 per cent by 2001.[9] The percentage of women members in the US House of Representatives has also increased progressively, from 4.1 per cent in 1977 to 13.9 per cent in 2001. Perhaps the most dramatic (and recent) story of direct political power concerns the US Senate. As of 2006 14 per cent of US Senators were female, rising from 9 per cent in 1996 and no more than two women (2 per cent) in any Senate prior to 1992. Putnam's analysis of political participation, in chapter 2 of *Bowling Alone*, needs this gendered dimension added, because his conclusion that 'the frequency of virtually every form of community involvement . . . declined significantly, from . . . petition signing . . . to . . . *running for office*' (Putnam, 2000, p. 41), is incorrect with regard to *women's* steadily increasing involvement in senior political office over the last three decades.

Finally, the projects in which some of these traditional organizations were involved, namely educational and social charity in the inner cities (particularly in the Progressive Era, as discussed in the last chapter), have been superceded by the post-war provision of a publicly funded educational system for all and a welfare state that attempted to meet the social needs of the poor under the auspices of government. Thus, the decline of traditional women's groups in the 1970s and 1980s, along with social service projects, is probably due, in part, to the rise of the welfare state as it began to address the social and educational needs of the less well-off that had previously been seen to by churches and community organizations. In addition, there were, quite simply, fewer women at home to meet such social needs over the last forty years.

The changing role of women in relation to the economic or business sphere and the diversity of professional associations available to them is also reflected in the decline in membership of one of these organizations: Business and Professional Women. Businesswomen can now choose from a variety of *professional* organizations. The *Women in Business Magazine* lists the National Association for Female Executives and the American Business Women's Association along with the BPW (Chin, 1994, p. 6). It is worth noting at this point, since the BPW, ABWA and NAFE open up consideration of not just 'civic' associations but 'professional' associations, that Putnam's analysis misses a very important dimension of the story with regard to women specifically.[10] While Putnam acknowledges

---

[9] The most recent figures are taken from the National Women's Political Caucus: see www.nwpc.org.

[10] In appendix 3 Putnam lists the civic associations, followed by the professional organizations, which he discusses in his chapter on 'Connections in the workplace' (pp. 83–5).

that professional associations (as distinct from civic organizations) are the 'singular exception to the general pattern we have seen of declining membership', he concludes that this pattern is not what it appears because the *relative* number of members is still shrinking in relation to an increasing pool of professionals in each group. Thus, for Putnam, professional organizations turn out to have 'followed a surprisingly familiar path' to that of civic associations (p. 83). Their membership grew after the Second World War, peaked in the 1970s, and then declined. This image, however, does not reflect professional *women's* experience over the same time period. Across the board, women's membership in professional organizations has simply grown as the obstacles to their inclusion in different professional communities dropped away.

The American Bar Association, which calls itself the world's 'largest voluntary professional association', is a good example. Prior to 1996 the ABA did not keep track of female membership, but between 1996 and 2000 the proportion of women rose from 24.8 per cent to 27.4 per cent, or, in numbers, from 84,000 to 100,000.[11] It would be safe to assume that the trajectory in the twenty-five years preceding 1996 was even steeper, since between 1971 and 1995 the percentage of women lawyers increased from 3 per cent to 24 per cent[12] (Curran, 1995). Finally, at least along gender lines, rather than women's representation in the ABA being lower than their representation in the general legal population, 'women's representation on the 39 member ABA Board of Governors in 2002 (28.21%) exceed their representation in the profession'.[13] Thus, for women, the story of major professional organizations such as the ABA over the last forty years is not one of decline but growth, in both absolute and relative terms.

Beyond the simple numbers this growth is important, for it challenges the *negative* interpretation that Putnam gives to the growth of these professional groups over civic associations. Putnam concludes that the general shift from chapter-based service organizations to mass-member professional associations is a generally negative development from the perspective of social capital building. But, for women, this shift represents something else: empowerment, and with it the chance to network professionally. The increase in the numbers of women in the ABA reflects greater equality between men and women in the legal profession. Consequently, like politics, the fact that the membership of a traditional business

---

[11] Figures supplied by the ABA, June 2002.
[12] Reprinted with permission from *Facts About Women and the Law*, copyright 1998 American Bar Association; all rights reserved.
[13] News release, 'Goal IX updates cites women's progress within ABA', www.abanet.org/media/jan99/goalix.html; accessed 6 June 2002.

association, such as the BPW, has declined while the number of women joining professional organizations such as NAFE, ABWA and the ABA has increased is a positive reflection of paths that were previously blocked to women being opened up.

In the last of the six traditional women's associations, the Order of the Eastern Star, women cannot join this organization in their own right but can affiliate only if they are related to a male Master Mason.[14] Needless to say, such a derivative membership constitutes a formidable barrier to present-day women, who see themselves as individuals in their own right rather than people whose status is defined in relation to a male relative. Again, the decline of membership in this type of organization may not be negative, but *positive*, from the vantage point of women's equality.

Thus, it is true that all six of these traditional women's organizations have declined in membership; but the question remains: is this necessarily a negative thing? While these traditional women's organizations have attempted to adapt to the shifting circumstances, their original purpose, it can be argued, has been overtaken by women's changing economic and political role, including full-time work and direct access to political or economic power through more formal means, such as becoming candidates for election, political party officers and delegates, or holding senior business offices, respectively. The projects with which these organizations were involved in the Progressive Era have also been overtaken by the post-war welfare state. Even within the voluntary sector, the decline of these traditional groups may not be an overall decline at all, if other kinds of groups that appeal more to contemporary American women have supplanted them. Thus, if one were to measure women's involvement in different kinds of voluntary associations (other than traditional ones), a different picture would probably emerge. One such study of voluntary organizations, carried out in the United Kingdom, suggests that this is indeed the case. Peter Hall, in his analysis of British social capital, finds the British trends to be contrary to Putnam on the general question of decline, with one notable exception. 'With the exception of traditional women's organizations, there has not been a substantial erosion in association membership over the long term' (Hall, 1999, p. 422). Hall concludes that these groups that 'tend to be oriented towards homemakers have experienced the most striking declines in recent years' (p. 421). It is not surprising, therefore, that women would choose not to join these kinds of organizations when other paths have been opened up to them, through second wave feminism.

[14] See the website of the OES under 'What is the Order of the Eastern Star?', www.oescal.org/whatisit.htm; accessed 1 June 2002.

The PTA: new challenges

One of the most important organizations that Putnam lists amongst his civic associations is the Parent–Teachers Association, singling it out for special consideration in his chapter on civic participation. The PTA grew out of the Congress of Mothers, and while it is no longer an exclusively female association I have included it here because its origins are the same as the other groups, the factors affecting its downturn are similar, and it has been studied more than any of the other organizations listed. The PTA provides us with several further lessons, regarding both the question of decline in civic engagement and its 'negative' character. The PTA is an important story, as Putnam suggests. 'The explosive growth of the PTA was one of the most impressive organizational success stories in American history . . . the PTA's collapse in the last third of the century is no less sensational than its earlier growth' (p. 56). The first point regarding the question of decline is the one Putnam himself makes, namely that the decline may not be as large as it appears. 'Some part of the decline in rates of membership is an optical illusion . . . many of the missing local PTAs reappeared as local PTOs' (pp. 56–7).[15]

The shift from a nationally based PTA to locally based PTOs may be an important trend for social capital theorists, depending on how strong the trend is, because it means that parents are not so much dropping out of the social network around their schools and children as creating networks that are focused around the school itself. The number of parents who have shifted from the PTA to PTOs is difficult to estimate. The PTO Today website claims that there are some 80,000 K-8 (primary school: kindergarden through to the eighth grade of schooling) parent–teacher groups.[16] Mary Lord concludes that, while membership in the PTA has decreased, 'parent involvement in education has [not] declined. Instead, it has found new outlets, unaffiliated parent–teacher organizations, or PTOs, and activist groups like "Mothers on the Move" and Parents for Public Schools (PPS)'[17] (Lord, 1999, p. 64). This latter group, the PPS, claims to have 'an organizational presence in 15 states'.[18] Everett Ladd concludes that parents are as involved in their children's education as

---

[15] Parent–teacher organizations are locally based groups created around a particular school and only loosely affiliated, if at all, with other organizations.

[16] See www.ptotoday.com; accessed 7 June 2002.

[17] The Parents for Public Schools organization is a national organization of community-based chapters that supports public education. The 'founding PPS chapter was formed [in 1989] to combat white, middle-class flight from the public schools' (Lord, 1999, p. 64).

[18] See www.parents4publicschools.com; accessed 10 June 2002.

previous generations, using Gallup polls to show that attendance at school board meetings and direct involvement in parent group events at local schools are stronger than ever (Ladd, 1996, pp. 5–8). One final argument regarding the decline in the PTA relates to changes in the size of the school age (particularly K-8) population. Ladd argues that the shift downwards follows a decrease in the number of children in primary schools; therefore, it may be a decline in the population rather than levels of parent participation that is being measured (p. 6).

While the numbers of parents involved in their children's education may not have declined as much as it appears, the question remains: why are parents no longer joining the PTA, and is this decline in membership a negative development? The reasons why parents have chosen either to create PTOs or organizations such as the PPS, or simply dropped out of the PTA, appear to be twofold: money and politics. On the financial front, some PTOs resent having to send some of their money to a national PTA rather than spending all of it on local concerns. The feature article in an issue of the PTO magazine asks: 'Do we want to spend our group dollars outside of our school? Or do we want to focus exclusively on our school where our kids are?' (Sullivan, 2000, p. 2). This shift represents not an inclination on the part of parents to disengage in their children's education but, rather, a change of view as to the most appropriate vehicle through which their interest, and financial resources, should be funnelled.

On the political front, there are challenges both from the left and the right to the PTA. Many conservative members of PTOs see the PTA as too focused on a 'liberal' political agenda rather than providing support for local fund-raising and parent–teacher relations. Thus, the PTA is challenged in an editorial of the *Christian Science Monitor* along the following lines:

By its own admission, the National PTA says membership has been 'static' for the past decade. This fact alone should send a signal to this more than 100 year old organization that it would do well to stick to bettering relations between parents and teachers, and leave the pursuit of a social agenda alone. (*Christian Science Monitor*, 2001)

In response, Lois Jean White, the first African-American woman to head the national PTA, is unapologetic in her defence of the politics of the PTA, stating: 'Our founders were activists, not fund-raisers. They probably never baked a cookie or sold a candy bar . . . unfortunately we've been shackled with that responsibility . . . [W]e're education advocates . . . our role is to make the public aware of the ills in schools and *in society*' (Lord, 1999, p. 63, emphasis added). This latter allusion to the ills 'of society' is an oblique reference to some controversial positions taken by the PTA on gay and lesbian rights, vouchers and gun control.[19] Some also see the PTA as being too close to the teachers' unions. To put it in simple terms, more traditional or conservative parents and educational advocates view the PTA as having gone well beyond its mandate, and no longer representing the 'true' interests of parents in their local communities. Charlene Haar, president of the conservative Educational Policy Institute, claims that the PTA 'represents fewer than 10 percent of US parents' (Lord, 1999, p. 62).

It should be borne in mind that the critics of the PTA are not only conservatives. Questions have also been raised from the opposite direction, namely whether the PTA is too *traditional* or *conservative* in both its membership and outlook. Susan Crawford and Peggy Levitt (1999) argue that one of the key challenges for the PTA (and other civic associations) is to adapt to contemporary conditions: 'Organizations that operate as if their membership continues to be the predominantly white, middle-class, stay-at-home mothers of previous decades find themselves increasingly irrelevant in today's world' (p. 250). They argue that social and demographic changes in American society have had an enormous influence on civic associations such as the PTA, and that they, in turn, have been slow to respond. Two significant elements in this demographic change, pointed to by Crawford and Levitt, are gender and race.

Changing gender roles have had an enormous impact on membership of the PTA. 'In sum . . . mothers working full-time and single mothers are less likely than homemakers to participate in such organizations . . . [T]he leaders of the PTA are right to be concerned about the impact of two-career families and single motherhood on membership rates' (Crawford and Levitt, 1999, pp. 270–1). For most of its life, the PTA has directed its promotional material at 'middle-class wives and mothers who did not work outside the home' (p. 263). Crawford and Levitt point to some important changes that have taken place recently within the PTA that should address this problem, including targeting fathers as well as mothers for membership, running aftercare programmes for children, holding meetings in the evening and during breakfast hours to accommodate working parents' needs, lobbying the Department of Education to create family resource centres and encouraging employers to allow for flexible lunch hours for parents who wish to visit or volunteer at their schools (pp. 281–3). All these initiatives are geared towards finding time and flexibility for working parents caught in a time crunch, but they are recent and piecemeal.

---

[19] 'The Texas PTA believes it lost members in the 1990s by lobbying against the carrying of concealed weapons and by promoting sex education' (Crawford and Levitt, 1999, p. 276).

Gender is not the only factor in the declining membership of the PTA. 'Minority group members participated at lower rates than whites' (p. 272). While the PTA has, over the last two decades, reached out to racial minorities, it is clear that moves to become more diverse ethnically may have come at the cost of traditional members. This conclusion is brought into sharp relief by the fascinating analysis, carried out by Crawford and Levitt, on the amalgamation of the national PTA with the national Congress of Colored Parents and Teachers during the 1960s and 1970s, and its impact on PTA membership. Although amalgamation should have meant an increase in members, racial politics resulted in a significant decline in the nine states that resisted integration until 1970. Of the nine states (Alabama, Arkansas, Florida, Georgia, Louisiana, Mississippi, North Carolina, South Carolina and Texas), all but two witnessed much larger declines than the national average. For example, in the academic year 1970/71, when the national average declined by 5 per cent, Mississippi declined by 40 per cent, South Carolina and Louisiana by 13 per cent, and Alabama and North Carolina by 11 per cent. As Crawford and Levitt conclude: 'Twenty-eight percent of the total national membership loss in 1970–71 came from just seven southern states' (pp. 277–8). There is an important lesson to be drawn from these statistics: while social capital declined during this period in terms of absolute numbers of members, a far more important objective, that of racial integration, was achieved. Again, the idea that such a decline in social capital is wholly negative must be seen in the broader social context of racial politics, and gains, in terms of justice, coming from a more inclusive association.

The story of the PTA may be one not so much about declining parent involvement as one of increasing demands for input at the local, community level and political challenges from both the right and left. There is no question that there will be a cost to the public education system if the unified voice of a national PTA is weakened by members leaving to form more locally defined groups, but it is equally true that there is also a price to be paid in terms of local control and a diverse, pluralistic approach to education by an ever larger national PTA that seeks to speak for all. How one reconciles these conflicting demands of social solidarity and a diverse population are exceedingly difficult and go well beyond any specific association to democratic theory as a whole.

The Women's Bowling Congress: a window into female athletics

The Women's Bowling Congress is Putnam's only measure of women's involvement in sporting activities amongst civic associations during the twentieth century.[20] By using this indicator as the measure of participation in women's sports, Putnam misses an extraordinary and dramatic story of exponential growth in civic engagement over the last thirty years in the area of female athletics. Since the passing of Title IX of the Education Amendments of 1972, a federal law that prohibits sex discrimination in any school activity, the participation of girls in sporting activity has grown exponentially. One of the best sources of collated information on women's participation is the Sporting Goods Manufacturing Association, which has published two reports (1998, 2000), both entitled *Gaining Ground: A Progress Report on Women in Sports*. Putnam refers to the earlier report in his chapter on informal social connections, where he states that youth sport participation has declined over the last several decades (pp. 110–12). But, beyond the SGMA, there are numerous other sources of information, from high school data to NCAA reports, to the Amateur Athletics Union to the Girl Scouts of America. We shall draw on all these sources in examining the case for an explosion of civic participation under the rubric of female athletics.

Putnam admits that women in sports represent an important 'exception to this general picture' of decline, but goes on to dismiss (in a footnote) the impact of Title IX on women's sports because it is limited to the six to eleven age group (p. 461, fn. 50). Putnam bases this conclusion on one sentence from the 1998 edition of the SGMA report on women's participation in sports.[21] This conclusion is contradicted, however, by many

[20] Bowling is a particularly odd sport in which to measure civic engagement in the athletic arena, because, at both high school and college, bowling represents a small fraction of total female athletes (0.20 per cent of female college athletes, 0.16 per cent of high school athletes, calculated from statistics taken from the National Federation of State High School Associations and National Collegiate Athletic Association). There is, however, an interesting story concerning black female athletes, particularly at the college level, for they represent the vast majority of female athletes in this sport – a point I discuss at the end of this section (NCAA, 2003b).

[21] The sentence from the SGMA report reads: 'Except in the 6–11 age group, there has been little change in the overall percentage of females who play sports frequently. The gains in numbers of participants reported here largely match the growth in the population' (p. 3). Two points are worth making here. First, this sentence refers to females who play sports 'frequently', as opposed to several other measurements in the same report that demonstrate an exponential increase in the number of females who have joined teams across all age groups during this same time period. For example, the same SGMA report concludes that between 1971 and 1990 the ratio of girls involved in high school sports increased from 1:27 to 1:3 (p. 1). Secondly, the 1998 report, quoted by Putnam, has been superceded by the more recent and even more dramatic results in the 2000 version of the report, as described below. Finally, one trend documented in both reports that bolsters Putnam's idea that people are tending to 'bowl alone' as opposed to bowling in leagues is the increasing recent trend of women joining individual as opposed to team sports, such as running and bicycling and – at the more extreme end – marathons and triathlons. Ian Adair reports in one local environment that the percentage of female triathletes between 1995 and 2002 grew from 31 per cent to 43 per cent (Adair, 2002).

sources, including the NCAA, SGMA (in other parts of the 1998 report and, even more strongly, in the 2000 version), National Federation of State High Schools, Amateur Athletics Union and newspaper accounts of female athletics. They all conclude that, from pre-adolescence to professional leagues, women's athletics has been growing explosively since the mid-1990s, and that this trend will continue into the foreseeable future. *Gaining Ground* (2000) summarizes the overarching story in the following way:

> A fundamental change has occurred in the way we think and act about females and sports. Just as little girls learned a generation ago that they could grow up to be doctors, in the 1990s they discovered that they can also grow up to be athletes. While this change certainly was made possible by the passage of Title IX in 1972, it didn't occur until the 1990s. Of course, the transformation is not complete, *but the trend is vast and undeniable.* (SGHA, 2000, emphasis added)

Because many of these sports did not exist for women at the beginning or even in the middle of the twentieth century, they do not form part of Putnam's measurements in the way that the WBC does.

Beginning with the six to eleven age group: girls' activities in pre-adolescent sport have increased significantly in the 1990s (for example: 15 per cent in baseball, 41 per cent in softball, 20 per cent in soccer).[22] In contrast to Putnam's conclusions, this trend also holds true for high school girls as well. As statistics provided by the NFSHSA demonstrate, in 2000/2001 high school girls were involved in organized sporting activities at record levels (2,746,181). This increase, measured from the introduction of Title IX, is dramatic. Using figures supplied by the NFSHSA and the Department of Education, the American Women's Sports Foundation estimates that, between 1971 and 2001, 'the ratio of girls involved in sports *expanded from 1 in 27 to 1 in 2.5*, while boys remained steady throughout these thirty years at 1 in 2'. To put it another way, female participation in high school sports has increased 850 per cent since the passage of Title IX.[23] *Gaining Ground* (2000) reports that the number of female athletes increased by 40 per cent on high school varsity teams just in the 1990s (the 1998 SGMA report also indicates a 31 per cent increase in the first half of the 1990s). Overall, the numbers of high school girls playing soccer increased in the 1990s by 112 per cent; softball, 55 per cent; swimming, 51 per cent; and cross-country, 46 per cent. At the college level, participation by women in collegiate activities increased

---

[22] See 'Women's sports and fitness facts', at www.womenssportsfoundation.org; accessed 12 June 2002.

[23] See www.womenssportsfoundation.org; accessed 15 May 2002.

128 per cent across all three divisions of the NCAA between 1981 and 1999 (NCAA, 2003a).

Beyond schools and colleges are growing numbers of club teams as well, meeting at the weekend or in the evening. Again, a more thorough analysis might demonstrate the full extent of this social capital building and networking, but some figures provide a sense of the trend in this area. The American Athletic Union, which, according to its website, is one of the 'largest, non-profit, volunteer sports organizations in the US [and includes] nearly 500,000 participants and over 50,000 volunteers', is divided into fifty-seven distinct associations. These associations annually sanction 'more than thirty-four sports programmes, 250 national championships, and over 10,000 local events'.[24] The number of girls who have registered for the AAU basketball tournaments increased 264 per cent between 1990 and 1998, exceeding the number of boys who chose basketball for the first time in 1997. Yet another source of female athletic participation is the Police Athletics League, which serves half a million youths, aged five to eighteen. The organization has 'over 300 law enforcement agencies, servicing over 700 cities and 1,700 facilities'.[25] Amongst PAL-sponsored basketball tournaments for girls, the number of girls registered expanded from 16,000 in 1991 to 43,000 in 1997, representing 168 per cent growth (SGMA, 1998, p. 13). The Amateur Softball Association reports an increase of 62 per cent in the number of female teams in youth league softball between 1986 and 1996. Little League softball participation reflects a similar pattern of growth: from 30,000 in 1974 to 400,000 in 1997 (SGMA, 1998, p. 14). Finally, the Girl Scouts have endorsed girls participating in sports. According to the Girl Scouts' 1999 Annual Report, 'every day, all around the country, girls participated in sports and fitness events as part of GirlSports 2000. 100,000 girls in 3000 councils, spanning 50 states . . . participated in 2,300 events' (Girl Scouts, 1999). By the next year, this number had grown to over 5,000 local sporting events for girl scouts (Girl Scouts, 2000).

Finally, the growth of both professional and elite amateur female sports is important, not only in and of itself but for its modelling effect on young girls. 'As opportunities open for elite athletes and their exploits become known, they inspire millions of others to experience the benefits of becoming an athlete' (SGMA, 1998, p. 19). In America specifically, the gold medal wins for US women's basketball, softball and soccer teams in the 1996 Atlanta Olympic Games had intangible but profound impacts on young female viewers. The extent to which girls are exposed to such role models depends on media coverage, but there are signs that this

[24] See http://aausports.org.   [25] See www.nationalpal.org; accessed 12 June 2002.

has also begun to grow. To begin with elite amateur sports: the addition of several new sports to the Olympic Games is an important measure of elite female athletics. In the 2000 Summer Games in Sydney, eight new sports (water polo, weightlifting, pole vault, hammer throw, modern pentathlon, trampoline, triathlon, and tae kwon do) were added.[26] As a point of comparison, at the turn of the last century, just before the Women's Bowling Congress was formed, women competed in only two Olympic sports: golfing and tennis.

In the professional arena: the Women's National Basketball Association was formed in 1997 and expanded from eight teams to sixteen in 2000, though as of 2004 it has thirteen teams. Attendance grew over this same time period. In 1999 the league attracted 1.96 million fans (300,000 more than the previous year). The Women's World Series in baseball was held for the first time in 2001, with four international teams competing; its most recent tournament was in 2004. Within the last seven years, the Women's Professional Football League started with eleven teams and had expanded to twenty by 2003, though it dropped down to fifteen by 2004;[27] the Women's United Soccer Association began a league with eight teams.[28] Finally, media coverage of some of these sports is also increasing. ESPN announced in 2001 an eleven-year $160 million contract to expand coverage of women's sports into Division II NCAA sports, including basketball, soccer, softball, swimming, volleyball and track events.[29]

These statistics are important not only to demonstrate the growth of women's involvement in sports at all levels but because such growth in *organized* women's sports represents a gold mine of civic engagement and participation.[30] For every one of those athletes at the elementary, secondary, collegiate, elite and even professional level, there is a network of parents, friends, sponsors, clubs, coaches, games, tournaments, refereeing associations and specific sporting organizations that grow up

---

[26] It is worth noting that some of these sports are demonstration sports and may (or may not) be part of future games. Secondly, some of these new sports are new for men as well as women, so they are not simply reflecting the increase in women's involvement at the highest levels of sport but, rather, the expanding definition of sport itself.

[27] See www.womensprofootball.com; accessed December 2003.

[28] *USA Today*, 11 October 2000; *New York Times*, 1 February 2001; *Sportbusiness Journal*, 2001. It needs to be made clear that these women's sports leagues, to the extent that they exist, are very fragile. Indeed, the WUSA folded in September 2003 (Straus, 2003), though in December 2004 it announced it would be relaunched (see www.wusa.com/news/?id=1723). The professional volleyball league was also forced to cancel its 2003 season due to a lack of financial resources.

[29] *USA Today*, 27 September 2001.

[30] The SGMA reports also document the growth in fitness, aerobic classes and in-line skating, largely individual sports that, consistent with Putnam's 'bowling alone' thesis, may improve individual health but do not contribute as much to social capital building. We have concentrated, therefore, on organized sports for girls and women.

alongside the athletic involvement itself. Unlike many professional and even college-level men's sports, women's sports still largely require fund-raising, volunteers and community support. All this activity (as anybody who has spent time chatting with fellow parents on the sidelines of a game, or working the concession stand at a tournament, will attest) is an important form of community building and civic engagement. If we accept the Women's Sports Foundation conclusion, that currently some-thing like one in two high school girls, as opposed to one in twenty-seven in 1971, are involved in sports, then a veritable gold mine of social capital has developed over the last three decades. In sum, none of this 'civic par-ticipation' in women's athletics is measured in Putnam's analysis beyond that of the bowling league, through the WBC.

Two final important points. First, women's athletics provides us with a very important lesson as to the importance of the state and/or courts in unleashing certain kinds of social capital, particularly where there are profound historical obstacles to the full inclusion of all US citizens. In other words, the Tocquevillean idea of *voluntary* association, where the growth of social capital is left to itself, may not be strong enough to overcome the forces of exclusion and discrimination that have pre-vented subordinated groups of people, in this case women, from entering many public arenas, such as athletics. Thus, there is no question that Title IX (and the court cases that ensued) proved to be the critical factor in the flourishing of female sports, and, consequently, the social capi-tal that forms around them.[31] Secondly, social capital building through sports has the potential to be one form of bridging capital across eth-nic and racial divides, as Putnam points out in the concluding chapter of *Bowling Alone*, but there is still some distance to go on the full inclu-sion of a diversity of athletes, most particularly female athletes of colour (p. 411).

In the previous chapter we saw how ethnic exclusion both restricted and shaped the nature of social capital accumulation in the Progressive

---

[31] It is worth noting that Title IX, despite the benefits to women, is a controversial piece of legislation. One of its negative downsides has been its impact on men's sports other than the most popular ones – baseball, football and basketball. In recent years Title IX has been challenged in court by several men's athletic associations, including the National Wrestling Coaches Association, College Gymnastic Association and the US Track Coaches Association, along with other groups representing male athletes, who argued that Title IX is unconstitutional since it forces certain male sports to close down (such as wrestling) and therefore effectively discriminates against these particular male athletes. The lawsuit was dismissed by the Department of Justice on 29 May 2002. The Women's Sports Foundation raised concerns about this decision because the motion to dismiss did not explicitly defend the legality and validity of Title IX. 'The government simply told the Wrestling Coaches Association to sue the colleges and universities that discontinue the sport' (see www.womenssportsfoundation.org; accessed 12 June 2002).

Era, particularly with reference to women's civic engagement. Statistics from the NCAA suggest that female ethnic minorities still lag behind their male counterparts in terms of participation in sports at the collegiate level. While black men represented 17.9 per cent of all male student athletes at the college level as of 2002–2003, only 10.5 per cent of female athletes were black.[32] A report commissioned by the Women's Sports Foundation on race and Title IX (Butler and Lopiano, 2003) concludes that, while male athletes of colour in NCAA varsity sports were proportional to their presence in the student body (22 per cent), female athletes of colour were under-represented (14.8 per cent) relative to their numbers in the student body (24.9 per cent) (p. 5). The specific position of African-American women, who have to overcome the historical discrimination of both race and gender, should be given some careful examination. Once again, it may not be enough simply to depend on 'voluntary association' to overcome such obstacles but, rather, truly inclusive bridging social capital may once again require the state to implement an initiative equivalent to Title IX for female minority athletes. The Women's Sports Foundation recommends that all sports organizations collect participation data 'disaggregated by gender, race, disability and sport', and what is needed with respect to minority female athletes is a 'National Strategic Plan' in which 'groups primarily concerned with issues related to gender, race, ethnicity and disability . . . partner with the USOC, national sports governance organizations . . . to collaborate on the development of a strategic action plan to address the issue of sports segregation' (Butler and Lopiano, 2003, pp. 20–1).

There is an ironic footnote to the story on minority women's athletics, and strangely enough it brings us back to bowling. For the NCAA Committee on Women's Athletics has recommended, in the last few years, that four emerging sports should be put on the 'fast track' to championship status: water polo, ice hockey, squash and bowling. While the first three are recommended because they represent sports with the most number of female athletes apart from the existing championship sports, the last is recommended 'to increase the opportunities for female ethnic minorities'. Cheryl Levick, chair of the CWA and senior administrator at

---

[32] See NCAA (2003b). It is worth noting that the gap between men and women minority athletes varies in accordance with Division I, II, and III as well as specific sports. Most importantly, there is a significant gap in the statistics between male and female athletes of colour, particularly African-Americans. In 2002/3, in Division I, 24.6 per cent of male athletes were black, whereas only 14.8 per cent of female athletes were black; in Division II, 21.8 per cent of male athletes were black, but only 11.9 per cent female athletes were black; in Division III, 8.7 per cent of male athletes were black and only 5 per cent of female athletes were black. Thus, while gender equality may have grown within the athletic world, there are still gaps to be addressed, or minority women will not benefit from Title IX to the extent that they should.

Stanford University, comments: 'Bowling does not have the same numbers as the other sports do, but we're also looking at diversity issues. Bowling has a large number of ethnic minority participants' (Hawes, 1999). This understates the situation: in 2001/2, 82.2 per cent of the female athletes in this sport were black (NCAA, 2003b; Butler and Lopiano, 2003, p. 6). In a report issued at the end of 1999, the CWA recommended that the first NCAA championship occur in 2003/4, even if the required minimum of forty institutions was not met. 'This should be done to provide additional championship opportunities for minority females. Bowling currently is sponsored by 23 institutions, of which 20 historically are black colleges and universities' (NCAA, 1999). In April 2003 forty-two sponsoring institutions signed up, allowing the sport to reach NCAA championship status, and a six-member Championship Committee was announced in August that year.[33] The first championship was held in April 2004.

Hadassah, Moose (Women) and Girl Scouts are the last three associations in Putnam's list of women's organizations. They differ from the other eight, in that they have not declined in membership in the same way that the other organizations have. Indeed, if you look at the *graphs* in Putnam's appendix 3, these three organizations are virtually the only ones that have grown amongst *all* the associations (pp. 440–4). The pattern for Hadassah and Moose (Women) is one of steady growth from 1940 to the 1990s and then a decline. There is an important gender gap in the changing membership in both Moose (Women) and the Girl Scouts compared to their corollary male organizations. Male Moose membership has declined dramatically, from 1.307 million in 1991 to 935,000 in 2001, while female Moose membership during this same period has declined by much less, from 546,000 in 1992 to 506,000 in 2002.[34] Similarly, when you separate out the Girl Scouts from the Boy Scouts in terms of membership, which Putnam does not,[35] it turns out that the former

---

[33] *NCAA News*, 23 June 2003; *College Bowling USA News*, 20 August 2003, available at www.bowl.com (accessed December 2003).

[34] The male membership figures are from the August–October 2003 Moose Magazine Online 'Convention Issue', in which Director General Donald Ross lays out the dramatic decline amongst male Moose members. The female membership figure for 2002 is taken from the February–April 2003 issue of the same magazine, in the article entitled 'Sailing into the future'. This article also includes the following statement, which speaks to the different patterns of membership: 'Women's Moose membership is 52.8% of the amount of men's membership [in April 2002]; ten years ago, the same figure was just 41.8%.' The online magazine is available at www.mooseintl.org/moosemagazine; accessed December 2003.

[35] Putnam does not separate out Boy Scouts from Girl Scouts in his graphs. It is worth noting that his statistics (going up to 1997) predate the controversy surrounding the Boy Scouts over the exclusion of gays, and the efforts made by the Girl Scouts to attract a more diverse membership – as will be discussed shortly.

has increased in membership to its highest numbers ever while the latter has been in decline (Ladd, 1996, p. 14). These striking counter-examples to the overall pattern of decline, as well as the existence of a gender-gap, make these organizations particularly worthy of further investigation, for they may hold some insights as to how civic participation may be built in the future even in traditional organizations and how such solutions may need to be both gender- and culture-specific. It is a question that Putnam might have asked: what is it about these three organizations that causes them to exhibit a different pattern from the others? The reasons for growth are different in each case, but all three provide useful insights as to the impact of culture and gender on the nature of civic engagement in contemporary, and future, America.

Hadassah: the rise of identity and advocacy politics

Hadassah is the 'Women's Zionist Organization of America'. The growth in this organization after the Second World War, and then from 1970 to the early 1990s, is a reflection of two trends: the rise of identity and advocacy politics. The term 'identity politics' refers to the notion that groups are organized less around universal 'ideas' that transcend ethnic or cultural difference and more around the promotion of a self-consciously cultural, ethnic or religious identity.[36] Such identity politics are more often than not tied to specific kinds of advocacy, for identity-based associations almost always grow out of a history of discrimination, subordination and exclusion. Thus they advocate for the preservation of their group and identity against forces that may seek to discriminate against, eradicate or assimilate them. Needless to say, the history of the Jewish people in the twentieth century speaks very much to the idea of a persecuted group, particularly after the Second World War. Hadassah also reflects a specific *gender* identity, since it is focused on Jewish *women* in particular.

This shift from service to advocacy is given voice in Hadassah's self-description in the *Encyclopedia of Associations*. In 1984 Hadassah described its mission as the provision of 'many community services in US and Israel'. By 2002 this had changed to read the 'Women's Zionist and Jewish membership organization [that] promotes health education, Jewish education and research, volunteerism, social action and *advocacy*

---

[36] The actual number, as noted in the *Encyclopedia of Associations*, is a peak membership of 385,000 throughout the 1990s until 1999. In the last few years, interestingly, this figure has dropped, standing currently at 306,000. This decline is worth further investigation. Nevertheless, the increase in membership through to the late 1990s is quite different from that of other organizations.

in the US' (2002, emphasis added).[37] Hadassah's shift from a service agency to more of an advocacy organization is rooted not only in its commitment to the 'centrality of Israel' and to 'strengthen [its] partnership with Israel' but also in the domestic issues that affect religious minorities, such as the separation of state and Church, as well as women's issues, such as domestic violence.[38] The growth of identity and advocacy groups is a broad trend within civil society, and like the Women's Bowling Congress, which gave us a window into the broader question of women's athletics, I want to use Hadassah as a window into the rise of identity and advocacy politics, particularly in light of the critical scholarship by leading academics such as Theda Skocpol (1999, 2002, 2004) and Robert Putnam, who argue that the shift from service to advocacy is largely a negative development. Let us consider the critique first, before we examine two specific cases of this new kind of civic advocacy in more depth.

Skocpol has written extensively about transitions in American civic life. In recent articles she laments the shift from older, chapter-based service federations to what she calls a 'civic America dominated by centralized, staff-driven *advocacy* associations' that are eroding 'bridges between classes and places' (1999, p. 500).[39] She appeals for the return to an older form of association, rooted in seemingly 'universal' values that bridge different groups, regardless of cultural background or gender. As we have seen, however, in the previous chapter, such 'universal' projects are often culturally specific in reality (Protestant-American) and carry with them particular implications for those groups of Americans who deviate in some sense from these shared norms. Putnam, in a similar kind of analysis in his chapter on social movements in *Bowling Alone*, suggests that, while the large scale civil rights movements of the 1960s were positive since they tended to create more civic participation, the move towards 'social movement *organizations*' is, in his own words, 'another matter' (p. 153). Like Skocpol, Putnam describes these newer associations as 'often Washington-based, full-time, professional, staff-run organizations,

---

[37] This is not to say that Hadassah is *only* an advocacy organization, for it continues to pursue its long-standing work to support social services and healthcare projects, but various events during the twentieth century – from the Holocaust, to the creation of the state of Israel to UN resolutions on Zionism – created a changing political environment that has fostered both a stronger sense of identity politics and the need to lobby Washington from this particular cultural/religious, gendered perspective.

[38] See www.hadassah.org/about; accessed December 2003.

[39] Indeed, Skocpol made this the subject of her APSA presidential address in 2003 (published in *Perspectives on Politics* the next year). It is important to note that Skocpol is not referring specifically to Hadassah in her comments, but Hadassah, nevertheless, provides us with an interesting case study on this growth in both advocacy and identity politics *within* an older organization.

with "social entrepreneurs" cultivating comfortable conscience constituencies' (p. 153). In answering the question on the civic legacy of the
1960s social movements, Putnam states that the 'civil rights movement
was receding by the 1970s and the women's movement began to decline
after the defeat of the ERA [Equal Rights Amendment] in 1982' (p. 155).
He then largely limits his discussion of social movement organizations
that grew out of this period to environmental groups, and casts them as
largely recruit-driven, hierarchical, symbolic associations (pp. 155–8). At
the conclusion of this discussion he compares the 'old-fashioned' associations listed in appendix 3 with these more recent forms of organizations,
clearly preferring the former to the latter.

At the heart of this vision (for both Skocpol and Putnam) is an
older vision of civic society constituted by 'grass-roots organizations' that
'involve their members directly in *community*-based activity' (Putnam,
2000, p. 53). Both Skocpol and Putnam make a connection between
civic society, 'community' and 'grass-roots' or 'chapter-based' organizations. The community that underpins this version of civic society is a
geographically defined place: the local neighbourhood, with all its multiple constituencies, rather than a group of people that might span a large
geographic space but be tied by similar experiences to social rather than
geographic factors (for example, the gay community, the Jewish community or the disabled community). The definition of 'community' has been
debated at great length by both political and philosophical communitarians over the last twenty years (Etzioni, 1995, 2000; Sandel, 1984). What is
clear, at the beginning of the twenty-first century, is that there are many
different kinds of communities, including ones that do not necessarily
share a geographical location and yet may be described as a community
nonetheless.[40] If one accepts this definition of 'community' then what,
in turn, constitutes 'community-based activity' will necessarily alter. If
the meaning of community-based activity changes, then the nature of the
relationship between the membership and its goals will also change; this
does not necessarily mean that these people are any less 'members' of
their groups than the traditional organizations. Thus, Putnam's generalized assumption that members of newer kinds of advocacy associations
are more 'consumers' than 'members', who tend to be united by 'symbolic ties' rather than 'real ties to real people' (p. 158), points to a failure
to acknowledge different kinds of communities and the specific nature of
the relationship between such communities and their membership. While

---

[40] Amitai Etzioni argues, for example, that 'community' can be defined by two criteria:
a shared moral culture and social bonds of affection. Thus, for Etzioni there is such a
thing as a 'gay community', which may not be located in a defined geographical place
but nonetheless shares a moral culture and a social bond (2001).

the ties between members of, for example, the 'gay community' may not be like 'the personal ties among the guys' in the 'local American Legion', they are nonetheless 'real ties' that stretch across geographical boundaries. Moreover, the gay community has a very different relationship to the larger civic society in America exactly because of their historical experience of exclusion and discrimination (to the extent that state referenda in the 2004 election overwhelmingly rejected same-sex marriage, the issue of discrimination can be described as not just historical but current as well).

Skocpol's critique of the shift towards advocacy in associational life is based on a number of different elements, which she tends to combine in her analysis but need to be separated out if we are to understand fully whether 'advocacy' is the negative shift that both Putnam and Skocpol perceive it to be.[41] Skocpol begins by distinguishing between three types of associational politics that emerge after the Second World War (1999, 2004). The first group consists of associations that are 'organizing for equality', namely minority and women's associations. As figures from Debra Minkoff demonstrate, women and racial ethnic groups shift from service orientation to advocacy after 1970. These organizations, which seek to bring about legislative change, are frequently based in Washington or New York (Skocpol, 1999, pp. 471–2). The second group of advocacy associations is public interest or citizens' organizations, which are also largely based in Washington (ranging from environmental groups to organizations devoted to reforming politics or ending child poverty). Finally, there are trade and professional associations, which grew in absolute numbers after the Second World War but have declined in recent times. Interestingly, Skocpol concludes that business associations have declined during the last four decades relative to the total number of American associations, from 42 per cent to 17.5 per cent (2004). This reinforces her thesis that advocacy, based on the first two constituencies, is taking over associational life. Civic life, she argues, has changed from one focused on the local 'community' to one based in Washington seeking legislative change; from one that bridges across sub-communities to one that focuses on a particular identity; from one that is based around 'shared values' to one that increasingly sows dissent and division over long-accepted norms; from one that is chapter-based to one that is bureaucratic and litigious. All these changes, in sum, constitute a largely negative shift in American civic society, according to Skocpol.

---

[41] Putnam writes about this transformation in his chapter on social movements, limiting himself to the environmental organizations without looking at other types of advocacy-oriented groups that might also have grown out of the 1960s, including the gay/lesbian, disability or women's associations.

Unlike Putnam, and Skocpol, I would argue not only that the meaning of 'community' needs to be rethought but that the transformation in civic engagement, from service to advocacy politics, should be seen in a much more *positive* light than they allow.[42] The shift from service to advocacy is rooted in the decision by some advocacy groups to move beyond simply servicing the needs of the marginalized and address why such needs exist. This change in orientation and the response it elicits is succinctly summarized in the famous words of Helder Camara, the Archbishop of Recife, Brazil: 'When I feed the poor they call me a saint. When I ask why the poor have no food, they call me a communist.'[43] The shift towards advocacy, in other words, represents the politicization of marginalization, where civic engagement is not simply about serving those who have been marginalized by mainstream society but advocating changes that will improve their position or status. Thus the shift towards advocacy, when seen from the perspective of those who have been, for a variety of reasons, excluded from, or felt the discrimination of, the American 'civic community', is a positive development towards a more just and inclusive community. Identity politics are key, for political advocacy over the last forty years has been concerned not only with the poor but with those groups that have been discriminated against based on religious, cultural or gendered identities. In the spirit of Camara, this shift towards advocacy on behalf of a particular identity should not be seen as politically suspect but a call for justice via broad political and societal change.

At the heart of this new identity politics is a paradigm shift in democratic theorizing about justice, from a Rawlsian distributive paradigm that sought to address the needs of the least well-off economically to a principle of the recognition of difference that not only embraces but protects and preserves cultural diversity and specificity.[44] This latter notion of justice, called the 'politics of recognition' by Canadian philosopher

---

[42] This is not to say that all aspects of this shift in civic life are positive. As Skocpol points out, some advocacy associations are centralized, less than democratic, 'staff-driven' and tend to see their supporters as customers rather than members. Her critique (and that of Putnam's) is an important one, which needs to be taken up by every association (particularly those seeking gender or cultural justice) to ensure that the cause does not supercede the principles of participation and democracy. On the other hand, as I argue shortly, for gay and lesbian and disabled Americans alike, this kind of centralized and legally oriented organizational form was critical to *opening up* civic society to these particular groups of American citizens.

[43] 'Brazil's Helder Camara, champion of the poor, dies at 90', Agence France Presse, 28 August 1999.

[44] Several political theorists have described the need for a paradigm shift in thinking about justice within democratic theory over the last two decades, from a distributive model (Rawls) to a 'recognition of difference' model (Taylor, 1994; Young, 1990; Fraser, 1998).

Charles Taylor, claims that many of society's injustices arise not only from an inequitable distribution of economic goods but from the lack of recognition, or misrecognition, of certain group identities in mainstream society.

The thesis is that our identity is partly shaped by recognition or its absence, often by the misrecognition of others, and so a person or group of people can suffer real damage, real distortion, if the people or society around them mirror back to them a confining or demeaning or contemptible picture of themselves. Nonrecognition or misrecognition can inflict harm, can be a form of oppression, imprisoning someone in a false, distorted, and reduced mode of being. (Taylor, 1994, p. 25)

Two obvious historical examples of 'misrecognition' that led to particular forms of advocacy politics are racial equality through the growth of civil rights organizations and gender empowerment through the growth of feminist organizations. I would like to consider in more depth, however, two other specific (but often overlooked) examples of civic engagement via identity and advocacy: the community of people with disabilities and the American gay and lesbian/queer community.[45] In both cases, people in these communities faced the strongest forms of exclusion in the first half of the twentieth century, as discussed in the last chapter, including policies of eradication (either through court-sponsored sterilization, in the case of mentally disabled Americans, or psychotherapy to 'create' heterosexuality, in the case of homosexuals) based on one aspect of their identity. In response to this history, the 1970s and 1980s ushered in the rise of advocacy politics by lesbian/gay organizations as well as associations representing Americans with disabilities against some powerful counter-forces. In both cases, this growth in civic participation seems to be overlooked by Putnam and Skocpol, absorbed as they are by a generalized view that advocacy associations and divisive battles over identity are largely negative developments in a generally declining American civic community, or that the struggle for civil rights ended with the fight over racial and gender inclusion in the 1970s.

---

[45] Queer theorists express concern that the designation of 'gay and lesbian' tends to marginalize transgendered, bisexual and transsexual individuals, as well as dichotomizing sexuality into 'hetero' versus 'homo' sexuality when there is in fact a multiplicity of sexualities in existence that do not easily fit into such a binary opposition (Butler, 1990; Phelan, 2001). They also suggest that queer theory must go beyond an appeal to civil rights within existing norms of liberal civic society to a more radical appeal to 'queering' citizenship (Butler, 1990; Phelan, 2001). This is a powerful critique of the way in which identity is constructed through language. My central concern in this chapter is the ways in which the gay/lesbian/queer community has been both excluded from civil society and liberal institutions (such as marriage and the military) and subject to pressure through civic society to 'normalize' their behaviour, as well as how this community has resisted such forces of exclusion and assimilation.

Let us begin with Americans with disabilities. In the early part of the twentieth century the idea that disability was an 'affliction' of God, and therefore something that simply had to be borne by the afflicted, can be seen in many of the words that were used in relation to the disabled: infirm, feeble, invalid, cripple, incapable. For anybody so labelled, he/she was beyond any possibility of returning to a 'normal' body or 'mind'. This notion of affliction gradually gave way to notions of rehabilitation throughout the twentieth century. The growth of rehabilitation, and with it the language of 'handicapped' as opposed to 'crippled', was an important cultural shift, and rooted, according to Henri-Jacques Stiker, in the First World War. As injured and disabled soldiers came back from the front, it was necessary to find a way to reintegrate them into society: thus 'rehabilitation' was born. Nonetheless, rehabilitation 'implies returning to a point, to a *prior* situation, the situation that existed for the able but one only postulated for the others' (Stiker, 1999, p. 122). Thus, individuals with disabilities are to be integrated back into society, through physical, medical and therapeutic means. As such, disability came to be seen as a medical problem for the 'individual', who with the right therapy might be transformed into a 'normal' human being.

These two strong currents regarding disability (namely pity and medical rehabilitation) dominated much of the twentieth century in America, and are reflected in both the mainstream civic associations dealing with disability and the state's approach to the disabled up until the advent of the civil rights revolution, as manifest in the fight for the Americans with Disabilities Act in the 1980s. Thus, during the first half of the century there were a handful of disability associations that grew out of the twin ideas of rehabilitation and medical recovery. The National Amputation Foundation grew out of the First World War to service amputee war veterans in their rehabilitation back to work. Goodwill Industries, founded in 1902 by a Methodist minister, sought to provide working opportunities for people of 'limited employability'.[46] The National Easter Seal Society was formed originally as the National Society for Crippled Children, by Edgar F. Allen in 1919, to spearhead a drive to create medical facilities for children with disabilities. In 1929 the National Easter Seal Society developed a separate international organization, which was renamed Rehabilitation International in 1972 (Fleischer and Zames, 2001, p. 11).

A second group of organizations, which arose in the first half of the twentieth century, tended to focus on people (more particularly children) with disabilities as victims to be pitied. Charities were born around a

---

[46] This information is provided by the organizations themselves or through the *Encyclopedia of Associations*.

specific disability and its cause (rather than effect). Organizations from the March of Dimes to the United Cerebral Palsy Association to the Muscular Dystrophy Association adopted a charitable view of people with disabilities along with a 'medical model' of disability: the goal was to raise funds either to find a cure or prevent a particular disability altogether. From the beginning, these groups found that 'emphasizing children proved to be an effective way of raising funds' (Fleischer and Zames, p. 10). In its most extreme form, particular associations took pity to a new height with the advent of television and the electronic telethon.

The techniques used in later years by the telethons were far more blatant and undignified. Real children with disabilities were paraded across the stage as objects of pity, while the amount of money raised was flashed on the television screen. (Fleischer and Zames, p. 10)

These organizations are classic examples of traditional service-oriented and locally federated associations. They raised enormous amounts of money to provide resources for further research into the relevant disabilities and were often the only organization outside the family to give support to individuals and their families living with various kinds of disabilities. But there were also troubling aspects to these philanthropic organizations, seen from the perspective of those who lived with a disability.[47]

First, they tended to focus on disability as something to be pitied; moreover, some scholars have argued that the tendency to use children (who presumably generate more sympathy) to raise funds tended to negate, at least in the general public's mind, the reality of adults who continued to live with the same disabilities. Secondly, because the focus was on finding the *cause* of the disability, money was often raised to fund research in order to try and prevent the disability in the first place. The ethical questions raised by this objective are, in the era of the human genome, particularly profound. For example, the Muscular Dystrophy Association used funds raised to research genetic screening to eliminate MD altogether. It is ultimately ironic, as Fleischer and Zames note, that 'Jerry's kids are . . . raising money to find a way to prevent their ever having been born' (p. 11). The ethical issue revolves around whether disabilities (and which kinds) should be seen through a cultural lens, as part of the diversity of human life in all its multiple forms and therefore something that should be preserved, or through a medical lens, as a 'disease' that needs to be eliminated.

---

[47] To their credit, some of the older disability organizations have recognized the need for independent living and self-advocacy, and made changes to reflect this paradigm shift in American society.

Some service organizations, such as Goodwill, created special 'enter-prises' or workplaces for mentally disabled people. Again, at the time these were often the only alternatives available to families with disabled members, but the thrust of such special enterprises was to separate off individuals from the mainstream of society. The state reflected the same underlying idea of segregation in the development of 'special educa-tion' classes. Thus, from the perspective of many 'service' associations dealing with disability up until the 1980s, people with disabilities were either patients to be rehabilitated, victims who required charity or people for whom separate spaces needed to be created. People with disabili-ties were often the 'objects' or causes (around which these associations developed, either as patients for rehabilitation or victims for charity) rather than subjects or self-advocates – in a word, *members* – of their own associations. As we shall see, the civil rights movement to whom the framework and impetus for making possible the transition from object to subject; from being a person to whom 'help' or charity was pro-vided to being a citizen with rights and a member of the mainstream community.

The American state's relationship to people with disabilities (before the Americans with Disabilities Act was passed in 1990) was also defined by the principles of pity, rehabilitation and segregation. For example, in the Rehabilitation Act of 1973 the focus, as the name would suggest, was on rehabilitating the 'disabled' to be 'normal'. Within this piece of legislation, however, specifically Section 504, were the seeds of a new paradigm for disability, that of civil rights rather than medical rehabili-tation.[48] This section and the fight by then President Nixon to water it down provided an important source of civic engagement for people with disabilities, as 'the battle over Section 504 regulations gave voice to the disability community' (Young, 1997, p. 23).

Thus, over the last three decades, beginning with Section 504 of the Rehabilitation Act of 1973 and culminating in the Americans with Disabilities Act, disability groups (and the number of lawyers employed to further their cause) have grown in number and strength. At the heart of this growth is the goal of *independent* membership in American society (defined in terms of citizenship), as opposed to *dependent* living (on either medical or social welfare or charity). As a result, many of the newer disability organizations began with a twofold strategy: supporting individuals with disabilities to become independent and integrated into mainstream society, coupled with pushing the larger society to make the

---

[48] Section 504 is described as 'the provision with the most far-reaching repercussions, provided civil rights for people with disabilities in programs receiving federal financial assistance' (Fleischer and Zames, 2001, p. 49).

necessary accommodations to allow for such independence. This latter goal of accessibility is an important shift, because it represents a reconceptualization of the nature of disability: rather than being defined as *an individual's* problem (either an affliction or medical obstacle to be rehabilitated), disability became a social and political question of how laws and institutions have failed to counter the obstacles to full citizenship in the physical environment. To change such long-standing structures and the philosophies that underpinned them, the disability community found it necessary to amass a strong and focused lobby in Washington.

This transformation over the last two decades from service to advocacy and empowerment is represented, in associational terms, by the shift from community-based service and philanthropy organizations, such as Easter Seals (founded 1919), Goodwill Industries (1902) and the March of Dimes (1938), to advocacy organizations, such as the Disability Rights Education and Defense Fund (1979), the National Council on Independent Living (1982), the Disability Rights Center (1976) and the American Disability Association (1991). The pattern of growth in these associations is very different from the trend described by Putnam in *Bowling Alone*. The *Encyclopedia of Associations* list seventy-five organizations under 'disability', 64 per cent of which (forty-eight) were founded between 1970 and 1990. Thus there was an enormous growth in associational life around the issue of disability during this period, and much of it was centred on advocacy, rights and independent living. Unlike earlier organizations, many of these were run by and for people with disabilities – that is, they were truly members of these advocacy associations, as opposed to being the 'cause' for previous service-based organizations. Perhaps most importantly for the larger American community, it was only as a result of these advocacy-based organizations that the Americans with Disabilities Act was passed in 1990.

Two important points arise out of this disability story. The first is that, despite all the civic engagement that developed around civil rights and the ADA, this civic participation is not acknowledged or measured by Putnam in either the civic participation or social movement chapters, despite the fact that they have been growing and their impact has been profound. As Senator Tom Harkin has said of the role of disability organizations in making the ADA law:

Within a few weeks the ADA will become the law of the land because of the vision of the disability community. You knew in your hearts what we now write into law – that discrimination based on fear, ignorance, prejudice, and indifference is wrong. It is true that I am the sponsor of the ADA and my colleagues are cosponsors. However, the ADA is first and foremost the outcome of the extraordinary efforts of the disability community. This is your bill, and you earned it. (Young, 1997, p. 11)

Although it is difficult to measure, the ultimate impact of the ADA on civic engagement is enormous, both through the involvement of people with disabilities in specific disability-related associations and, more importantly, through the increased level of accessibility that people with disabilities have to join *any* community organization, which might have been completely inaccessible prior to the ADA. There may even be some crude evidence, from the *Encyclopedia of Associations*, to support the idea that advocacy is now in decline since the ADA was passed, while other kinds of activities for people with disabilities is on the upswing. While the 1970s and 1980s witnessed an explosion in the number of disability-related associations formed (due to both the civil rights reorientation and the fight for the ADA), in the 1990s only a few organizations related specifically to disability were founded, and the majority of those in the first half of the decade. This might be regarded as a sign of decline in civic participation amongst people with disabilities – or it could represent the development suggested above, that people with disabilities, having won the fight to be included as equals in society, are no longer forming associations related to their disability alone but, rather, with the greater accessibility of buildings and transportation (as a result of ADA), are choosing to participate in other kinds of civic activities, unrelated to their disability. If this is indeed the case, it would represent an important victory for the idea of inclusion within American civil society. The one exception to this mainstreaming of civic activity would be the growth of disabled sports associations that serve to facilitate competition amongst disabled athletes. As with female athletics, this emerging area of athletic involvement needs to be incorporated into the overall story of civic participation at the beginning of the twenty-first century. The 2002 edition of the *Encyclopedia of Associations*, for example, lists thirty different disabled sports organizations, which would no doubt also be reflected in the growing number of disabled athletes, from the level of Paralympics to local, community-based activities.[49]

Beyond the actual measurement of the civic participation of the disabled is the value of advocacy for this particular group of Americans. Put simply, it is not the negative shift suggested by Skocpol and Putnam at all if one accepts that the ADA has been a net benefit to civic life in America, even though *all* the characteristics of advocacy listed by Skocpol are present among the disability rights organizations: that they changed from service to advocacy and legally oriented organizations; that they often based themselves in Washington rather than local communities in order

---

[49] All the figures in this paragraph are taken from the *Encyclopedia of Associations* (2002), Vol. I, *National Organizations of the US*, part 2, pp. 1281–90.

to lobby for the ADA; and that they focused on their particular 'identity' and what was specifically required for people with disabilities to have equal access. Finally, they challenged the existing norms of American society's view of disability in a divisive battle over the meaning of 'disability' and the norm of 'inclusion'. All these aspects of civic engagement were not only positive but also necessary if people with disabilities were to gain the important legal tool of the ADA in their quest for independence and full citizenship. This need for a strong advocacy role that was powerful, centralized and focused was particularly acute given that the opponents of the ADA included the 'National Federation of Independent Business, the US Chamber of Commerce . . . the Restaurant Association, Greyhound buses . . . as well as conservative elements in the Republican Party' (Fleischer and Zames, 2001, p. 99).

The gay/lesbian/queer community represents another form of advocacy politics based on a historically subordinated identity.[50] As with the disability community, in the last thirty years there has been an explosion of organizations representing gay and lesbian people and advocating legislative change on issues ranging from the right to marry, hate crimes, military service and adoption rights. Increasingly the gay/lesbian community has turned to advocacy within the American community in order to ensure equal civil rights, regardless of sexual orientation.[51] Like disability, homosexuality was seen largely through a medical lens for most of American history, as something that should be eradicated, suppressed, rehabilitated, pitied or cured. It is clear that Sigmund Freud, from a letter he wrote to an American mother who had sought advice regarding the possibility of 'curing' her homosexual son, in which he concluded that psychoanalysis might not bring about the desired results, did not really doubt that homosexuality was 'abnormal' or an appropriate subject for 'treatment'.

By asking me if . . . I can abolish homosexuality and make normal heterosexuality take its place. The answer is in a general way, we cannot promise to achieve it . . . It is a question of the quality and the age of the individual. The result of the treatment cannot be predicted. (Kaplan, 1997, p. 76)[52]

---

[50] There is a growing literature on the gay and lesbian rights movement and organizations; see Rimmerman et al. (2000) and Button et al. (1997).

[51] This is not to say that gay men and lesbians have always been mutually supportive or have the same goals. Indeed, as Diane Helene Miller suggests: 'At times, the two movements' goals have coincided and they have joined together to pursue mutually beneficial ends . . . on other occasions, the two groups have worked with a complete disregard for each other or even at cross-purposes' (Miller, 1998, p. 2).

[52] Freud's view of 'normal' sexuality should be seen in the wider context that he wished to challenge the American psychiatric community's 'moralizing tendencies' and to avoid seeing homosexuality as either a 'vice' or a 'crime' (Kaplan, pp. 75–7).

This fundamental view of homosexuality as abnormality, 'illness' or a disease to be cured (if possible) was the catalyst for the growth of the gay/lesbian associations of the 1970s. As with disability, the focus was on challenging how society defined 'normal' and the pressure through a myriad of scientific enterprises to make those who were 'abnormal' conform to society's norms.

The emergence of a renewed movement for lesbian and gay rights and liberation in the wake of the Stonewall Rebellion of 1969 very quickly focused attention on the ways in which medical, psychiatric, and psychological judgments and institutions contributed to the marginalization of lesbian and gay male citizens. (Kaplan, p. 74)

Consequently, almost all the gay/lesbian associations listed in the *Encyclopedia of Associations* have emerged in the last thirty years. Many of them are associated with the medical or psychiatric communities, schools and universities; others are associated with the families of gay men and lesbian women (including the 80,000 membership of Parents, Families and Friends of Lesbians and Gays, founded in 1981). But, once again, like the disability community, there are numerous organizations devoted to civil rights. The National Gay and Lesbian Task Force and the Lambda Legal Defense and Education Fund (both founded in 1973) are both focused on defending the civil rights of gay persons.[53] Given the historical subordination of gay men and lesbians, it is, again, not surprising that these organizations, formed after Stonewall, would adopt an advocacy model to overcome the enormous obstacles to their full acceptance and inclusion in the American community – a project that is ongoing. While Putnam acknowledges Stonewall and its significance in his chapter on social movements, he fails to recognize or measure the many organizations that grew out of this event and give voice to the gay/lesbian/queer community.

Like disability, gay and lesbian associations faced (and face) formidable opposition, in particular from the Christian right (Rimmerman, 2002, pp. 122–54). Interestingly for Putnam's thesis, Rimmerman suggests that the gay and lesbian movements need to 'develop their own sophisticated grassroots mobilizing and organizing strategies at the local and state levels' if they are truly to challenge the Christian right, who are very organized at the local level, through their churches. Thus, Rimmerman supports Putnam's notion of the need for *grass-roots* organizations, but not so much to build community as a tactical device to do battle over incommensurable values. The critical point here is that it may be impossible

---

[53] *Encyclopedia of Associations* (2002), Vol. I, *National Organizations of the US*, part 2, pp. 1312–16.

to build both communities simultaneously, to *bridge* their differences. Just one example: a vote taken in June 2002 by the Anglican diocese of Vancouver to allow bishops to bless same-sex unions has split the Church, both within the community and the world at large – a rift that is deeply felt by both sides and may be irresolvable for the foreseeable future.[54] There are at stake, on both sides of this argument (traditional Church versus same-sex unions), deeply held and *incommensurable* values; advocacy and rights for certain groups of people may thus ultimately be antithetical to more traditional notions of community building, particularly if they are rooted in a specific theological view.[55]

Moreover, as some commentators have noted, there is an equally compelling story to be told within the American gay community about local civic engagement and AIDS. As Denis Altman, in his review of *Bowling Alone*, entitled 'Case to the contrary', comments:

It is striking that [Putnam] totally omits one of the most remarkable examples of the creation of social capital in recent US history, namely the community-based responses to AIDS. Starting with safe-sex programs . . . and encompassing the creation of large support and educational organizations . . . and a huge range of cultural and political responses . . . AIDS generated an extraordinarily broad response . . . This response was essentially the product of a pre-existing sense of shared *identity* and community of gay people around their sexuality. The very idea of People with AIDS grew directly out of gay liberationist ideas of 'coming out' and asserting an otherwise *invisible identity*. (Altman, 2001, pp. 3–4)

Finally, it is important to recognize that within both the gay/lesbian and disability communities there is diverse opinion as to the best way to advance the interests of historically marginalized groups. An important distinction can be drawn between those who plead for inclusion (within an overarching liberal paradigm of everybody is the same regardless of race, gender, disability or sexual orientation) and those who advocate a more radical view of either sexuality or 'disability' that argues for the need not simply to be included in the existing community but to change the very norms by which American society is currently governed. Thus, for example, queer theorists such as Judith Butler (1990) and Shane Phelan (2001), as well as Deaf theorists such as Lennard Davis (1995, 1997)

---

[54] The North American Anglican/Episcopalian Churches are largely on the same side on this particular issue (in support of gay clergy and blessing same-sex marriages), but the divisions within the Church are deep.

[55] It is worth noting that, in the section directly following his analysis of the environmental associations, Putnam discusses the recent growth of the Evangelical Church in the United States and, more importantly, that 'the traditional repugnance . . . for political involvement [has been] gradually reversed' (p. 161). The rise of political and conservative Christianity needs to be seen not only as a source of social capital but, simultaneously, as a potential obstacle to civic engagement, particularly for gays and lesbians.

and Harlan Lane (1997), argue – as Charles Taylor has – that equality of treatment is not enough; rather, justice requires the recognition of difference and protection of cultural diversity from either the dominant culture of 'heteronormativity' or 'Oralism' respectively. Put simply, rather than attempting to live in accordance with majority norms that may do damage to their sense of self or community, the politics of queer and Deaf activists involves resistance to these norms and the active preservation of a unique cultural identity.[56]

Thus the Deaf community, who see themselves as a linguistic minority group rather than individuals with disabilities, require not so much inclusion in a hearing or 'Oralist' world as respect for and preservation of cultural difference. Similarly, queer theorists such as Phelan argue that sexual minorities are really not members or citizens at all (beyond the formal meaning of the term) but rather 'strangers', who are 'neither us nor clearly them, not friend and not enemy, but a figure of ambivalence who troubles the border between us and them. The enemy is the clear opposite of the citizen, but the stranger is fraught with anxiety' (Phelan, 2001, p. 5). Exactly because queer Americans are 'strangers' in American communities, the simple idea of inclusion and equality as same treatment advocated by gay/lesbian rights activists does not get to the heart of the problem. Phelan concludes that

strategies of equality . . . must always be attuned to the difference between equality and sameness. The position of the [sexual] stranger is not only difficult it is rewarding. Let us not abandon it for a citizenship that abandons others and suffocates that in each of us that does not fit; instead, I hope to help imagine and enact a postmodern citizenship of solidarity . . . in which many bodies, many passions, many families, many workers, find a place. (Phelan, 2001, p. 8)

The key in both cases is not simply to adapt oneself to the existing norms of American community and citizenship but to challenge the norms themselves, from a position that is both outside and within American community.

Thus, identity politics (whether it involves advocacy for inclusion through same treatment or diversity and difference through preservation of difference) sits uneasily with Putnam and Skocpol's vision of a larger shared community. In the short term, identity politics (aimed either at equality for gays and lesbians or inclusion for the disabled, or, even more so, the recognition of difference demanded by queer theorists and Deaf cultural advocates) sow very divisive seeds indeed for the 'American' community and its 'shared values' as they have long been understood.

---

[56] For the distinction between 'deafness' as a disability and 'Deafness' as a linguistic or cultural minority designation, see Lane (1997).

While Skocpol and Putnam claim that what is missing in America today is the 'sense of brotherhood or sisterhood and shared American citizenship' that once animated earlier civic organizations (Skocpol, 1999, pp. 500–1), advocacy groups (particularly those looking for inclusion/respect of difference) are demonstrating by their growing numbers that such a call for solidarity and 'shared citizenship' based on universal norms or values is premature. Advocacy for these groups is rooted in a continuing sense that the American 'community' should either not solidify until it reflects a set of norms that is truly inclusive and/or mutually respectful of all *or*, from some perspectives, that it should *never* fully bridge the differences between the majority and minority because of the inherent power that the former has over the latter.

Ultimately, the assumption underpinning the social capital literature is that unity and the overcoming of difference should be the overarching objective of American democracy, and civil society should not be a site of contestation as transcendence.[57] Accordingly, civic associations dedicated to such goals are the true builders of community, whereas those groups that seek to advocate a particular minority point of view (against the dominant model) or that emphasize difference or engage in potentially divisive legal tactics over certain key issues are seen as negative forces for both a stable democracy and the accumulation of social capital. But the question at stake, particularly for these historically marginalized groups, is not just whether we can build a community and social capital but, rather, whether we can build a *just* community and *just* social capital. To put it another way, it is not just the amount of connectedness that matters but also the *nature* of those connections: to what extent do certain kinds of communities or connections serve either to empower or to dis-empower particular individuals or groups?

Ultimately, for equity- or diversity-seeking groups, there is no solidarity or set of values upon which the American community may yet combine to share, for the very terms and conditions of 'community' are still under negotiation. Whether it will ever be possible to reconcile a multicultural and diverse population with the socially cohesive republican ideals of the American community is the very stuff of current debates in democratic theory.[58] This question becomes particularly acute in light of

---

[57] Another way of putting this is the basic suggestion by Skocpol, albeit one originally coined by Tocqueville, that the 'knowledge of how to combine' is 'vital to democracy' (1999, p. 462).

[58] Much of the literature on multiculturalism and liberalism (Taylor, Barry, Kymlicka, Eisenberg), deliberative democracy (Habermas, Cohen, Dryzek) and agonistic theories of democracy (Schmitt, Mouffe) is engaged in this very question. There is, of course, a profound danger to such 'factionalism' and division within any community, as American thinkers going back to the founding of the United States have argued. The answer to

11 September 2001 and the research done subsequently by Putnam on the inverse correlation between social capital and cultural diversity. This concrete question will be explored in more depth in the penultimate chapter of this book.

Finally, it is important to note that the shift towards Washington-based legal associations underlines the belief for some of these equality-seeking identity groups, such as the gay/lesbian and disabled organizations, that the power of the *state* and *courts* is required to address the profound *political* issues that arise in relation to the historical and current discrimination experienced by minority cultures. Thus, the idea that civil society is the key to restoring democracy rings hollow for those still seeking justice. Gay and lesbian Americans who wish to be participants in such basic liberal institutions as marriage or the military may organize around these issues in civic society but, ultimately, they require the coercive power of the law to change existing discriminatory practices, as a counterweight to a society that may still deny same-sex couples the right to marry or join the military openly. To this end, the state and superior courts are potential tools in changing the prevailing norms and create communities that are just, respectful of difference and, where appropriate, inclusive.

To return to where we started: Hadassah may not seem, at first glance, to conform to the kinds of organizations that Skocpol and Putnam are critiquing since it is an old, service-based federation.[59] In many ways, however, Hadassah reflects exactly the kind of shift in its own organizational structure and mandate critiqued by Skocpol and Putnam. While it is an organization built upon traditional concerns with health and social welfare (a continuing mandate), there has been, as suggested above, an increasing emphasis on advocacy, identity politics (both gender and religious minority) and lobbying in Washington. For example, their official website is organized around a number of political campaigns, from supporting the interests of Israel and Jewish people around the world, to fighting domestic violence, to legislation on hate crimes and equal pay.[60] Hadassah in its work in Israel also recognizes the dangers of divisive politics. Their support for such projects as the Jerusalem Hadassah Medical

---

current-day versions of identity divisions, however, is not to wish away such divisive politics but to embrace them in the search for a truly inclusive *and* mutually respectful and diverse community.

[59] In fact, Putnam uses Hadassah as an example of an 'old-fashioned' organization in his analysis of environmental associations because the former is constituted by 'real ties to real people', as opposed to the symbolic ties of the latter (p. 158). While it is true that Hadassah has local chapters, it nevertheless is different from the other organizations for two reasons, as discussed: its increasing emphasis on advocacy, and the focus on a particular religious, gendered and cultural identity.

[60] See www.hadassah.org; accessed December 2003.

Centre, which treats all patients, regardless of religious or national identification, is one such example:

Medicine, the motto goes, is a bridge to peace, and every patient gets equal treatment here. The hospital is one of the few places left in Israel where you still see Jews and Arabs together. There may be no greater equalizer than a waiting room. Throughout Hadassah, you'll see Jews helping Arabs, and Arabs helping Jews. (CBS, 2003)

On the issue of gender identity, Hadassah has developed specific programmes with regard to Jewish *women*, taking seriously the objective of gender empowerment. As Bernice Tannenbaum, a past national president of Hadassah and founder of Hadassah International, comments:

On many levels we have moved forward – with a foundation to raising the self-esteem and leadership potential of women and girls in the United States and Israel; with scholarship through the Hadassah-Brandeis Research Institute on Jewish Women; with the Hadassah Leadership Academy. (Tannenbaum, 2002)[61]

In addition, ethnic identity is a primary focus of this organization. In particular, they have been active in attempting to overturn the 'Zionism is racism' resolutions at the United Nations during the 1980s, and more recently lobbying against the general tenor of the debate and resolutions passed at the UN Conference in Durban, South Africa. Hadassah has also recognized in its formal structure the multiple identities amongst Jewish women (including age, disability, profession and marital status). As one member, Laurie Weitz, describes her decision to join Hadassah:

What hooked me was the organization's ability to constantly reevaluate itself and adapt to the changing, multiplying and diverse needs of Jewish women. We have remained strong because of our tremendous efforts to be relevant to our members. (Weitz, 2002)

Finally, Hadassah has taken an increasingly active role in Washington. It is clear, from the perspective of Hadassah members, that if one wants to challenge the ways in which the United Nations or some member states characterize Zionism or Israel, it is necessary to engage the State Department in one's efforts. Beyond foreign policy, Hadassah has also been active on the domestic policy front in protecting minority religious rights. One particular example is their strong support for a separation of state and religion, through opposition to public vouchers for private

[61] Hadassah is the largest Jewish organization in the United States, with a membership of 306,000 in 2002, compared to 250,000 for B'nai Brith, 50,000 for the American Jewish Congress and 70,000 for the American Jewish Committee (*Encyclopedia of Associations*, 2002). These figures suggest that Jewish *women* prefer to join an organization emphasizing *both* gender and culture.

religious schools, and the School Prayer Amendment to the US Constitution. They also advocate on behalf of women in areas such as domestic violence. This shift towards advocacy, Washington lobbying and identity politics is part of a broader trend in civic life in America, as described above. While there are some negative aspects to these changes, there are enormous positive implications as well. Moreover, as Hadassah demonstrates, the commitment to advocacy (for Zionism and Israel) can also be accompanied by a commitment to cross-cultural causes and peace (the Jersualem Medical Centre).

Moose (Women): one solution to the time crunch

The Moose (Women) organization[62] is an interesting case of a traditional women's association, growing out of a fraternal organization, that has tried to evolve with the times. Like Hadassah, it contradicts the generally sharp downward trend in growth over the last three decades. Its membership, however, has grown for very different reasons. Membership amongst women rose from 1940 (with a plateau from 1950–70) until the 1990s. Male membership, on the other hand, increased rapidly from 1940 to 1950, was relatively steady until 1980 and then went into a decline, which became precipitous after 1990. What led women to buck the pattern described by Putnam in *Bowling Alone* and continue to join Moose (Women) while men (after 1990 in particular) dropped out? Why the dramatic gender difference over the last two decades?

Presumably a survey of members might provide a more exact answer, particularly with respect to what caused the decline amongst men in the 1980s, but there is one important change in the organization, described on its own website, that may help to explain the pattern of the 1990s.

In the early 1990s, the Moose organization decided to rethink the entire idea of what a fraternal facility and its programs need to be about in the 21st century – de-emphasizing our Social Quarters, and placing greater emphasis on programs designed to appeal to every segment of our members' families in facilities called Family Centers.[63]

---

[62] The Moose organization is made up of 1.5 million men and women (in the United States and a handful of other countries). It was founded in the late 1800s as a fraternal organization for men to socialize but added to its mandate at the beginning of the twentieth century a service orientation towards children and seniors. 'The main endeavors of the fraternity remain Mooseheart, the 1,000-acre Illinois home and school for children in need, and Moosehaven, the 65-acre Florida retirement community for senior members in need.' In the 1990s, as discussed later, the Moose organization had a formally mandated change in direction from fraternal 'social quarters' to 'family centers'. See www.mooseintl.org (accessed December 2004).

[63] From www.mooseintl.org (all other quotations are taken from this web page).

In their vision statement, this transition is articulated as a need to appeal to young families by changing the Moose lodge into a Moose home, 'a center of family activity'. In clarifying what this change means, the director general suggests that the 'family center' should be seen as an alternative to 'family eateries', where 'members and their families can relax and enjoy themselves over food and a modest amount of drink'. The explicit purpose of this transformation was to attract younger members with families. This is particularly important for women members, as Tonie Ewoldt, Grand Chancellor of the Women of the Moose, comments: 'We must be receptive to new ideas . . . we must be accepting of new members, especially young members with children – they are our future' (*Moose Magazine Online*, 2002). The key change here is an acknowledgement of the real time and energy constraints on women, who are constantly balancing the public and private, by providing a place where parents, particularly mothers, who still have a disproportionate responsibility for childcare, can overlap their civic and family responsibilities. If they can bring their children with them when they go to engage in civic or associational activity, the energy and time to participate in community service is freed up for women (and parents more generally) rather than stretched still further. This is one of the keys (along with ways of overlapping civic activity and paid work) to unleashing the civic potential of women.

It is worth noting that there may be a direct trade-off between male and female membership with the switch from fraternal 'social quarters' to 'family centers', in other organizations as well as this one. In a paper presented at the conference 'Whither Social Capital?' at London South Bank University, Kwok-fu Sam Wong (2005) made the argument, with regard to mainland Chinese migrants in Hong Kong, that such social fraternizing among men is critical to social networks, employment and the creation of venues for economic and social mobility. Thus, one must be careful, in thinking about how to include women more fully in civic activities, with regard to the implications for men across different kinds of cultural groups.

At the same time, the Moose organization addressed the old language of exclusive gender-segregated fraternalism through the goals of integration and equality in relation to its female members: 'Fraternalism means . . . a fuller, more substantive recognition of the Women of the Moose as our equal partners' (*Moose Magazine Online*, 2003b). At the May 2003 international convention the director general, Donald Ross, in his keynote address, spoke about the decline in male membership and suggested that the organization should think about shifting from a gender-segregated membership to a 'family membership', which would mean a joint male–female leadership for the order (*Moose Magazine Online*, 2003c). Finally, during the 1990s Moose International also developed 'Home Chapter' membership for women, which meant that female members did not have to be affiliated to a male Moose member in order to belong (*Moose Magazine Online*, 2003a).

The Moose fraternity thus provides some insights, in a very traditional organization, as to how membership and the nature of actual lodges can change in order to accommodate better the changing role of women along with their families. Once again, such changes are not without costs, as social quarters are replaced by or supplemented with 'family centers' (as the decline of male membership might suggest), but these changes reflect a more inclusive approach to organizational structures and activities than was the case in the past.

Girl Scouts: a success story

The Girl Scouts organization is unique out of all eleven female civic associations studied. While the last two (Hadassah and Moose) both showed growth in the 1990s, their membership tailed off over the last half of the decade. The Girl Scouts continued to grow during this period, reaching their highest membership numbers in the most recently available data. As of 2003 3.8 million American females were involved in the Girl Scouts, made up of 2.9 million girls and 986,000 adults.[64] Everett Ladd documented this growth in his critique of Putnam's decline thesis in 1996, pointing at that time to the rebounding numbers of adult members in Girl Scouts, from a low of 534,000 in 1980 to a then high of nearly 900,000 in the early 1990s (Ladd, 1996, p. 15). Ladd suggests that the drop in adult volunteers in the 1960s and 1970s was due to 'the change in women's labour force participation' but provides little evidence to support this conclusion (pp. 4 & 15). One might ask: why would it rebound in the 1990s, given that women are still in the paid labour force (at even higher levels than before)?

A more convincing argument lies in the capacity of the Girl Scouts movement to adapt to the changing times and appeal to an evolving American public, particularly a diverse population of girls and their mothers. Like Moose (Women), the Girl Scout movement had a fundamental shift in emphasis during the 1980s and 1990s, embracing, in particular, the concepts of gender equality and diversity in very concrete and

---

[64] These are raw membership figures; they do not incorporate growth in the overall size of the relevant constituency, as Putnam does. Nevertheless, they represent a significant increase in the number of members, particularly when seen in comparison to comparable Boy Scout numbers (Girl Scouts, 2003, p. 12; available at www.girlscouts.org/who_we_are/facts/pdf/2003annual_report.pdf; accessed December 2004).

profound ways. In other words, diversity and equality were not simply marketing tools used to sell the existing organizations but, rather, principles that changed the Girl Scouts in almost every way imaginable, from their basic oath, to the cover of those famous cookies, to their long-standing uniforms to their programmatic goals. This transformation stands in stark contrast to the Boy Scouts of America, who have fought to maintain a very traditional set of values rooted in a long-standing oath and with an organizational style that tends to be top-down. We now examine this contrast and the impact of these differing philosophies on each group's membership, beginning with the transformation of the Girl Scouts in the 1990s.

One key change in the Girl Scouts movement in the 1990s in relation to religious and cultural diversity was the decision in 1992 to make 'God' optional in the Girl Scout promise, 'when Muslim and atheist Scouts balked at reciting the Girl Scout promise' (Tyre, 2001, p. 51). In the latter half of the 1990s the leaders of the Girl Scouts movement considered further ways in which diversity could be encouraged within the organization. In 1998 Marsha Johnson Evans was appointed as executive director. As a former recruiter for the navy, 'she was the mother of the 12-12-5 affirmative action policy, a mandate to make the Navy look more like America – 12% African-American, 12% Hispanic and 5% Asian/Pacific' (Lopez, 2000). In 2001 the Girl Scouts launched a programme entitled 'For every girl, everywhere', emphasizing a commitment to greater diversification within the movement. The organization wanted to increase its membership amongst ethnic minorities, but was particularly concerned about the small percentage of Hispanic-Americans within the organization (6.6 per cent of its members, compared to 17 per cent in the general population in 1998). What is fascinating about this particular initiative is the means chosen to achieve the ends. Rather than selling the 'Scouts' as a given package to the Hispanic-American population as a whole, the Girl Scouts looked at how *they* could change their own ways of doing business to reflect better this cultural milieu, as well as giving greater local control to the leaders to tailor Girl Scout groups and membership drives to appeal to the specific community in question. As Marty Evans, national executive director of the Girl Scouts, comments: 'It's a grassroots enterprise, and the grass is different in every location' (Taylor, 2002, p. 19).

Examples of modifications in the organization included changing the green Girl Scout uniforms, because 'to a Hispanic mother, they may stir up memories . . . of US immigration officials' (Taylor, 2002, p. 19). They also looked at ways in which Latin American traditions could be absorbed into the Scouting mainstream. For example, on 24 April 2001 Girl Scouts across the United States participated in a national observance of El Dia de los Niños (The Day of the Children), based on a traditional Latin American holiday. The Girl Scouts also created a 'Cultural awareness training program' that focused on relationships within a multicultural community. The idea was not simply to translate the existing formula of Scouting into Spanish but, rather, to transform it into something that was sensitive to this particular culture. As Varela Hudson, the market specialist who helped the Girl Scouts on this campaign, commented: 'It's all part of . . . being "in-culture" rather than being simply "in-language"' (Taylor, 2002, p. 19). The efforts seem to be paying off, as the membership of Hispanic-Americans in the Girl Scouts is growing each year. In 2000 the African-American membership increased by 3.2 per cent, Asian/Pacific islander membership increased by 3.5 per cent and the numbers of 'girls of Spanish/Hispanic origin increased by . . . 10.3%' (Girl Scouts, 2000, p. 16). In the 2003 Annual Report the growth in Hispanic membership over the previous year was given as 13.6 per cent, African-American membership 1.1 per cent and Asian/Pacific islander 5 per cent (Girl Scouts, 2003, p. 12). It is worth noting that the Girl Scouts movement is one of the few organizations that readily provides a breakdown of members based on ethnicity. This allows them not only to set targets for ensuring a membership that is reflective of the general American population but, perhaps most critically, it also provides a real sense of the degree to which this organization is a force for 'bridging' as well as 'bonding' social capital. Trying to get accurate numbers for bridging capital is a problem that Putnam himself bemoans in the first chapter of *Bowling Alone*.

Beyond ethnic multiculturalism, Girl Scouting, like its male counterpart, has had to face the issue of homosexuality in relation to its membership. While the Boy Scouts have chosen, as a national organization, to exclude all gay men or boys from their groups, Girl Scouts have taken a different approach. The Girl Scouts policy is to let each of its 300 plus local councils decide for themselves rather than imposing a policy from above. Some argue that such a policy 'sidesteps the issue', a 'kind of Junior League "don't ask, don't tell"' (Tyre, 2001, p. 51) that could still result in a lesbian counsellor being fired. Others, including the leadership of the Girl Scouts, see it as a fundamentally democratic policy that recognizes a diversity of views but leaves it up to the local community to decide. 'Christie Ach [a spokeswoman for the national organization] says that in a grass-roots organization . . . the "norms of each community" must determine whether gays can be excluded' (Tyre, 2001, p. 51). Beyond this policy with regard to membership, however, both specific local councils and the national leadership have been supportive of resources that reflect and embrace diverse kinds of families, including same-sex couples (Berkowitz, 2001; Lopez, 2000).

Finally, Girl Scouts have also embraced a new emphasis on girls and strength,

aimed at providing the public a contemporary view of Girl Scouting . . . cutting-edge program activities for girls continue to be created and carried out, including *Girl Sports*, Girl Scouting Beyond Bars, Girls at the (Science) Center, Strength in Sharing (a program to teach girls about philanthropy), and Money Smarts.[65]

In 1996 the Girl Scouts launched the *Girl Sports* initiative, encouraging girls and adults to host sports and fitness events in their local communities. In 1999 2,300 sporting events were held with 100,000 participants. By 2000 this had grown to 5,000 different events. In addition, the Girl Scouts movement supports the annual National Girls and Women in Sports Day, with a variety of athletic activities (Girl Scouts, 2002). This emphasis of female fitness and strength has even had an impact on those famous Girl Scout cookies.

On the newly designed boxes, consumers will see Girl Scouts playing high-adventure sports, exploring careers as aviators, firefighters, broadcast journalists and veterinarians. The message displayed on each box reads, 'You'd be surprised what a Girl Scout cookie can build: strong values, strong minds, strong bodies, strong spirit, strong friendships, strong skills, strong leadership, strong community.' (Girl Scouts, 2001)

Thus, Girl Scouts are changing, and it would appear that this changing mandate (rather than the ratio of women in the paid labour force, as Ladd suggests), together with the increasing emphasis on empowering girls, local democracy and increasing diversity, has led to an increase in membership, particularly amongst ethnic minorities. This result is in stark contrast to its corollary organization, the Boy Scouts of America, whose membership over the last few years has been in decline. As Andrew Stephen comments, 'The American Boy Scouts are facing a mounting crisis: [in 2000] membership has dropped by more than 4% on the West coast, by 8% on the East Coast' (Stephen, 2001). The question immediately arises: why are the Girl Scouts expanding and the Boy Scouts contracting?

While the Girl Scouts have embraced the changing multicultural nature of America, the Boy Scouts have adopted a different approach. Perhaps the issue that illustrates these differences best is the Boy Scouts' exclusionary policy on homosexuality. In 2000 the US Supreme Court upheld

---

[65] See www.girlscouts.org; accessed 22 June 2002.

the Boy Scouts' right to exclude homosexuals from their organization. It was a divisive battle. Steven Spielberg resigned from the national advisory board and several sponsors cut or withdrew funding (Stephen, 2001). While some Americans saw the Boy Scouts as intolerant and discriminatory, others saw them as champions of traditional American and Christian values. Nevertheless, the impact on membership of the decision is clear. Statistics taken from their Annual Reports suggest that there was a 5 per cent decline between 1999 and 2001 (from 3,195,429 to 3,049,000) in the combined membership in Cub Scouts and Boy Scouts (ages eleven to seventeen). The 2003 Annual Report shows that the membership numbers have continued to decline, falling to approximately 2,897,000 combined Cub Scouts and Boy Scouts.[66]

The questions facing the Scouting movement are not only whether to create an inclusive organization but, equally important, the extent to which 'values' should be shared by all local councils and be imposed from 'above'. Unlike the Girl Scouts, who allowed local organizations to make their own decision on this issue, the Boy Scouts issued an edict that described the exclusion of gay men as part of 'the bedrock of Scouting values'. In other words, there is a set of values to which *all* Boy Scouts *must* subscribe. These values are set in stone (bedrock) and cannot, therefore, be changed by any shift in ethical views or the appeal by any particular subset of the American community. If new members want to join the Scouting community they must conform to these existing traditional values, and local councils must also subscribe to them. Moreover, the anchor for the Boy Scouts, according to the 'Bedrock of Scouting Values' page of the Boy Scouts of America's website, is a belief in God. 'The bedrock of Scouting's values is literally and figuratively . . . duty to God.'[67] Once again, the Girl Scouts, who have made the reference to God optional in their pledge, allow for more flexibility, and therefore greater levels of tolerance, in their organization. It is the duty to God (according to the Boy Scouts leadership) that leads to the exclusion of gay men and boys from the organization. 'Scouting is in accord with the teachings of the world's great religions and is committed to the concept that sexual intimacy is the providence of a man and a woman within the bonds of marriage.' It is disingenuous to suggest that all Christianity, let

---

[66] See www.scouting.org; accessed December 2004. The figures for membership were taken from the 1999, 2001 and 2003 Annual Reports, combining Cub Scouts and Boy Scouts. Copies of the Annual Reports from 1997 to 2003 can be found at www.scouting.org/nav/enter.jsp?s=xx&c=ds&terms=annual+report. See also France (2001).

[67] See 'The Bedrock of Scouting Values', at www.scouting.org/excomm/values/bedrock. html; accessed 21 June 2002.

alone all religions, endorse this particular view of sexuality. Under the guise of 'shared bedrock values', a group of Americans who wish to be included in the Boy Scouts continues to be excluded.[68]

Thus, the Boy Scouts provide an example of an organization that continues to be top-down, focused on a singular set of traditional values, exclusionary in principle and unwilling to bend to an increasingly diverse American community. The Girl Scouts represent the mirror image, embracing a grass-roots, multicultural and diverse but inclusive vision of American society as the basis for both their organization and membership drives. There is an important broader lesson to be learned by those who seek to build civic associations and, through them, civic participation in the future. An organization of any kind that builds itself upon a particular 'bedrock of shared traditional values' that cannot accommodate, let alone embrace or respect, the increasingly multicultural plurality of our times will not only fail to attract new members but, more importantly, will constitute, as the Boy Scouts do, an obstacle to a fully inclusive, and therefore just, American community. The encouraging news, from the vantage point of the United States as a whole, is that this model of community, at least in terms of membership, seems to be in decline, while the opposite, as represented by the Girl Scouts organization, is growing.

Beyond the eleven associations: new kinds of civic participation

Beyond the eleven associations listed above, there are other kinds of activities, not represented in these formal organizations, in which working women have increasingly invested their time and energy. This is certainly the view of Peter Hall in his analysis of social capital in the United Kingdom, in which he concludes that women are the single most important factor in increasing participation in the community over the last four decades.

---

[68] In the closing paragraph of chapter 23 of *Bowling Alone* (p. 401) Putnam refers to the Boy Scouts as a model for the twenty-first century, but then seems to imply that we may need to 'reinvent' a twenty-first-century equivalent. It is unclear whether Putnam is suggesting that the Boy Scouts are outdated or not. It seems strange that he makes no reference to the fact that this organization has explicitly excluded a group of men and boys from their organization due to their sexual orientation (which would draw into question whether they *are* a good model for future civic organizations to follow). Either way, Putnam overlooks the better example of the Girl Scouts, as an organization that has evolved with the times, not in need of replacement by a twenty-first-century equivalent, but a model that is more appropriate to today's diverse, multicultural society.

One of the most striking features of the British data is that, while community involvement by men increased slightly (by about 7%) between 1959 and 1990, the community involvement of women more than doubled (increasing by 127%) to converge with the rates of men. In short, *social capital has been sustained in Britain largely by virtue of the increasing participation of women in the community.* (Hall, 2002, p. 37, emphasis added)

These findings are significant in themselves, for they fundamentally challenge the decline thesis, particularly in relationship to women. Hall's conclusions with regard to gender pose an important question for Putnam's thesis: why should there be such a radical difference between the United Kingdom and the United States on civic engagement, and amongst women in particular? I would argue that there is not such a difference, but that Putnam's model understates women's civic engagement because he measures old rather than new kinds of civic engagement in his choice of survey data and he holds education constant (which has particular gendered implications). Putnam uses survey data from DDB Needham, the General Social Survey and the Roper Social and Political Trends archive across all the years studied in his measurements of civic activity, Hall uses Almond and Verba's Civic Culture analysis for 1959; Barnes and Kaase's Political Action survey data for 1973; and, most importantly, Inglehart's World Values survey data for 1981 and 1990.[69] By using the same survey Putnam is able to claim comparability over time. Hall, on the other hand, is introducing different categories into his comparative analysis.[70] However, by using the World Values survey data, Hall includes within his analysis both professional associations and advocacy associations (such as environmental and human rights groups) and religious (as opposed to Church) organizations, capturing the changing religious affiliations in Britain. Through his choice of surveys, Hall is able to address both the growth in 'post-materialist' civic associations, particularly for those groups in society who are marginalized, and new kinds of civic activity.

In addition, Putnam's argument regarding a generational decline in civic activity (a younger generation of women is less engaged than an

[69] Hall summarizes the general shift in group membership in table 1-1 (1999, p. 423; see also 2002, p. 26). He refers to his sources in footnote 19 (1999, p. 423), including the Civic Culture survey: Almond and Verba (1963); Political Action survey: Barnes and Kaase (1979); and World Values survey: Inglehart (1990).

[70] For example, only the Political Action survey includes political parties (question 82 in Almond and Verba, 1963, p. 11) as one of the 'groups' being measured (unlike the other two surveys). This would probably cause the figures for 1973 in table 1 of Hall's analysis (1999, p. 423) to be higher, in terms of associational membership, than other years that reflect surveys that did not include party membership as part of the count for civic participation.

older generation of women) is profoundly shaped (and, I would argue, misrepresented) by his decision to hold education constant. The enormous increase in women's enrolment in post-secondary education over the last forty years is a story of growing equality and justice, leading to increased civic participation, that should be highlighted rather than hidden, as it suggests that the way to increased social capital may be through educational policy. Hall's and Putnam's conclusions are analysed fully in the next chapter, when we discuss generational change as one of the causes Putnam identifies for the decline in civic participation. Suffice it to say for now that Hall's diametrically opposed conclusions on the growth of women's social capital in Britain are the result of a number of factors (including state policies encouraging voluntary activities), but key amongst them are the role of education and the fact that the surveys he uses are updated and therefore able to capture new kinds of civic activity.

Hall's and Putnam's conclusions have been challenged by feminists, who argue that they both overlook new kinds of female civic activity. One under-represented area cited by both Theda Skocpol and Vivien Lowndes is 'child-centred activities'. As Skocpol concludes:

Newer types of involvements – such as parents congregating on Saturdays at children's sports events, or several families going together to the bowling alley . . . may not be captured by the GSS questions. As many fathers and mothers have pulled back from the Elks Clubs and women's clubs, they may have turned not toward 'bowling alone' but toward child-centered involvements with other parents. (Skocpol, 1996)

The care of children (and related activities) is gendered because women are more likely to be involved in these activities, and by relying on the GSS data one excludes *women's* civic activity in particular. Thus, as Lowndes argues in her critique of both Putnam's and Hall's analysis of social capital, there is an implicit bias in the lists of organizations used to measure civic participation towards male-oriented activities.[71] In particular, she is critical of Hall's 'relegating to a footnote increases in time spent on childcare' (Lowndes, 2000, p. 534). If these social networks 'produced and reproduced through a range of familiar activities . . . for instance, the "school run", childcare "swaps", baby-sitting, shared children's outings, emergency care, and the taking and fetching and watching of children in *their* school and club activities', as well as more formalized groups, such

---

[71] Lowndes is too quick, however, in suggesting that athletic activities are singularly male-dominated in every context. In the United States, the impact of Title IX (as discussed earlier) means that women's sporting activity is an important source of social capital (although it is still under-counted and under-analysed), and women's sports have grown internationally as well.

as 'playgroups, after-school clubs, post-natal support groups, "mums and toddlers" mornings', were included in the analysis of social-capital-forming activities, Lowndes concludes that a truer picture of social capital accumulation amongst women, particularly younger women, would emerge (p. 534). The reason these types of activities are not counted by either Putnam or Hall, according to Lowndes, is because they continue to be seen as part of the 'private sphere' of family and care-giving rather than the public sphere of 'civil society'. 'Child-care activities . . . are regarded as domestic rather than civic or community matters' (p. 535).

The third kind of social capital that has grown over the last three decades is informal small groups. Women find this kind of more flexible and informal structure easier to reconcile with the heavy schedule of a working mother. Robert Wuthnow argues that measurements of civic activity, particularly amongst women in the United States, must take into account this small group activity, from

home Bible study groups, prayer fellowships, house churches; therapy groups, a wide array of self-help and twelve-step groups . . . and other groups such as book discussion groups and hobby groups . . . Although some of these groups are likely to have been captured by the GSS questions about membership in voluntary associations, many go under different labels, do not consider themselves to be 'organizations', or in surveys fail to evoke responses unless mentioned specifically. (Wuthnow, 2002a, pp. 91–2)

He compares a Harris poll in 1984, in which only 3 per cent of the American population said that they were involved in a self-help group, to a 1992 Gallup poll, which found that 10 per cent of the public were participating in a self-help group (pp. 92–3). The problem with these types of groups, according to both Wuthnow and Putnam, is that they may not contribute to civic engagement beyond the individual's involvement in the specific group. Wuthnow concludes that the evidence suggests 'that support groups are part of the wider retreat of social capital from marginalized categories of people, rather than an antidote to this trend' (p. 100).

Conclusions: normative and empirical dimensions of the 'decline' in civic participation

Having looked at all eleven women's civic associations identified by Putnam, we can answer the questions we posed at the outset of this chapter and draw some conclusions about the normative and empirical dimensions of the 'decline' thesis in civic participation, as it applies to women and cultural minorities. First, is there an empirical decline in the

membership of these associations? Yes, there is a decline in absolute numbers in eight of the eleven associations over the last three to four decades,
but a general increase in the last three organizations. The answer to the
empirical question appears, at least on the surface, to be a clear-cut one
in the affirmative, at least for the majority of the organizations under
consideration. The theory of decline, however, is fundamentally undermined when one poses two critical supplementary questions. First, have
the organizations themselves declined, or is the decline in the 'relevant
population' from which these organizations draw their members? Secondly, are there new kinds of civic activity, engaged in by women, that
have been overlooked by Putnam?

As Putnam himself points out in the introduction to his analysis of
civic participation, it is critical that in measuring membership in civic
organizations it is done in relation to changes in the relevant population
(Putnam, 2000, p. 450, fn. 15). The problem is how to define a 'relevant
population' – a question that is fundamental to Putnam's, and a gendered,
analysis of civic activity. Should one compare organizational decline in
relation to the overall population of American women or particular subsets of that group? Putnam states that he measures the membership in
Hadassah against the changing population of Jewish women (as opposed
to all women) in the United States, and presumably he measures the
numbers of Girl Scouts against the relevant age population. Thus the
principle of dividing women into subsets depending on the nature of
the organization is one endorsed by Putnam; but can, or should, this principle be extended to other kinds of populations? For example, the first
six organizations we have examined may be measured in relation to all
American women (in which case you have a clear case of decline) or in
relation to a subset of American women from which these organizations
largely draw their membership, namely 'traditional women', or full-time
homemakers (a population that was in decline throughout the last half
of the twentieth century). Putnam may be just measuring a decline in
the population of traditional homemakers rather than a decline in the
civic participation of women overall. Peter Hall's argument in relation to
women's social capital in the United Kingdom makes exactly this point
when he concludes that there is only one group of organizations that
constitutes an exception to social capital growth amongst women in the
United Kingdom over the last thirty years, namely traditional women's
organizations, precisely because they 'tend to be oriented towards homemakers' (Hall, 1999, p. 422).

Similarly, the PTA's decline may, in their appeal to 'white, middle-
class, stay-at-home mothers', also reflect, in part, a decline in this same
population (Crawford and Levitt, 1999, p. 250). Some might argue that

measuring a population called 'traditional women' would necessarily be more subjective than measuring the American female population, or even the subsets mentioned above, namely Jewish or Girl-Scout-aged females.[72] While this may be true (although there would be relevant data that would give one a good indication of this change in population), the problem of measurement should not stop us from admitting the validity of the principle once it is accepted that organizations represent particular subsets of populations that can either grow or – as important in this case – decline over a span of decades.

Moose (Women) and Hadassah have bucked the trend and reflected a different pattern of growth over the last fifty years. It was suggested that these increases might be due to the fact that these organizations appeal to the growing population of women who face a time/work crunch and/or reflect a general trend in American society towards more political forms of advocacy and identity politics, respectively. The Girl Scouts, with their emphasis on girl power, multicultural diversity, local democracy and inclusion, have gone from strength to strength in recent years. As has been suggested, this organization – particularly when compared to its male counterpart, the Boy Scouts – provides many lessons on the future of civic associations, and community more broadly, in the United States in light of a diverse society and the principles of multiculturalism and gender equity. Thus, the decline of women's involvement in civic associations may not be a general pattern at all but simply a reflection of an evolving society in which those organizations keeping up with the changes continue to attract members while those that do not fall behind. The positive stories emerging out of traditional organizations such as Hadassah, Moose (Women) and the Girl Scouts also suggest that historically subordinated groups are changing the rules of associations as their own lives, families and communities change.

Beyond these eleven organizations, this chapter has also provided evidence that there are many new kinds of civic activity that women are engaged in that Putnam, in his choice of organizations, simply has not measured. We have shown that one area completely overlooked by Putnam is the pattern of growth over the latter half of the twentieth century in specifically *women's direct* involvement in politics, as opposed to the indirect paths provided by more traditional women's organizations. Similarly, the growth in professional organizations, specifically of female members, is not addressed. Nor is the growth in women's athletics beyond

---

[72] Although the measurement of this group would indeed be more subjective, there are ways it could be done, including relevant data on the numbers of women working outside the home over the given time period, or women who consider themselves to be 'traditional' homemakers.

the WBC, not only in terms of the number of female athletes involved but the social capital that forms around them, from T-ball to the Olympics. The fourth area of social capital building that has been overlooked or misrepresented is the associations growing out of the civil rights movement, including ethnic/cultural and women's groups, but also disability and gay/lesbian associations. Fifthly, as Lowndes suggests, child-related activities are another untapped source of growing social capital building (Lowndes, 2000). Finally, Wuthnow has argued that small groups represent an important new form of community activity not accounted for in the formal organizational measures (Wuthnow, 2002). In essence, women, particularly of a younger generation, are expending their energies on *new forms* of activity. Ultimately, the empirical case made by Putnam, until it includes these other kinds of civic activity, is unconvincing. It may well be that women's civic participation has not *declined* so much as *changed*, or, if Hall is to be believed, *increased*, and these changes are inextricably tied to the revolution that occurred in women's lives during the second half of the twentieth century.

The normative question underlying this chapter is equally important. Even if there is a decline in these civic associations, is this necessarily a bad thing? As the analysis suggests, the decline in the six traditional associations may not be as negative as thought, if seen within the context of a population of independent women who are choosing to get involved more directly in politics and business, and are engaging in different kinds of civic and political activity, as well as from the perspective of a multicultural society that has evolved past organizations founded on the membership of a racially or religiously privileged population. The decline in the PTA may be a more complex question, and the normative value of its decline depends, as has been suggested, on the degree to which one believes such associations should emphasize local control and diversity or a unified national political force for public education. Similarly, the decline in membership of the WBC may not be a negative phenomenon if it reflects women choosing (and being able) to engage in other kinds of sporting activities. Finally, the growth in identity and advocacy politics, seen as a negative development by Putnam and Skocpol, can be seen, instead, from the perspective of historically subordinated groups as a reflection of their empowerment and the particular needs of their communities, as well as a positive outcome of their struggle for fuller inclusion and/or respect in the larger American community.

4   The causes of 'decline' in social capital theory

Having considered the evidence for a 'decline' in civic participation and assessed its validity for women, in particular, through a close examination of the eleven relevant civic associations, we turn to consider in this chapter the *causes* that Putnam suggests are behind the 'collapse' of American community. Given that the previous chapter concluded that there may not be a decline in civic participation at all so much as a change, one might well ask: why bother with Putnam's causal explanations at all? There are two reasons. First, in addition to the decline in participation, Putnam's analysis is also attempting to provide a causal explanation for a decline in *trust* (the other critical component of social capital). As the following chapter argues, while participation may only have changed, generalized trust has clearly declined; to the extent that Putnam's analysis might provide explanations for this decline (or not) makes my analysis of 'causes' in this chapter necessary. Secondly, it is important to analyse these causal explanations in their own terms to see if they hold together logically based on the studies provided (television), to compare them in relation to competing theories (generational change) and to make explicit any assumptions implicit within the analysis that might have an adverse impact on women or cultural minorities (dual-career families).

In section 3 of *Bowling Alone*, entitled 'Why?', Putnam breaks down the causes for the 'decline' in social capital in the following way: dual-career families (10 per cent); generational change (50 per cent); television (25 per cent); and mobility/sprawl (10 per cent)[1] (pp. 283–4). We

---

[1] It is worth noting at the outset that, while the question of cause appears to have changed for Putnam from his earlier versions of the social capital thesis (1995a, 1996) – when television was the singular culprit for civic decline – to *Bowling Alone* (2000), where he includes these several different factors, the degree to which generational change is a cause separate from television is unclear, as shall be discussed. To the extent that Putnam himself claims that generational change is not so much a cause as the effect of some 'anti-civic X-ray' from the 1950s forward (as well as the pro-civic influence of the Second World War), television remains dominant in his theory of civic decline in *Bowling Alone*. As such, the relationship between television and civic participation, and the case studies in which Putnam anchors his causal connection, is considered in some depth in this chapter.

consider the first three of these reasons in turn.[2] Throughout this analysis of causal explanations, a gendered and cultural lens is again deployed to see whether the claims made by Putnam are universal and equally true for all groups of Americans. As shall be demonstrated, gender differences are an important but under-analysed factor in the case of generational change and misrepresented in the case of dual-career families. With respect to cultural minorities, the causal explanations provided by Putnam are particularly weak in relationship to the lack of *trust* – as opposed to participation – in certain minority populations, such as African- or Hispanic-Americans. If we are to take seriously Putnam's causal analysis of the decline in social capital, we must ultimately accept that the reason why ethnic minorities have fallen off even more precipitously than other Americans in levels of trust is due to television, suburbia and dual-career families. The more likely culprits for what I call the 'gap', as opposed to the decline, in trust will be analysed more fully in the next chapter.

Dual-career families: is part-time work the answer?

Putnam argues that one of the contributory factors (10 per cent) to the decline in social capital over the last three decades has been the increasing numbers of dual-career families. Putnam is probably underestimating the impact of this change on the nature of individual family lives as well as the collective life of the community, given that some of the other factors he mentions, including the impact of suburban sprawl and the increased level of television viewership, especially amongst the young, are probably also partially the effect of changing gender roles in addition to dual-career families. In the case of television, harried parents (particularly mothers) often find the television a useful tool to allow them some time in the late afternoon or evening to prepare dinner or do the other domestic chores necessary for the following day. Similarly, suburban sprawl would not have the same impact if there were still women at home sharing coffee in the neighbourhood or volunteering at the local charity. The important point about the impact of changing gender roles is that this time crunch cannot be solved on an aggregate individual basis; collective, even societal, solutions must be found if time is to be carved out between the public sphere of work and the private sphere of family for civic participation.

---

[2] The issue of mobility and sprawl is not specifically analysed in this section, in large part because Putnam's conclusions seem sound. The only point that might be added to his analysis is whether the attributes of suburbia are a cause or effect of changes. Thus, do gated communities lead to a decline in trust, or does a decline in trust lead to gated communities? Are there deeper causes at work here: the changing nature of the American economy; a growing disparity between the rich and the poor? These other potential causal explanations will be taken up in the next chapter.

There is an important reason why Putnam does not wish to overstate the impact of dual-career families: for fear that people understand him to be holding women responsible for the decline in social capital. Putnam comments: 'I explicitly disclaim the view that working women are "to blame" for our civic disengagement' (p. 201). Although he does not wish to blame women, he clearly puts them in a different category from men in his analysis of the pressures created by dual-career families. His analysis of time and money in chapter 11 of *Bowling Alone* focuses exclusively on the decisions that *women* make in terms of home and work, assuming either that men do not face these same questions or that it is not worth asking them.[3] From the outset, this analysis of work and family in relation to the time available for social capital is gendered and continues a long tradition in this literature of assuming that women should absorb more of the responsibility for balancing these dual demands and taking the lead in building social capital, as shall be discussed.

Despite his disclaimer that he does not want to 'blame' women, Putnam does argue that the full-time employment of women is a key factor in the 'reduction' of American civic engagement. 'Full time employment [of women] appears to cut home entertaining by roughly 10 per cent, club and church attendance by roughly 15%, informal visiting with friends by 25%, and *volunteering by more than 50%*' (p. 195, emphasis added). He then goes further, revealing the extent to which he continues to see women as the natural 'leaders' in social capital building, and men as the 'followers': 'With fewer educated, dynamic *women* with enough free time to organize civic activity, plan dinner parties, and the like, *the rest of us* too have gradually disengaged' (p. 203, emphasis added). The implication is that, if only *women* had more 'free time', they could once again take up the lead for fostering civic engagement, and men would assume their 'natural' role as followers in the social and civic volunteer realm.

The problem that immediately arises for Putnam is this: if women are to lead this revitalization of civic society, then how are they to find the time, especially when most studies continue to show that women are working outside the home and doing disproportionate amounts of work in the home? One possibility, implemented by the Moose organization (as discussed), would be to provide facilities that allow parents to overlap their responsibilities for childcare and civic engagement. Another possibility, to be discussed in more depth in the concluding chapter, would

---

[3] To be fair, Putnam is using a data set that asked these questions only of women. Nevertheless, it is troubling that women alone were required to answer them, since both men and women must make choices between family and paid employment. Moreover, I have my doubts that, if men *had* been asked and had answered in the same way, it would be suggested that men, as a group, should be encouraged to work part-time.

be to look at the state's role in restructuring the work/family balance.[4] In chapter 11 of *Bowling Alone*, however, Putnam suggests a different solution for this time crunch: lessen the amount of time that women spend in the paid labour force. The ideal, he argues, would be for women to work part-time. The important caveat, for Putnam, in order to square his recommendation with the principle of women's equality in having the same right to choose full-time careers as men, is to argue that women actually *want* to work part-time rather than full-time. In order to back up this claim, he uses data from the DDB Needham Lifestyles survey. Like earlier times in American history, women are being asked to assume a disproportionate responsibility for leading the charge on civic engagement by reducing their involvement in the paid labour force; but, unlike earlier periods, Putnam argues that women's sacrifice will not be expected or forced on them, but readily agreed to by women themselves.

Setting aside, for the moment, the loss to society of women's work in the paid labour force or the danger involved in the increased economic dependence of some women on their domestic partners, let us for the moment just consider Putnam's argument regarding women's preferred 'choice' to work part-time. His proposal is premised on the notion that the increase in women's employment since the second wave of feminism is really about financial security rather than the empowerment or fulfilment of women. 'Virtually all the increase in full-time employment of American women over the last twenty years is attributable to financial pressures, not personal fulfillment' (p. 197). This claim is contentious, as Putnam knows, and thus he sets out to demonstrate that women are largely working full-time out of 'necessity' rather than 'choice' and would ultimately prefer, given a choice, to work part-time, using data provided by the DDB Needham Lifestyles survey. There are a number of problems, however, with the collection of this data, the conclusions he draws from it and the inferences made for future policy directions.

The first problem is that Putnam uses only one source of research to back his conclusions, stating that he 'could find no other archives that contain the over time information on women's work preferences necessary to confirm it' (p. 476, fn. 29). This single-source reference should be considered in light of his 'core principle', articulated in chapter 1 and at the end of the book in appendix 1: 'Never report anything unless at least two independent sources confirm it. In this book I follow that same maxim' (p. 26). 'No single source of data is flawless, but the more numerous and diverse the sources, the less likely that they could all be influenced

---

[4] More recently Putnam has also talked about family leave policies to tackle the time crunch; these will be discussed in more detail in the concluding chapter.

by the same flaw' (p. 415). Given the profundity of the conclusions that he wishes to draw from this analysis, namely that women should give up their hard-earned struggle for economic equality, there is even more reason for Putnam to respect his own rule, even if that requires doing independent survey work on *men's* answers as well as women's to such questions.

The second important problem, to which Putnam himself admits, is that DDB Needham Lifestyles surveys do not use random samples of the population, but are based on the replies from those individuals who choose to answer the mailed-out questionnaires. Putnam points out, in appendix 1, that there are some general biases built in to this kind of survey: 'non-English speakers and ethnic minorities are less likely to be represented than "middle Americans", in the order of a ratio of 1 to 5–10' (pp. 420–2). As was pointed out in chapter 2, the experience of African-American women in relation to work and home is often very different from that of white American women. The fact that they are under-represented is a problem in the findings quoted by Putnam. Secondly, parents are over-represented (by 10 per cent), single people under-represented (by 10 per cent). In terms of women, therefore, mothers are over-represented, while single-career women are under-represented (p. 421). If the conclusions drawn from this survey are that women work out of financial necessity rather than personal fulfilment, it is not hard to see how this skewing towards mothers over single women might introduce a bias in favour of seeing the motivation for work as more the former than the latter. A final bias that could also factor into the results is the fact that women who are engaged in jobs that are more satisfying are probably less likely to fill out questionnaires than those who have boring jobs and more time to respond to questionnaires.

The biggest problem, however, is that Putnam's conclusions do not necessarily follow from the data he is examining. The original question asked on the survey of women is: 'Which of the alternatives . . . best describes what you do, along with the *main* reason behind your choice?'[5] (p. 476, emphasis added). Women are provided with six possible

---

[5] The full question is: 'In today's society, many women work at home as full-time home-makers, and many women work and are paid for jobs outside the home. Other women combine both worlds by working part-time. Which of the alternatives below best describes what you do, along with the main reason behind your choice? (1) Full-time homemaker, because I get personal satisfaction from being a homemaker and do not care to work outside my home; (2) full-time homemaker, because I feel I should be at home to take better care of my children, even though I would like to work; (3) employed part-time, because I get personal satisfaction from working at least some time outside my home; (4) employed part-time, because the money I earn at my part-time job helps out the family finances; (5) employed full-time, because I get personal satisfaction from my job; (6) employed full-time, because the income I earn contributes to the family finances' (p. 476; fn. 28).

answers, twinned in accordance with their current occupational status: full-time homemaker (1) and (2); part-time worker (3) and (4); and full-time worker (5) and (6).[6] With reference to full-time workers, the two relevant answers to this survey question regarding the 'main' motivation for work are (a) 'because I get personal satisfaction from my job' or (b) 'because the income I earn contributes to the *family* finances' (p. 476, emphasis added).[7] Putnam concludes that those women who answer (b) are working 'not because they want to, but because they *have to*' (p. 200, emphasis added; see also figs. 47 & 48, pp. 197–8). Nonetheless, it is completely plausible (indeed likely) that a woman's *main* reason for working could be financial and yet she could still *want* to work full-time. To conclude on the basis of her answer that she is working not because she wants to work but because she has to is simply wrong. Indeed, if someone asked me that exact question with the two available choices, I would have to say that the *main* reason why I work is to support my family's finances (even if the job was no longer satisfying I would continue to work), but that does not mean I am working because I 'have to'. And it certainly does not mean that I would prefer to work part-time. Putnam goes further, suggesting that these 'unhappily' employed women are a growing trend: '[M]ore and more women are *by necessity not by choice* [working full-time]' (p. 200, emphasis added). Thus, through a slippery kind of reasoning, he has changed the meaning of the answers given to support the call for part-time work and still square it with women's right to choose. Thus he concludes: '[F]rom the point of view of civic engagement, part-time work seems like a "golde. mean"' (p. 200).

The real issue, of course, for Putnam, rooted in a functionalist view of social capital, is that full-time work, particularly for women (who are the leaders in civic engagement), 'inhibits social connectedness' (p. 200). This is the nub of the problem. If more women worked part-time, they would be available to do the kinds of social capital building they did in

---

[6] The assumption underlying all these answers is that women are absolutely free to choose their occupational status: there is no sense in this analysis that women are constrained by history or the expectations of their community or their husbands about their roles.

[7] In addition, there might be *other* reasons for working part-time or full-time, such as the social life to be enjoyed through work, the opportunity to get out of the home, the desire to contribute to the economic life of the community or country, or the need to be financially independent in the case of divorce. None of these reasons falls easily into either of the two suggested categories, which means that the real 'main' reason for working might not even be represented by these two choices; and, even if women (given a variety of choices) stick with family finances or personal satisfaction as the *main* reason, it might (amongst a plurality of reasons) account for only, say, 25 per cent of the reason for working. I point this out because I think it undermines Putnam's suggestion that the two answers given are the only possible ones and, moreover, that they represent a mutually exclusive situation in which women work *either* out of choice (personal satisfaction) *or* out of necessity (contributing to family finances).

the past. Putnam seems to assume that the problem is the number of hours worked by women, but Robert Wuthnow has made the case that the problem should not be seen so much as a part-time versus full-time question as a childcare/work issue.

> The reason women who work full time are less likely to give time to voluntary organizations has much more to do with their off-work responsibilities than with the sheer number of hours they spend on the job. Those who have children at home are significantly less likely to volunteer than those who do not. (Wuthnow, 2002b, p. 76)

In other words, the issue may not be hours of work at all but, rather, the reconciliation of care-giving at home, paid work and civic activity, and the structural changes that would be necessary (rather than the individual choices that women should make) to allow for the overlapping of different kinds of responsibilities.

Moreover, the shift from full-time to part-time work may benefit civic associations, but what happens to the benefits that previously accrued to society through women's full-time paid work, and what happens to the woman herself once she is made more economically dependent on and therefore vulnerable to her spouse?

Ultimately, when placed in the larger social capital theory literature, this argument is a deeply worrying acceptance of gender inequality, masked in choice but nonetheless continuing to embrace the traditional view that women should be the ones to invest time and energy in civic activity in order that their families and others in the wider community might benefit. To understand how this gendered aspect of social capital building is endemic to this literature, we will return to James Coleman's original and groundbreaking article, which Putnam himself claims 'laid the intellectual foundations for the study of social capital and its effects' (p. 302). Coleman argues that social capital is different from other kinds of capital in one regard: those who invest in either physical or human capital are the ones who 'reap its benefits', whereas

> [m]ost forms of social capital are not like this . . . The kinds of social structures that make possible social norms and the sanctions that enforce them *do not benefit primarily the person or persons whose efforts would be necessary to bring them about*, but benefit all those who are part of such a structure. (Coleman, 1988, p. S116, emphasis added)

The example immediately following this statement makes clear who those 'persons' are likely to be: 'For example, in some schools where there exists a dense set of associations among some parents, these are the result of a small number of persons, ordinarily *mothers who do not hold full-time jobs outside the home*' (S116, emphasis added). He goes on to say, like Putnam, that women must be able to choose to work full-time for 'personal' reasons, but these decisions will result in a net 'loss' of social capital. 'The withdrawal of these activities [of the working mother] constitutes a loss to all those other parents whose associations and contacts were dependent on them' (S116). This hearkening back to a previous time, when women did not work outside the home and civic engagement was much stronger, carries within it a message for women that the decision to be fully independent economic actors is a *negative* development from the perspective of social capital building. Coleman's ultimate conclusions are that maternal employment will, 'by weakening the parent–child relationship that encourages children's identification with parental goals and values, hinder children's future socioeconomic attainment' (Parcel and Menaghan, 1994, pp. 972–3).[8] While Coleman is making the case in terms of children and Putnam in terms of community, both are ultimately arguing, based on their functionalist theory of social capital, that society would be better off if women did not work full-time.

What is particularly worrying in *Bowling Alone* is that, while the acceptance of gender inequality is explicit in prior versions of social capital theory such as Coleman's, the gendered implications of Putnam's analysis are often hidden in non-gendered language. For example, Putnam concurs with Coleman's analysis that the educational benefits of social capital are 'eroding because both the Church and the family have lost strength and cohesion' (p. 303) in his chapter on education and children's welfare, but makes no reference to Coleman's explicitly gendered implications from this shared conclusion. Similarly, Putnam adds 'and men too' *in parentheses* at the conclusion of his chapter on time and money (p. 201), suggesting that men too should be allowed or encouraged to work part-time, but it is at best token given that the rest of his analysis leading up to this conclusion focuses entirely on women and the choices they make. Finally, when Putnam comes to lay out his 'agenda' in the last chapter of his book, his call for 'part-time work' is suddenly transformed into a non-gendered recommendation. 'For many *people*, we discovered, part-time work is the best of both worlds' (p. 407, emphasis added). It was not 'people' who were discussed in chapter 11 but *women*. More recently, Putnam has suggested that a 'radical expansion of the Family and Medical Leave Act' may be the answer.[9] The idea of extended family leave is an important and potentially valuable suggestion but it too has inequitable gendered consequences, as Paul Kershaw has shown,

---

[8] Coleman's thesis elicited a sizeable literature debating the importance of maternal employment, its effect on women's capacity to build social capital in the home, and the impact on children's welfare (Parcel and Menaghan, 1994; Belsky and Eggebeen, 1991; Ferber and O'Farrell, 1991).

[9] 'Lonely in America': interview with Robert Putnam, www.theatlantic.com/unbound/ interviews, 21 September 2000.

unless – as has been done in Norway and Sweden – the state puts some paternal requirements into taking parental leave.[10] It is hard to tell whether Putnam is hoping that, in some utopian future, social capital will indeed become non-gendered, or whether he is aware that explicitly gendered recommendations, like those of Coleman's, simply would not be acceptable in a contemporary American society dedicated to equal rights. Either way, the issue of gender (in)equality cannot be wished away. Without a wary gendered lens, these conclusions may well appear to be without gendered implications, when in fact both history and the literature suggest the contrary.

Generational differences: decline or change?

Putnam describes generational change as the 'most important' factor in the decline of civic engagement, and provides some powerful evidence in chapter 14 of *Bowling Alone* to support this hypothesis (pp. 247–76). In table 3 (p. 252) and figure 71 (p. 253) Putnam 'presents patterns of change among four different age groups over the last quarter of the twentieth century' (p. 250) in activities ranging from reading newspapers to running for political office. He concludes that, 'in virtually every case, disengagement was concentrated among the younger cohorts and is slightest among men *and women* born and raised before World War II' (p. 251, emphasis added). His central point here is that baby boomers are *less* civically engaged; older Americans (born between the wars) are *more* civically engaged.

The first issue to be raised is the extent to which new forms of political or civic activity are being measured in his generational analysis. In the last chapter, we looked at this exact question through membership figures in eleven organizations in order to examine Putnam's general thesis of civic decline. This section considers the other set of data that Putnam uses to support his civic decline thesis, namely survey questions about participation in formal organizations, in order to answer a second question regarding generational change as causal: if survey questions use older forms of civic activity as the measure of civic participation, is there a bias in the data towards an over-representation of civic activity amongst older Americans and an under-representation in the civic activity amongst younger Americans? If so, then not only may the actual decline be smaller than

---

[10] Norway was the first country (1992) to reserve a set number of weeks' leave specifically for the father, which cannot be transferred to the mother of the child; Sweden followed suit in 1995, and has expanded its scheme subsequently (*European Industrial Relations Review*, 2001, 'Maternity, paternity and parent benefits across Europe', vols. 330–1, cited in Kershaw, 2005).

it appears (as argued in the last chapter) but the causal theory of generational change will also be brought into question. In his generational analysis in chapter 14, Putnam is depending upon a particular database, namely survey answers to questions posed about group membership from three different surveys: the DDB Needham survey, the Roper Social and Political Trends archive and the General Social Survey.[11] In order to answer the questions raised above, it is necessary to consider the specific wording of the surveys with respect to both questions and categories.

Peter Hall's study in Britain is, once again, an important counterexample to Putnam's. While in the last chapter we used Hall's analysis to examine the decline in participation particularly with respect to traditional women's organizations, in this chapter his analysis provides contrasting conclusions with respect to generational change.[12] Hall concludes that there is little generational effect in the United Kingdom: baby boomers are just as likely to participate in associational life as those born before the Second World War (Hall, 1999, p. 430). Perhaps most significantly, Hall argues that there is an important gender gap, with women's civic engagement during the period 1970 to 1990 roughly doubling while men's grew only slightly, suggesting that a younger generation of women is twice as likely to participate as an older generation (p. 437).[13] As with the question of overall decline addressed in the previous chapter, the question here is: why should there be such an opposing pattern *in generational change* between the United Kingdom and United States in the period studied? I am going to suggest two reasons for the differing results: Putnam's decision to hold education constant in studying generational change, and the different surveys consulted by the two scholars. In the end, I argue that Hall's analysis provides a better picture of generational patterns in participation, most particularly in relation to women and cultural minorities.

Let us begin with the role of education in generational change. Figure 71 (Putnam, 2000, p. 253) demonstrates in a very dramatic fashion the decline 'from generation to generation' of civic engagement. Putnam

[11] See Putnam's table 3 and figure 71b (pp. 252–3). There are several different kinds of measures in table 3 and figure 71, including political and religious participation. I am particularly interested in participation in civic organizations, as represented by the measurement in figure 71b with respect to regular attendance at clubs (DDB Needham survey) and group membership (GSS) (see p. 432 for sources).

[12] I am grateful to Peter Hall for comments he made on this section. Although he had no singular source of data that spanned the same period in the way that Putnam had for the United States, and the decision to use different surveys was, therefore, the only one available to him, necessity became a virtue in this instance, because Hall better captures the generational changes in activity through the updated survey questions.

[13] See also Maloney et al. (2000) for another example of analysis suggesting that the level of civic participation is increasing in the United Kingdom.

notes that, 'to clarify generational differences, figure 71 holds constant the educational composition of the various birth cohorts' (p. 483, fn. 9). He does this because he claims that he wants to be able to measure not simply the growth in overall educational attainment but how civic engagement changed independently of educational attainment.[14] It is unclear why we should be interested only in civic activity affected by causes other than educational attainment. As Hall comments: 'Putnam . . . control[s] for education on the premise, *which I do not fully share*, that it is the propensity of civic engagement independent of the effects of education that should interest us most' (Hall, 1999, p. 431, emphasis added). Putnam argues that his control for education is analogous to controlling for population size in measuring membership in formal organizations, but this analogy does not fit. In the case of the latter, it makes sense to control for population because one wants to isolate changes in participation from demographic growth. In the case of the former variable (education), however, there is a potentially *causal* relationship with participation. As such, providing data that does not hold education constant allows the reader to explore education as a potential solution to the problem.

One could argue, as Putnam does, that putting controls on his generational analysis allows him to isolate what causes the decline (by excluding education as a causal factor). There are two problems that arise with this. The first, as Hall points out, is that controlling for education 'tends to raise the involvement reported for earlier generations' (Hall, 1999, p. 431). As such, figure 71 in *Bowling Alone* tends to exaggerate visually the curve of the decline, since earlier generations have higher levels of reported involvement (as education is held constant), which is problematic not so much for those scholars who understand this kind of empirical analysis but certainly for the general reader, who does not understand what such controls mean and assumes the dramatic curve downward is a simple measure of decline. Putnam could have provided the same data on generational change *without* controlling for educational attainment (as Hall does) to see the specific impact that education has on civic participation by comparing the two sets of data.[15] Hall finds that, if education

---

[14] As John Helliwell and Putnam state in a research paper on education and social capital (1999), 'Education is one of the most important predictors – usually, in fact, the most important predictor – of many forms of political and social engagement. Over the last half century (and more) educational levels in the United States have risen sharply. In 1960 only 41% of American adults had graduated from high school; in1998 82% had' (Helliwell and Putnam, 1999, p. 1).

[15] See Hall (1999, tables 3 & 4, pp. 430–1) for his results on participation with and without a control for education (over three generations and at different ages). When education is not controlled, Hall finds an increase in participation. When he standardizes educational attainment across generations the line tends to flatten out, because it 'tends to raise the

is not controlled for, participation goes up in the last three generations; if education is held constant, participation holds steady.

This leads to the second problem in controlling for education, which is that it tends to push the analysis away from how the state (through educational policy) might impact civic participation and towards civic society itself. To put it another way, if educational attainment *offsets* other factors causing a decline in participation, surely this should be highlighted as a possible solution to the problem, particularly if it proves to be strong enough to counter other forces that cause a decline, as Hall finds in the United Kingdom. This is a point that should be highlighted in the search for solutions to a lack of civic participation. As Hall concludes, educational policy is critical to the growth of social capital in the midst of opposing forces. 'The radical transformation that took place in the British educational system between the 1950s and 1990s is of great significance. In large measure, it seems to have sustained the level of associational involvement in Britain despite countervailing pressures' (p. 435). Thus, in a strange way, Putnam's holding education constant causes the reader to look elsewhere, away from the state and towards individual citizens, for possible solutions to civic 'decline'. Ultimately, the import of Hall's arguments is that the 'revival' of community may not lie in bowling leagues at all but state policies that make greater educational opportunities available to all.

Finally, the increase in educational attainment in recent generations has particular significance for women and cultural minorities. Hall states with respect to education and gender: 'The importance of the educational revolution wrought in Britain over the past three decades is especially apparent in the case of women . . . between 1959 and 1990, the community involvement of women more than doubled . . . the data suggest that the greater access which women *secured to high education is by far the most important factor*. By 1990, 14% of women had some post-secondary education, compared with barely 1% in 1959' (p. 437, emphasis added). Figures taken from the US census suggest that there has been a comparable growth in the percentage of women enrolled in post-secondary education: in 1990 18 per cent of American women had completed four years of post-secondary education, whereas in 1959 only 6 per cent had.[16]

---

involvement reported for earlier generations' (p. 431). Thus, he concludes, '[E]ven when respondents' level of education is held constant, the basic inclination of the vast majority of the British populace to join associations remains roughly the same today as it was in the 1950s' (p. 424).

[16] See US census, 'Percentage of people 25 years and over who have completed high school or college by race, Hispanic origin and sex: selected years 1940–2003', at www.census.gov/population/socdemo/education/tabA-2.pdf; accessed December 2004.

Again, seen through the lens of gender, controlling for education hides this very important story of equality for women, as well as the possibility that, like Hall's analysis in the United Kingdom, a younger generation of women actually increased its civic participation *exactly* because it is now able to participate fully in post-secondary education.

But the story of education may be even more dramatic in American society today in relation to ethnic minorities (who experience the lowest levels of participation). Thus, the 2003 US census suggests that the gap in educational attainment between white Americans, African-Americans and Hispanic-Americans is significant. According to the census, 85 per cent of white Americans have four years of high school education, compared to only 80 per cent of African-Americans and 57 per cent of Hispanic-Americans; similarly, while 27.6 per cent of white Americans completed four years of college, only 17.3 per cent of African-Americans and 11.4 per cent of Hispanic-Americans did. Thus, the potential for education to increase 'social capital' amongst ethnic or racial minorities would need to be analysed in relation to both gender and culture, but it would seem to follow (at least from Hall's study) that, if educational policy targeted those groups of Americans disproportionately disaffected, an increase in civic participation, at least, would probably follow. It is worth noting at this point that any changes to educational policy may or may not have an impact on trust. As Hall points out, while participation has expanded over the last three decades in Britain, trust has continued to decline, despite the increase in educational attainment. In the next chapter, we shall discuss some of the causes that might have led to a decline in trust.

A second reason for the profound differences between Hall's and Putnam's analyses with respect to generational change is revealed if one looks carefully at the surveys that each author uses to measure associational activity *and* the generational effect on civic participation.[17] While Putnam uses the *same* three surveys (DDB Needham, RSPT and GSS) for *all* the years analysed in his measurements of generational change, Hall uses *different* surveys for *different* years (Almond and Verba's Civic Culture analysis for 1959; Barnes and Kaase's Political Action survey data for 1973 and, most importantly, Inglehart's World Values survey data for 1981 and 1990).[18] All these surveys vary in the type of questions asked.

---

[17] Hall himself suggests that the main differences between the United States and United Kingdom, beyond the expansion of education (particularly amongst women), are the expansion of the middle class and British government policy to encourage the voluntary sector (Hall, 2002).

[18] Hall summarizes the general shift in group membership in table 1–1 (1999, p. 423; see also 2002, p. 26). He refers to his sources in footnote 19 (1999, p. 423).

By using the same survey Putnam is able to claim comparability over time. Hall, on the other hand, is introducing different categories into his comparative analysis, raising questions about their comparability.[19] In the end, however, despite the questions raised with respect to perfect comparability, Hall's method is to be preferred, as he gets at changes in civic activity that Putnam cannot.

There are specific reasons why the questions and categories on the GSS and Roper surveys used by Putnam could be considered dated. In some cases it is a matter of archaic language rooted in a different historical context. For example, the GSS refers to 'professional *societies*' (rather than professional *associations*); '*church*-affiliated groups' (rather than faith-based or *religious* associations); 'political *clubs*' (as opposed to political *parties* or advocacy organizations). In other cases, the specific civic group used in the questionnaire as an example of civic activity may bias the data. The most extreme example of this kind can be found in the RSPT question, under the political activity series (which Putnam uses for table 3 (p. 252)), regarding membership in 'good government' organizations (Brady et al., 2000, p. 10). The question posed by the interviewer is whether the respondent in the past year has 'been a member of some group *like the League of Women's Voters*, or some other group interested in better government?' (p. 20, emphasis added). As has been noted in previous chapters, using such a traditional form of civic association (LWV) as the specific point of reference is to focus interviewees on certain types of older organizations (namely formal, chapter-based, service-oriented, maternalist Progressive Era groups) as opposed to more recent types of civic or political participation and activity. There is a bias, in other words, in these questions towards measuring traditional kinds of civic activity. Because older Americans are more likely to be involved in an organization such as the LWV, and younger women are more likely to be involved in a local childcare board, there is an inbuilt bias as well in the generational patterns.

On the other hand, the 1981 and 1990 World Values surveys, used by Hall in his survey in the United Kingdom, reflect a more inclusive language with regard to organizations. For example, the list of voluntary organizations includes '*religious* or church organizations'; 'sports or recreation'; 'trade unions'; '*professional associations*'; '*conservation, the*

---

[19] For example, only the Political Action survey includes political parties (question 82 in Almond and Verba, 1963, p. 11) as one of the 'groups' being measured (unlike the other two surveys). This would probably cause the figures for 1973 in table 1 of Hall's analysis (1999, p. 423) to be higher, in terms of associational membership, than other years that reflect surveys that did not include party membership as part of the count for civic participation.

environment, ecology'; '*local community action on issues like poverty, employment, housing, racial equality*'; '*women's groups*' (emphasis added).[20] Within this list are a few important additions: religious organization (not just Church or Christian-related groups); professional *association*, not 'club' or 'society'; and environmental organization. These last two get at some of the growth in the new kinds of civic participation, described in the section above.[21] As such, Hall concludes that there is no 'baby boom' collapse in participation as suggested by Putnam. Wuthnow comes to similar conclusions with regard to the United States when he uses the 1981 and 1990 World Values survey:

> The result of this broader inclusion [human rights organizations and environmentalist groups] is that more of the American public appears to be involved in at least some group than in the GSS [which has a more limited number of groups]. Moreover, the proportion involved actually rises (from 73 per cent to 82 per cent) over the period. (Wuthnow, 2002a, p. 89)

The problem with Putnam's theory of generational change based on survey data is the same as his theory of 'declining' membership based on the analysis of civic organizations. If one does not account for all the *new* forms of civic engagement, then one will not get an accurate picture of how the *younger* generations (as opposed to the older ones) engage in civic life; moreover, the further one gets from the historical context within which the original questions were composed the more this generational effect will increase. In this sense, survey questions might go beyond even the environmental and professional associations listed in the World Values survey to include newer forms of civic participation (for example, organizations that have developed around all kinds of identity politics, civil rights and gender concerns, as well as new venues for civic participation such as childcare or small groups). If one could magically imagine, as was suggested earlier, that these categories were included and measured in previous surveys back to the 1950s, one would have a much fuller picture of the ways in which civic participation has both *increased* and *declined* across generations. For example, what would happen if one could include on all surveys dating back to the 1950s the following questions: 'Did you attend a Gay Pride parade in the last year?'; 'Did you partake in any civic activities relating to support for people with AIDS in the last year?'; 'Do

---

[20] These terms are taken from the World Values survey questionnaire (V19–36). For the full question, see Inglehart (1997, p. 396).

[21] Putnam, as has already been discussed, sees this shift as a negative development, and I have argued earlier that this is more positive than either he or Theda Skocpol suggest. The point here, however, is a slightly different one. It is simply whether or not the generational effect on social capital is as suggested by Putnam and whether such generational changes are the same for men and women.

you belong to a local childcare centre and have you engaged in fund-raising for this centre?'; 'Have you accessed a disability resource centre in the last year over issues of accessibility?'; 'Have you refereed, coached, played in or supported your daughter at a girls'/women's athletic event in the last year?' If these questions were asked and if one could compare them to earlier data sets, the trajectories for these types of civic activities would be in an upward direction; and one would get a better picture of how civic engagement changes in relation to the specific social conditions of a different generation. With all this data included, it is not clear whether or not one would still have a story of decline in the younger generation. Clearly, in the case of the United Kingdom, the answer, particularly in the case of women, would seem to be 'no'.

Finally, as stated at the outset, whether generational change should be considered a 'cause' at all is unclear. Putnam himself, in previous versions of the social capital thesis as well as in *Bowling Alone*, suggests that it is still necessary to find the causal factor that demarcated one generation from the other. 'To say that civic disengagement in contemporary America is in large measure generational change *merely reformulates our central puzzle . . .* [w]hat force could have affected Americans who came of age after World War II so differently from their parents and even from their older brothers and sisters?' (p. 266, emphasis added). While Putnam points to a number of possibilities, he tends to dismiss other causal explanations (p. 267), and ultimately arrives, in the 'reformulation of the puzzle', at two central causes: the Second World War's impact on older Americans and television's impact on younger ones.

The wartime Zeitgeist of national unity and patriotism that culminated in 1945 reinforced civic mindedness . . . So one plausible explanation for the strong generational effects in civic engagement that pervade our evidence is the replacement of a cohort of men and women whose values and civic habits were formed during a period of heightened civic obligation with others whose formative years were different . . . The long civic generation was the last cohort of Americans to grow up without television. The more fully that any given generation was exposed to television in its formative years, the lower its civic engagement during adulthood. (pp. 267 & 272)

While the former pro-civic ray (the Second World War) leads us to the idea that what might really be needed in this generation is a 'galvanizing crisis' (the implications of which will be discussed in chapter 6), the latter (anti-civic ray) seems to lead us back to television.

The role of television: is this the smoking gun?

Putnam once held television to be the 'prime suspect' (1996, p. 17), or the singular 'mysterious anti-civic "X-ray"', that split the civic generation from the anti-civic generation (1995b, p. 677). In *Bowling Alone*, he seems to suggest a more multivariate explanation of the collapse, with television now responsible for only 25 per cent of the decline. On closer examination, however, television still seems to be the largest contributing factor, as alluded to above, when one looks more closely at generational change. It is clear that television is the factor that creates the anti-civic ray of the post-war generations and is of growing importance as the younger generations grow in relation to the older ones. Putnam himself concludes that generational change and television might well be the same thing: 'Although more research is needed . . . it seems likely the effect of TV . . . and the effect of generation . . . are in some respects opposite sides of the same coin' (2000, p. 272). Thus, the 25 per cent that Putnam accords to television in his analysis needs to be supplemented by the impact of television covered under the rubric of generational change.[22] Ultimately, I would argue that television remains, in *Bowling Alone*, his main explanatory factor.

The toughest question for Putnam in relationship to television is whether the *correlation* he discovers between increased television watching and the decline in social capital is, in fact, a *causal* relationship. There is the possibility that the causal relationship goes the other way, or that both increased television watching and decreased civic participation or trust are caused by other factors altogether – a thesis suggested by Lance Bennett in the 1998 Ithiel de Sola Pool Lecture, as will be discussed in the next chapter (Bennett, 1998). Putnam argues that television has impacted on social capital in three separate ways: the displacement of time; psychological effects that inhibit participation; and specific changes in content that undermine civic motivations (p. 237). If we keep in mind that social capital is both participation *and* trust, the displacement effect on time may affect civic participation (although we question that assertion below), but it is difficult to see how exactly this could explain the decline in *trust*. The second suggested way in which television might impact social capital (the inhibition of participation) is explicitly linked to participation. This leaves us with the programmatic content of television as the explanatory factor for a decline in trust. While Putnam does not directly address this in the chapter on technology and mass media, there are ways in which the changing content of the media may have impacted both the decline in levels of social trust, as well as the gap in trust between the privileged and the marginalized. We shall address this in more depth in the next chapter, on trust.

---

[22] While Putnam says at the summing-up of all the contributing factors (p. 284) that there may be 'other factors lurking behind the "generational effect"', he provides no indication or evidence of what those other factors may be, beyond the Second World War and television.

Putnam admits that he is unable to claim definitively that television is the *cause* of civic decline but he does provide three 'proofs' in *Bowling Alone* in support of his causal hypothesis. The first is that the decline in social capital happened a decade *after* the 'widespread availability of television' (p. 235). There were still, however, an infinite number of other events occurring during this same time period; the relative timing establishes no causal relationship, but may rule out the converse: that civic disengagement caused an increase in the level of television viewing. Putnam cannot preclude, on the basis of this argument, the possibility that other factors may have been the cause of one or both. The second reason he gives is that, if younger people who watch more television are less civically engaged, this establishes a correlation (through the correlate of age) between television viewing and civic disengagement. Again, this does not preclude the possibility of other factors causing both phenomena (p. 235).

The third 'proof', described by Putnam as 'strikingly direct evidence about the causal direction', is a study of a Canadian community carried out before and after it gained television in 1972. 'From a range of intriguing studies . . . the most remarkable of these . . . emerged from three isolated communities in northern Canada in the 1970s' (p. 235). The study to which Putnam refers at some length was conducted by psychology professor Tannis MacBeth Williams and her team of researchers in three small towns in British Columbia in the 1970s. Their findings were first published as a book in 1986, and then condensed into an article in 1991 (MacBeth Williams, 1986; MacBeth, 1991).[23] It is worth noting at the outset that these communities were not located in *northern* Canada, as Putnam claims, but southern Canada (indeed, Multitel was near the US border). Nor were they *isolated* as Putnam suggests; indeed, MacBeth Williams is at pains to point out that the town of Notel is *not* isolated: 'This town lacked TV because it happened to be in a geographic blind spot, *not because it was particularly isolated*' (1986, p. 2).[24] The one community in question, Notel, due to its location in a valley, had no reception

---

[23] In 1986, when the book was published, it was under the name of Tannis MacBeth Williams. By 1991, when the article was published, Williams had reverted to her original name of MacBeth; hence the different names for the two citations by the same author. I would like to thank Tannis MacBeth for the detailed feedback she gave me on this chapter.

[24] This is important, for two reasons. First, because it means that whatever conclusions that can be drawn about the impact of television in Notel are not the result of suddenly being connected to the 'outside world' but the narrower variable of having television on a regular basis. Thus, it is a conservative test, scientifically speaking, according to MacBeth Williams, because the members of the community previously had access to television if they travelled a short distance. Secondly, it is important because the findings will be more generalizable if the community is typical of other towns around it, rather than being isolated and therefore able to represent only itself. See the section on generalizing from the findings (1986, p. 31).

and therefore no television until 1972, when it received one channel of the national public broadcaster, the Canadian Broadcasting Corporation. Notel was compared to another community (Unitel) that received one channel (CBC) for seven years, but got a second channel (also CBC, so the content varied little between the two channels other than local news) at the same time that Notel received its first channel. These two communities were also compared to a third community (Multitel) that had received four channels (CBC, ABC, NBC, CBS) for fifteen years. The research on these three communities involved many different studies but included surveys of activities as well as behavioural measures and observational analysis. The surveys of activities involved two questionnaires conducted in each phase of the study: one on participation in organized community activities (e.g. sports teams, club memberships, etc.), and the other on private leisure activities (e.g. knitting, social drinking, etc.) during the past year.

There are a number of problems with Putnam's use of this particular study as the linchpin in his causal thesis with regard to television and community involvement. First, MacBeth Williams's focus – and, indeed, the focus of most of the literature that Putnam cites on television – is on the impact on children and their behaviour rather than *adult's* activities.[25] Thus, while the findings are important and provide insights into the displacement of children's time, whether they can be extrapolated to provide causal links in terms of *adult* civic behaviour is another question altogether. Secondly, whether a community such as Notel, abstracted from both its historical and geographical context, can be used to extrapolate conclusions about communities in an entirely different country is also worth consideration. As MacBeth herself concludes: 'No single study can be definitive' (1991, p. 141). Yet, for Putnam, this study appears to be his definitive piece of evidence. Ultimately, the impact of television on adult community activity is, according to MacBeth, a very mixed story – not the strong unequivocal link suggested by Putnam. Let us consider her findings in more detail.

The introduction of television in Notel had a negative impact on active participation in community sports and attendance at community suppers, dances and club meetings. With respect to club membership, however, there is an interesting question raised by MacBeth regarding its effect of television in the long term. While the study found that Notel membership declined over the two years in question, Unitel's club membership *increased* over the same period. One of MacBeth's explanations

---

[25] Putnam provides a list of studies (p. 236, fn. 39) that are almost entirely focused on children's behaviour.

for Unitel's increase in club membership, consistent with studies carried out in the United Kingdom, is that Notel's experience with television was relatively short-term; over the long run, Notel (like Unitel) would probably see interest and membership revive. Thus, using earlier studies by Belson and Himmelweit et al., she surmises that interest and membership in clubs might decrease in the first year or two after the introduction of television, but ultimately increase after four to five years (MacBeth Williams, 1986, p. 168; Belson, 1959; Himmelweit et al., 1958).[26] Thus, the length of time for which a community has had television may be an important factor in determining participation in organized clubs. It may also be that the number of channels or the content available in Unitel is a contributing factor. In all these early studies the number of channels available was very limited, and usually restricted to a public broadcaster (BBC or CBC). Thus, if we compare Unitel (CBC) to Multitel (ABC, NBC, CBS and CBC), Unitel's club membership is similar to Multitel's at the beginning of the study but significantly higher at the end. This pattern suggests that it may not be television per se but the number of channels (one versus four), the length of time a community has had television (eight versus fifteen years) and/or the *content* of public versus private broadcasting that are the determining factors.

There is also a question of age segregation. It is clear that the particular age group disproportionately affected by the introduction of television, with respect to club memberships and general participation, is that of older members of the community (over fifty-five) (MacBeth Williams, 1986, p. 184). In particular, when age is correlated not just with participation but with involvement in key roles in organizations, MacBeth Williams finds that 'the arrival of television counteracted the normally expected increase in performances with increasing age' (1986, p. 177). It is important to recognize that this group somewhat skews the findings for changing patterns of adult community activity with respect to both participation and performance.

Finally, and most importantly, MacBeth Williams finds that the introduction of television had no impact on a whole range of activities in the

---

[26] Belson found in London that people's interest in organized clubs decreased in the second year after owning a television set but, by five years later, interest in clubs was greater than it had originally been. Another theoretical argument that MacBeth Williams draws on is psychological ecology, namely that 'settings constrain and influence people's behaviour' (1986, p. 159). In this case it may be that an organization will allow a decrease in participation in the first year after television is introduced, but over time, if the existence of the organization is threatened, organizational pressure will be applied upon the members to attend. If this is correct, it would provide evidence for Putnam's preference for bowling leagues over 'bowling alone', as the former might provide the kinds of constraints on people's behaviour that the latter does not.

community: religious activity, going to the park or playground, swimming, visiting the doctor, going to stores or offices. She also finds that television had little impact on what she calls 'civic activities', using as examples 'visiting the town hall', 'fund-raising events' or 'clean-up campaigns' (1991, pp. 128–30).[27]

There were no systematic differences among the towns in attendance at medical and religious activities, but there were some differences among the towns for involvement in open areas, businesses, civic affairs, educational (non-school) and other activities, *but the pattern of results suggested that television did not play a role in these differences.* (1986, p. 399; 1991, pp. 129–30, emphasis added)

MacBeth Williams's findings suggest that television may account for some decline in sporting activity, membership in organized clubs and community activities (particularly for seniors) and general levels of socializing. However, even in the one area that she finds most negatively affected (sports), television may still be of limited explanatory power if measured against the impact of other cultural factors, returning us to the first question of extrapolating from one cultural context to another. With respect to sports, television was introduced in Notel in 1972, the same year that Title IX was passed in the United States. If this had been an American community, statistics quoted in the last chapter on the impact of Title IX suggest that any negative impact of television on sporting activity specifically with reference to girls would have been far surpassed by the long-term effect of this piece of legislation.

What all this suggests is that television cannot be considered the 'smoking gun' or 'prime suspect' or 'mysterious X-ray' in the 'decline' of American communities but, at best, a contributing factor in the changes that have occurred; one that may, given the right set of historical factors, be superseded by other cultural or social forces. MacBeth Williams emphasizes the point that television should not be used as a simple time displacement causal theory, particularly with respect to adults:

As we have emphasized, a simple displacement hypothesis regarding the effects of television is inappropriate. In the case of leisure activities, other demands constrain the amount of leisure time available. For example, an individual with no paid work . . . might participate in many community activities . . . Detailed time budgets are required to ascertain more precisely the ways in which television, other leisure activities and paid and unpaid work responsibilities interact. Unfortunately, we were unable to obtain such information in this project. (1986, p. 176)

---

[27] It is important to note that MacBeth Williams's definition of 'civic' is far narrower than either mine or Putnam's, but this is a critical point, because what she is examining is the degree to which television impacts citizens' engagement in local civic issues – one of Putnam's key concerns.

Thus, while television has had an inarguably enormous impact on American culture, the specific and singular causal link suggested by Putnam with respect to either trust or civic participation is simply not there in the study singled out by Putnam himself to underpin his causal analysis.

The one aspect of television's impact on community proposed by Putnam that is worthy of closer examination (as alluded to above in the comparison between Multitel and Unitel) is the programmatic content of television. Given that 'participation in total community activities . . . was greater' in Unitel (only CBC) than Multitel (all the American private channels as well) in both phases but with a growing gap suggests that content may well have mattered even in 1972.[28] Since then the question of content has become even more germane. Over the last thirty years television has developed in ways that expose the viewer to more available channels, while simultaneously becoming more commercialized and, for a variety of reasons, tending to reinforce a negative view of human nature and politics. As Putnam himself points out, from confrontational talk shows such as Jerry Springer to the popularity of the contrived violence of professional wrestling, to the new 'reality'-based survival shows that all seem to revolve around pitting individuals against each other and then eliminating them, one at a time, from a social setting, television's negative effect may be the impact of such content on general levels of civility and trust. George Gerbner and his colleagues have described this as the tendency within television to create a 'mean world syndrome' (Gerbner et al., 1994). It should not surprise us if viewers were not to trust others in such a 'mean' world.

There have been a number of challenges to Putnam's television thesis along these lines of distinguishing between amount watched and content with regard to civic-mindedness. Pippa Norris, for example, has teased out the differences between television as a whole and the kinds of programmes watched. Norris concludes that those who view news and public affairs programmes are more highly correlated with civic and political participation than those who watch no television (Norris, 1996). Norris has

---

[28] The question of how different the content of public and private broadcasters were in 1972 could be debated. MacBeth Williams (1986) suggests that there might have been considerable overlap given that the CBC, in prime time, often broadcast American programmes (p. 20), but the CBC has always had a mandate unique to a public broadcaster, to ensure Canadian content while serving the Canadian public interest. In November 2004 Robert Rabinovitch, president and CEO of CBC/Radio Canada, stated in a presentation before the Standing Committee on Canadian Heritage what the mandate of a public broadcaster was: 'We developed some key strategic objectives for the Corporation, going back to our public broadcasting roots and focusing on the services that others cannot or do not provide. We focused on service, not ratings . . . on treating our audiences as citizens, not consumers' (see www.cbc.radio-canada.ca/htmen/speeches/20041115.htm, accessed February 2005).

also found that 'extensive and sustained negative coverage' of a particular topic (in her case the euro) is 'significantly associated with lowered levels of diffuse and specific support' for the broad subject under consideration (Europe) (Norris, 2000, p. 206). Put simply, negative news creates a negative public. Others have argued that changes in content, including a more cynical view of politics as a game of insiders, have poisoned the public's view of community *and* politics more generally (Patterson, 1993; Cappella and Jamieson, 1997). To this end, the programmatic content of not only television but talk radio (which gets only a brief mention in *Bowling Alone*) should be part of the analysis of media on levels of trust and connectedness to others for its potentially corrosive impact on civility, the levels of tolerance and acceptance of different groups of people in American society, as well as the sense given that *all* politicians are either inept or corrupt (Cappella and Jamieson, 1997; Hilliard et al., 1999). Hilliard et al. argue that talk radio provides the voice for the radical right wing and is an important contributing factor to the incivility between different groups: 'Talk radio in the United States is dominated by those who support the aims of militias, white supremacists and ethnic purists' (1999, p. 6). The central point here is that, if it is the content of television that is the problem rather than the amount of time watched, the solution seems to rest as much with those who are deciding on its format (i.e. the purveyors of mass media) as it does with the consumers. We shall explore this question in a little more detail in the last section of the next chapter, where we seek an alternative explanation for the pattern of decline in trust.

Methodological questions

Putnam's data and causal explanations for the 'decline' in civic participation raise a number of methodological questions. In the introduction, it was suggested that one of the reasons for using the idea of 'social capital' as opposed to the more generic notion of community building was because it provided an analytical tool that spoke to a variety of different social sciences under an economic paradigm of methodological individualism and quantifiable data. Perhaps most importantly, this economic methodology allows scholars such as Putnam (and other concerned actors) who wish to focus equally on the social and economic dimensions of human life to measure both with the same hard, quantitative edge. Thus, Western economic theorists studying industrialized economies as well as those searching for new strategies of Third World development have embraced 'social capital' as a way of bridging the divide, methodologically, between the social and economic spheres (Putnam, 2000, pp. 4–5).[29] His methodology, however, is not only a great potential strength in terms of its ambitions to transcend disciplinary divides but, as we have seen, also a source of acute weakness, to the extent that the methodology adopted is inappropriate to the subject studied.

The first methodological problem we encountered (in the last chapter) concerned whether the appropriate means by which to measure longitudinal patterns in civic participation over the last century was membership in the selected formal groups. Putnam's selection of organizations was based in part on their existence right from the beginning of the twentieth century through to the end (as required by a methodology that sought to measure aggregate growth across time in meaningful comparative categories). Thus, the methodological question for Putnam, where he uses formal membership to measure a decline in civic participation, is whether he can claim to be measuring decline in overall civic activity at all, or just a decline in the membership of the specific organizations that were founded at the beginning of the twentieth century. As I argued in the last chapter, the answer is that he is not measuring a decline in *civic participation in general* so much as a decline in the specific organizations chosen.[30] This question of measurement is particularly important for cultural minorities and women, because they formed many different kinds of new (and more informal) groups in the latter half of the twentieth century that are simply not included in the Putnam account.

A second methodological problem raised (in this chapter) by using survey data is that of whether comparability across time can be achieved if one uses a single survey; there are benefits, not least the inclusion of new kinds of groups, if one uses more contemporary surveys. This issue was addressed in relation to the different conclusions arrived at by Peter Hall and Robert Putnam with respect to the decline of civic activity and generational change. Putnam chose to use the same surveys across time (and protect a purer notion of comparability methodologically); Hall chose to use different surveys (and therefore different questions) in measuring civic activity. The methodological question is whether it is better

---

[29] For example, the World Bank uses the idea of a quantifiable social capital as a critical element in its case that one must (and now can) measure both economic growth and social cohesion and participation in developing countries.

[30] I am not the first to make this case. It is analogous to the argument made by Pippa Norris with respect to *political* participation: that it did not decline so much as evolve, in terms of 'agencies', 'repertoires' and 'targets', over the twentieth century (Norris, 2002). Douglas Baer et al. (2001) conclude, in the area of civic participation, that Putnam is really measuring no more than the decline in two main institutions rather than American society as a whole. 'With churches and unions excluded from the analysis, no decline [in participation] is evident in the US' (Baer et al., 2001, p. 269). Everett Ladd has argued, across the board, that Putnam is not measuring the right things (Ladd, 1996, 1999).

to retain your categories of measurement and know your comparison is sound, or to include an evolving inventory of groups more relevant to the contemporary context but at the expense of some of your comparative edge. Putnam makes the case for comparability in appendix 1: 'Survey questions must be (more or less) unchanging to capture change.' He particularly warns against comparing different surveys by different organizations. 'It is especially risky to compare results from questions posed at different times by different survey organizations' (2000, p. 417). As Putnam himself describes his methodology, he is aiming at doing 'social time lapse photography', ensuring that everything remains the same (survey questions, groups measured), other than the temporal dimension.

This question of comparability over time (and retaining static categories) versus capturing change over time (and changing categories) is a critical methodological question for those concerned with temporal patterns in political or civic activity. Warren Miller and Paul Abramson debate the trade-offs in *Public Opinion Quarterly* (Miller, 1990; Abramson, 1990) with regard to the introduction of new questions on the National Election Survey. While Abramson is careful in his conclusions to say that he is not arguing against new items being added, his analysis is permeated by an underlying assumption that a trade-off between methodological comparability and new kinds of questions is inevitable. Miller, in response to Abramson, recognizes these concerns, concluding: 'The Abramson article . . . reminds us how pervasive other problems of establishing comparability of measurement across time and space may be' (p. 192). Miller defends the decision to include new questions and eliminate outdated ones, based on the need to capture a new political reality.

As questions were added in the National Election Survey, additional categories of civic activity were added in the World Values surveys on civic participation raising exactly the same dilemma between comparability on the one hand and new trends on the other. Ultimately, I would argue, like Miller, that the inclusion of new categories and questions on surveys is not only appropriate but necessary if surveyors are not to build in biases towards older forms of civic and political activity. It may not be time-lapse photography, as described by Putnam, but it avoids more profound problems. Thus, Wuthnow and Hall's method is more sound, as it is better suited to capturing an overall picture of civic participation incorporating the changing forms of activity and membership. The alternative, as defended by Putnam and Abramson (choosing to use the same questions or the same set of civic groups in 1999 as in 1960), fails to capture the changing nature of civic life, as has been demonstrated in the last two chapters.

A third methodological question raised by Putnam's analysis is whether social capital can be measured with the same precision and level of objective quantification as economic or political capital.[31] The central difficulty is that, unlike economic and certain kinds of political categories, measuring social phenomena such as civic activity is a far more historically contingent and value-dependent enterprise.

The debate between Miller and Abramson is illuminating on this point. While Miller has no problem with the sections dealing with partisanship or political involvement (where the questions remain relatively constant), his concerns are to do with public policy and political attitude questions. Thus, Abramson concludes, there is 'a surprising decline in comparability during the 1980s, *especially in the study of public policy questions and political attitudes*' (Abramson, 1990, p. 178, emphasis added). The critical point here is that these areas of study (public policy and attitudes) are more historically contingent than partisanship or political involvement. One either supports (partisanship) or belongs to and works for (political involvement) the Republicans, Democrats or another party; the categories do not tend to change across time. On the other hand, public policy and political attitudes are more dependent upon changing social, economic and political environments. Most importantly, the designer of the survey must decide, with respect to these latter categories, whether or not to stay with certain questions or ask new ones: this can never be an objective science in the way that (relatively) constant categories such as partisanship can be.

Social capital, as a 'social' concept, like public policy, is historically contingent, and hence its measurement must evolve over time and be defined by the researcher. This has been shown in a number of ways in our analysis. The subjective nature of measuring social capital first emerged in the last chapter in trying to define the populations against which to measure the growth in organizations.[32] One is faced with the subjective task of defining the exact nature of the population being used as the point of reference. In economics, where one is looking at national economies, it may be possible to define the per capita number on the basis of census data. But, in the case of civic or social life, one must make subjective judgements about what constitutes the relevant social

---

[31] Some commentators (such as Marilyn Waring, 1988, 1999) would question the 'objectivity' of economic measures as well, but, for the purposes of this analysis, we are assuming that GDP and growth as measures of economic well-being are relatively stable in meaning over time, compared to the ever-changing nature of civic associations as the measure of social well-being.

[32] Putnam's methodology quite rightly requires that membership in organizations be a ratio of the population in order to ensure that any change is not simply the result of population increase.

group in question. One specific example, used in the last chapter, is the relevant population for the first six traditional women's organizations: should it be all American women, or just women who are traditional homemakers? In the case of the PTA, should one include all parents with children in school or compare the populations of those with children of a certain age who are more likely to be involved in the PTA (as Everett Ladd does)? In both these cases, there is an historical and contingent nature to the population under consideration. It would be possible, as Putnam does, to use the population of adult women, but, by using this seemingly 'objective' figure, is he actually measuring what he hopes to measure, namely the overall decline amongst women in particular groups, or, as Hall argues, the decline in population amongst a sub-population of women?

Another 'subjective' question is raised by the introduction of 'bridging capital' into Putnam's analysis: how does one 'objectively' measure what Putnam himself calls the most important dimension of social capital in diverse societies? The first issue is measurement itself, because surely it is necessary, if one wants to get at *bridging* capital, to measure not only the changes in overall membership in any given organization but also the growth (or decline) in *particular sub-populations* as well. The examples used in the last chapter of organizations that already provide this kind of data were the Girl Scouts of America, the Bar Association and the NCAA, all of which keep detailed membership records with respect to both ethnicity and gender. Thus, the growth in Girl Scout membership may be measured against the population of girls generally; but, if one wants to see the extent to which it is increasingly multicultural and therefore a form of bridging capital, one must also measure the change in the membership of specific cultural groups. The question of bridging capital therefore again raises a subjective set of questions. Which groups should be included, and how are they defined? What about the privacy of the individual members? To measure bridging social capital is not an easy task, for defining sub-populations involves any number of culturally bound value choices and ethical decisions. But, if one ignores these sub-categories and simply goes with an overall membership figure, it is difficult to see how bridging capital is measured at all over time. Once again, the measurement of social capital takes us towards a socially constructed idea of a sub-population.

Perhaps most important for my analysis, with respect to the social nature of the phenomena being measured, is the extent to which social capital theory should incorporate the different *meanings* that growth in particular kinds of associations may have for specific groups of people. If one does not recognize these social differences in meaning then the civic activity may either not be measured at all or its value *to that particular group*'s civic life will be missed in larger aggregate measurements. One example is the need to include disability and sexual orientation groups in one's calculus. While these associations are marginal in terms of their size relative to large civic organizations in the United States, they are at the same time exceedingly important to the possibility of even entering civic life for particular groups of the American population. Unless this socially constructed story is recognized, neither the attendant levels of membership in these associations nor the broader implications for the civic life of disabled or homosexual Americans will be recognized or measured.

Moreover, organizations have profoundly different meanings to groups (such as disabled Americans) depending on whether it is a service or a self-advocacy group: the methodological problem is that simple aggregate figures assume that the level of membership in one organization can simply be translated into an equal number of memberships in another. For example, the shift in membership from service organizations for people with disabilities, such as the March of Dimes, Easter Seal Society or Muscular Dystrophy Association, in the first half of the twentieth century to the rights-oriented disability organizations of the last thirty years has a meaning that mere number counting in terms of membership simply will not get to. Another example of how the actual calculus is affected by the social meaning of changing groups is the decision as to whether one should measure the increasing numbers of women in particular kinds of associations, such as professional associations. Putnam does not measure the numbers of men versus women in these organizations, nor recognize that such growth has a social meaning for men that is very different from what it is for women, which can be accounted for only if the specific social evolution of *women* in the twentieth century is acknowledged and incorporated into the analysis. If one does not then the particular narrative of half the American community is simply submerged under what the shift means to men, beneath the rubric of an ostensibly generalizable tale of decline and malaise for all.

Thus, what all these various examples demonstrate is that the social character of the material being analysed undermines the idea that a value-free methodological individualism and aggregate numbers can be used to measure social capital in an accurate and meaningful way without either excluding important aspects of social capital and/or making some important subjective decisions with respect to measurement and meaning. To attempt to tell the story of community in America in the twentieth century by methodologically removing any reference to gender, ethnicity or culture in either the measurement tools or the values ascribed to the changes recorded is not to create an objective and universal story along the lines of the longitudinal trends of GDP; rather, it is to obscure the political (meaning conflictual nature), sociological (meaning societal importance) and diverse cultural meanings of the changes that have occurred.

A final, and very different, methodological problem in Putnam's thesis of decline is the issue of circularity, or cause and effect. The question raised by some scholars is the following: 'Is social capital itself a characteristic of a flourishing society, or a means of achieving it?' (Baron et al., 2000, p. 29). Is social capital both an explanatory variable of 'trust' as well as the term used to describe that phenomenon? Alejandro Portes concludes:

> The fundamental problem with Putnam's argument [is] its circularity . . . Social capital is simultaneously a cause and an effect. It leads to positive outcomes, such as economic development and less crime, and its existence is inferred from the same outcomes. (Portes, 1998, p. 16)

The problem that Portes (and others) point to is an important logical flaw, but given the nature and complexity of social analysis it has been argued that it is exceedingly difficult to isolate variables and provide the kind of linear argument demanded by pure logic. The social nature of the analysis requires that we recognize that 'a social capital approach is relational, and requires us to look at social phenomena from different angles simultaneously' (Baron et al., 2000, p. 29). Boix and Posner (1998) suggest that one possible approach could be an equilibrium model of social capital, which would avoid the charges of circularity but might still leave the question of the origin of either 'virtuous' or 'vicious' circles unanswered. While it is true that the study of social variables can be understood only as part of complex systems and extracting them analytically and positing them as either causes or effects can be done only in a tenuous, relational and ultimately holistic manner, what I believe Portes and others are getting at in Putnam's analysis is a conflation of three very different phenomena under the rubric of 'social capital': civic participation, civic trust and political participation. As a first step in trying to address the problem of circularity, I would argue that it is critical that civic trust, civic participation and political participation be seen as independent phenomena rather than all being treated as part of the same 'syndrome', as Putnam describes them. In the next chapter I examine the phenomenon of trust independently of civic participation, and, rather than assuming (like Putnam) that the causes of one are necessarily the causes of the other, I attempt to develop an alternative causal theory for both a decline and a gap in civic trust, specifically.

Ultimately, with respect to causality, I will argue that it is necessary to go beyond the aggregate individual model presupposed by American social capital methodology to analyse the broader collective forces in society. If there is one aspect of social capital, particularly as it applies to political participation and social trust, that is overlooked in *Bowling Alone*, it is the profound gaps between the marginalized and the privileged, which persist over time. Such gaps suggest that the temporal dimension of participation and trust is not the only thing that matters in understanding the causes and patterns of what Putnam calls 'social capital' but that, rather, the collective experiences that groups of people go through historically, such as African-Americans or Native Americans or women, must also be analysed in order to help us explain why groups seem to respond and act as a collective identity in relation to civic society. Thus, all these variables that Putnam classifies under 'social capital' must be examined in the larger social, economic and cultural contexts within which they develop. In particular, both civic participation and, as we shall see, civic trust in the United States over the last forty years have been buffeted and changed, by the enormous forces unleashed by changes in the global economic system, the relations between different groups of American (along both gendered and cultural lines) and specific political events, magnified by the power of technology and – in particular – television, all of which have undermined (for good reason) American citizens' belief in their political leadership and their society.

Conclusions

As we have seen in this chapter as we have addressed the underlying 'causes' of decline, there is an implicit (and sometimes explicit) sense in Putnam's work (perhaps to avoid the charges of circularity or fuzzy social thinking) that he can indeed point to a direct linear causal progression in his argument. In essence, he argues that it is the increase in television and changing generational attitudes (supplemented by dual-career families and suburban sprawl) that lead to a decline in civic and social participation (which, in turn, leads to a drop in political participation and trust). This is the underlying story of collapse in American society as Putnam tells it. In this chapter we have examined three of the suggested first causes in more detail: dual-career families, generational change and television. As a result, this chapter (as well as the analysis in the previous chapter on women's participation in formal organizations) has raised a number of methodological questions for Putnam's analysis of both the decline in civic participation and its causes.

Ultimately, these three causes (dual-career families, television and generational change) are problematic for specific reasons, as described above, in explaining the decline of social capital. Underlying these specific problems are three general ones in Putnam's causal theory. The first is his tendency to aggregate a number of different phenomena together (declining civic participation, declining political participation and declining levels of trust in others) under one general rubric (social capital), assuming that they are a 'coherent syndrome' rather than several independent phenomena with independent causes. In order to understand what is going on, it is necessary to disaggregate these variables, *and their causes*. The second general problem (with regard to civic participation specifically) is Putnam's failure to look at and account for the contrary case in his causal explanation of decline: that is, traditional civic groups that have increased their membership, or new kinds of civic activity that have growing numbers of members.[33] Thirdly, by looking only at individual choices (through aggregate data) rather than deeper structural factors (the nature of the organizations themselves, or the wider community within which they operate) that allow the accumulation of social capital to develop in some ways and not others, Putnam's functional model does not allow for the possibility that it may not be aggregate individual choice that is changing civic society but these larger structural forces.

Wuthnow suggests exactly this possibility in his distinction between Putnam's 'erosion perspective', which focuses on the aggregate individual erosion of given organizations, and his own 'exclusion hypothesis', which looks instead to the organizations themselves as the cause for decline, particularly amongst the marginalized in society.

A possible reason for the decline in social capital is that existing social arrangements have become systematically more exclusionary, causing some segments of the population to feel unwelcome and to cease participation, or failing to provide the resources that people need to engage in civic activities. In contrast to [Putnam's] erosion perspective, the exclusion approach focuses less on the moral commitment of the laboring population and more on whether or not this population has the resources necessary for participating in organizations, as well as on the possibility that organizations are less than democratic in their actual functioning. *It raises the possibility that if people are no longer joining Kiwanis as often as they did in the past, it may be indicative of some problem with Kiwanis rather than with the population.* (Wuthnow, 2002a, p. 79, emphasis added)[34]

In the next chapter, I attempt to respond to these three general problems by disaggregating civic trust from civic participation, and look to the causal factors that might be involved in the decline and growing gap

---

[33] Putnam does consider the environmental movement as a new kind of activity but limits his analysis of counter-cases largely to this group.

[34] Wuthnow provides statistical evidence to support this claim, which demonstrates that nearly all the decline in associational memberships between 1974 and 1991 took place amongst those who were marginalized in society, by a variety of characteristics including race, socio-economic status, and number of children (2002a, pp. 81–2).

(between privileged and marginalized) in trust. This alternative causal explanation for the distinctive patterns with respect to trust will consider counter-examples (i.e. does trust increase at any particular time, and why?) as well as include the larger structural forces of exclusion pointed to by Wuthnow, and Bourdieu before him, as opposed to summarizing from the aggregate analysis of individuals, in order to understand these social phenomena properly.

5   Civic trust and shared norms

The focus, thus far, has been largely on civic participation; we turn in this chapter to two other critical dimensions of 'social capital' for Putnam, namely civic trust and shared norms.[1] Indeed, it is the *connection* between participation and trust that lies at the core of social capital's unique contribution to the study of politics and society.[2] As Pippa Norris and Ronald Inglehart comment: 'The core claim of Putnam's account [of social capital] is that face-to-face . . . horizontal collaboration within voluntary organizations . . . promotes interpersonal trust' (Norris and Inglehart, 2006, p. 2). While civic participation is the extent to which individuals join associations and can be measured by membership figures in voluntary associations as well as surveys of the general populace, civic trust is the degree to which people trust the generalized 'other' and is normally measured through public opinion analysis. The 'shared norms' that 'attend' trusting communities vary considerably in definition, as shall be discussed. At a minimum, Putnam explicitly argues for reciprocity and trustworthiness, but – as I shall argue – embedded in Putnam's theory is a much broader set of shared *cultural* norms that implies a thicker and more homogeneous kind of community than the minimalist definition might suggest. We begin by exploring the idea of 'trust' and incorporate the idea of shared 'norms' later in our analysis.

---

[1] I would like to thank both Eric Uslaner and Mark Warren for the helpful comments they provided me with for this chapter – any remaining errors are, of course, mine. I make a distinction between what Putnam calls 'social trust' and what I call 'civic trust'. Civic trust is the 'generalized trust' one has in strangers in one's community, as opposed to either trust in government or the broader category of social trust used by Putnam that includes trust in strangers but also includes the level of trust we have in people we know socially in our community. Civic trust is most closely aligned to what some theorists have called 'thin' trust in the generalized 'other'. These different kinds of trust and the importance of these distinctions for social capital are fully explored in Uslaner (2002).

[2] It should be noted that the participation side of social capital, for Putnam, goes beyond what I have called 'civic participation' (membership in voluntary associations) and also includes informal social interaction, religious participation and political participation. These other areas of community involvement are touched on in this analysis, but my main focus is on civic trust and participation.

There is an important distinction in the literature on trust between 'thick trust', the trust you have in people with whom you have interacted in the past, and 'thin trust', the trust you have in the generalized 'other' (Warren, 1999, pp. 8–10; Putnam, 2000, pp. 136–8). It is the latter form of trust – what I call 'civic trust' – that concerns Putnam and social capital theorists in their analyses of socially cooperative communities.[3] Social capital theorists tend to use one standard question to measure the changing levels of civic trust in any given society: 'Generally speaking would you say that most people can be trusted or that you can't be too careful in dealing with people?' (Putnam, 2000, p. 467, fn. 26). We begin with the empirical question as to whether civic trust is in *decline*, as Putnam claims. The data, as we shall see, bears witness to another dimension of civic trust, namely the *gap* in trust between the privileged and the marginalized. Thus, throughout the chapter we need to keep in mind these two empirical dimensions of trust: the decline and the gap. One final empirical dimension we address is the link made by Putnam between participation and trust, to see whether either a correlative or causal connection exists.

Then, as with our analysis of participation, we will turn from the strictly empirical question of trust to consider the normative issues raised by these findings: is a decline or gap in trust necessarily a bad thing? I begin with the answer provided by social capital theories as to why trust is a good thing both for the individual and the community, but then consider the possibility that *distrust*, under certain circumstances and from particular perspectives, might be an appropriate – or even good – thing. From this normative analysis of trust, I turn to consider an alternative causal explanation for both the decline and gap in trust. Examining both dimensions of trust will push us to look beyond the causal explanations provided by Putnam's social capital theory to consider a much broader set of economic, social and cultural forces unleashed in the United States since 1960. Through this causal analysis it will become exceedingly clear that the conflation of civic participation with civic trust in social capital theory obfuscates both the very different nature of each phenomenon and the different causes for the patterns that have emerged. Ultimately, what Putnam overlooks in his causal analysis of a decline in trust as opposed to

[3] Trust is equally important to economists, for similar kinds of reasons. As Robert Solow has commented, in a recent collection of articles published by the *World Bank* on social capital, 'The simple combination of rationality and individual greed that provides the behavioral foundations for most of economics will go only so far. There are important aspects of economic life and economic performance that cannot be analyzed that way . . . The story gets more interesting when it has to allow for the fact that a lot of economically relevant behavior is socially determined . . . one important example [is] trust' (Solow, 2000, p. 8).

participation is that the former, unlike the latter, is rooted in betrayal. It is necessary, therefore, in our alternative causal explanation to begin by looking for what might have led Americans to feel increasingly betrayed by their community or society over the last forty years (the decline question), as well as why some groups of Americans have a *deeper* sense of betrayal than others (the gap question).

Two empirical dimensions of civic trust: decline and gap

Civic trust, according to most of the literature on trust in America, has declined over the last forty years.[4] Putnam concludes, on the basis of survey data, that the level of trust that Americans have in each other fell during the last three decades of the twentieth century, from approximately 50 per cent in the 1970s to 40 per cent in the late 1990s.[5] Eric Uslaner uses the figures 58 per cent in 1960 and 35 per cent in 1994/5 (Uslaner, 1999, p. 131). Peter Hall has reported similar figures in the United Kingdom: in 1959 56 per cent expressed trust in others, and the young were more trusting; by the 1980s only 44 per cent expressed trust and the young were the least trusting (Hall, 2002, p. 44). Although I have argued that civic participation has changed rather than declined, I would concur with Putnam and other scholars that the change in civic trust truly reflects a decline over time. This decline is real because, unlike civic participation, the meaning of the term or the categories that encompass it do not change over time. Despite some of the difficulties with the question asked (Putnam, 2000, pp. 137–8), it is a useful longitudinal comparative measure of the extent to which Americans trust the generalized 'other' in their communities.

Thus, civic trust has indeed declined over time, but there is another dimension to civic trust that requires explanation, namely the gap in the levels of civic trust between privileged and marginalized groups, along gendered, cultural and economic lines. Hall, for example, finds in the United Kingdom that 42 per cent of women in 1990, compared to 46 per cent of men, expressed trust in others (the gap, although slight, has grown since 1959, when men and women were equally trusting at

---

[4] One exception to this consensus (and it is qualified dissent) is Orlando Patterson, who argues this pattern of trust is not as recent a development as Putnam suggests, with evidence of it as 'far back as the second half of the nineteenth century' (Patterson, 1999, p. 151). Moreover, even with the more recent general pattern of decline, there are 'striking oscillations', with the highest level of trust occurring during the Reagan presidency, which might suggest that trust is related to perceptions of optimism and/or economic growth (p. 171).

[5] Putnam uses the NORC General Social Survey and the National Election Survey (2000, p. 467, fn. 26).

56 per cent of the population). Patterson finds the same gender gap in trust (with women slightly less trusting than men) a persistent phenomenon in his analysis of longitudinal data in the United States (1999, pp. 173–4). While the gap between men and women is persistent, it is relatively small; differences in race/ethnicity, on the other hand, give rise to enormous gaps in trust within American society. Patterson refers specifically to the role of 'race' in measures of trust in America as being 'truly disturbing'.

The difference between whites and Afro-Americans is staggering: The mean percent of trusting persons among blacks for the entire period is only 17, compared with 45% for whites . . . [Between 1972 and 1994] whites [declined] from 51 to 38%, while blacks went down from 23% to the present extraordinary level of 15% of those who say others could be trusted. (Patterson, 1999, p. 190)

Indeed, the question that jumps out from Patterson's findings is not so much why there has been a *decline* over time, which looks relatively small in comparison, but why there is such an enormous gap *between* different groups of Americans that *persists* over time. For Robert Wuthnow, the gap in trust between the privileged and marginalized in America is a far more significant pattern in the data on trust than that of decline amongst Americans as a whole. 'Any discussion focusing only on decline in trust is missing the more essential fact that trust has been, and remains, quite differentially distributed across status groups' (Wuthnow, 2002a, p. 86). Even the decline over time must be seen through this filter of marginalization. 'To the extent that social capital has declined in the United States over the past two decades, a significant share of this decline has occurred among marginalized groups whose living situations have become more difficult during this period' (p. 101). As we shall see, recognizing this dimension of trust challenges Putnam's theory of social capital as a whole, for if this empirical dimension of trust can be explained only by reference to deeper socio-economic and cultural factors then his reliance on civic participation to solve the 'trust' problem will fall considerably short of the desired outcome.

One might well ask why Putnam is singularly focused on the question of decline rather than the gap, and there are probably three reasons. Methodologically, Putnam is focused on the issue of 'time' precisely because he uses longitudinal analysis. Almost by definition the data presents itself through a temporal lens. One cannot deny, moreover, that the temporal dimension to this story of trust is a significant one. Once taken up with this question of decline over time, the issue of gaps (within any particular time-frame) may recede from view. A second reason for focusing on the temporal dimension is the individualistic assumptions underlying the role of trust in social capital theory. If trust serves in the social capital model as an instrumental good necessary for *individuals* to cooperate with each other, then the unique patterns of trust *between and within groups* (as collective historical entities) is difficult to fit into this functional analysis, other than as an aggregate of individual experience. Finally, there is a tendency in Putnam's work to want to speak about the United States as a whole and its collapse rather than the story of particular sub-groups defined along either gender or racial lines. Thus, in order to recognize and explain the gap in trust, one must move away from a strictly functional analysis of America as a whole to a more sociological and historical analysis of the large economic, social and political forces that may have had differential impacts on particular marginalized groups of Americans. This in turn requires an explicit recognition of the contemporary reality of marginalized groups, such as African-Americans, as not simply an aggregate of individual lives but a collective experience. If one takes the *gap* in trust as seriously as the *decline*, the social capital analysis of trust may ultimately be turned on its head: the central question is not so much how we increase connectedness in order to build trust, but, rather, how we overcome a sense of betrayal and create trust in order to build healthy and connected societies.

Civic trust: its role in social capital theory

Having ascertained that there is both a gap and a decline in civic trust in America, the normative question is whether such a decline or gap is a bad thing. For Putnam and social capital theorists, the answer to this question with respect to decline is 'yes', for two reasons. The first is that trust serves as an instrumental good in social capital theory for individuals: the vehicle through which civic participation by individuals is transformed into a generalized sense of reciprocity and cooperation; it is the linchpin in securing many of the benefits of social capital. Putnam argues that 'the touchstone of social capital . . . the principle of generalized reciprocity' increases with trust, which in turn decreases the 'transaction costs of everyday life' (2000, pp. 134–5). This aspect of civic trust is important for individuals involved in both civic activities and economic transactions (Fukuyama, 1999). With a decline in civic trust, social and economic cooperation between individuals becomes more difficult. Thus, the decline in civic trust has a negative instrumental effect with respect to the interaction between members of a community.

Trust, it is argued by social capital theorists, also serves a public good, namely to make communities more socially cohesive and/or civically united. As the subtitle of *Bowling Alone* would suggest, Putnam's goal is the 'revival' of American *community and coming together*, not simply the betterment of individuals and participation. Moreover, his emphasis throughout this book is on a 'coming together' of community members around a common sense of civic life and shared norms. The question becomes how to reconcile a normative commitment to social cohesion or civic unity with a methodological commitment to individualism. The answer is: trust; a mechanism by which social networks can not only further the 'private' ends of individual self-interest, as described above, but also serve the goal of civic unity simultaneously. Putnam argues that an increase in trust and cohesion will curtail the 'fraying of the social fabric'. Let us turn to look at each of these aspects of civic trust in social capital theory (civic participation/self-interest and civic unity/community building) in more detail.

Civic participation and civic trust: serving 'self-interest rightly understood'

Underpinning social capital theory is a central premise: that participation and trust have a correlative, even *causal*, relationship. The extent to which civic participation is the causal (as opposed to correlative) element in the decline of civic trust is ambiguous in Putnam's scholarship. In *Bowling Alone*, Putnam is cautious with regard to the causal direction: 'The causal arrows among civic involvement, reciprocity, honesty and social trust, are as tangled as well-tossed spaghetti. Only careful, even experimental, research will be able to sort them apart definitively' (p. 137). Ultimately, however, he does suggest that they are something akin to a 'coherent syndrome' (p. 137). At the same time, using John Brehm and Wendy Rahn's analysis as evidence (Brehm and Rahn, 1995), he seems to suggest that civic participation *should* be seen as the independent variable. 'Sorting out which way causation flows – whether joining causes trusting or trusting causes joining – is complicated . . . although John Brehm and Wendy Rahn report evidence that the causation flows mainly from joining to trusting' (Putnam, 1995b, p. 666).

This general causal direction is apparently reaffirmed in the introduction to a more recent collection of articles: 'Dense networks of social interaction *appear to foster* sturdy norms of reciprocity . . . Social interaction . . . [encourages] people to act in a trustworthy way when they might not otherwise do so' (Putnam, 2002b, p. 7, emphasis added). The causal question is absolutely critical, because if one sees the independent variable as civic participation then the solution to a decline in trust is the fostering of increased participation and connectedness within communities, rather than addressing directly the lack of generalized trust amongst Americans (and marginalized Americans in particular). Ultimately, the causal assumptions of Putnam are reflected in the normative thrust of *Bowling Alone*, which, in its recommendations for the future, focuses on participation rather than trust. In the final chapter, Putnam describes ways to increase connectedness, assuming that trust is sure to follow. If, however, there is only a correlation between these variables (participation and trust) then the decline and gap in trust may not simply be the result of a lack of participation but symptoms of a more deeply rooted problem in American society, the causes of which lie in recent history. Before we consider this alternative possibility for explaining either the decline or the gap in trust, we will first examine this aggregate model of civic trust and civic participation in social capital theory in more detail.

First, both the correlative and causal connections between participation and trust can be challenged on a number of grounds. If one examines international data, it is certainly far from clear that even a correlation exists. Ronald Inglehart (1990) concludes that, compared to other countries, the level of civic membership in the United States is high but the level of trust is low, suggesting that there are reasons other than civic membership in the United States that must explain the higher levels of distrust. Conversely, people in Scandinavian countries generally do not join groups but, nevertheless, are amongst the most trusting of people: is there something in these countries, beyond civic activity, that would help to explain their relatively high levels of trust? Andy Green and John Preston also conclude, from their study, that 'associational membership and social trust do not co-vary cross-nationally' (Green and Preston, 2001, p. 247).

Putnam is largely concerned with the United States in *Bowling Alone*, so international evidence may be of limited use, but even in the American context recent work on the specific kind of trust that animates social capital, namely 'thin' or generalized trust, suggests that there may be more important factors in explaining the decline. Putnam's claim that individuals' participation creates civic trust assumes, by definition, that trust is affected by individual experiences in the world. Intuitively, this seems to make sense: the more one has social connections in one's community the more one is likely to get to know others, and therefore to *trust* others; on the other hand, the more one is disconnected from one's community, and does not experience relationships with others, the more likely one is to *distrust*. Put simply, an individual's trust is the aggregate product of one's individual experiences with others, and the more connected one is the more trusting one is.

The main advocate for this point of view is Russell Hardin (2002), who argues that a micro-level explanation of aggregate individual *experience* is crucial in explaining trust. Hardin concludes that judging the trustworthiness of others should be seen as an expression of 'encapsulated interest', allowing Hardin to extend the rational choice theory of individual interest to his understanding of 'trust' in others. Because the other's interest is encapsulated in one's own interest, increasing one's vulnerability to another makes sense, even from a rational choice perspective, if you know the other individual. It is critical, therefore, in Hardin's account that, before deciding whether others can be trusted, one has knowledge about their motivations. It would follow, as Putnam argues in *Bowling Alone*, that the more connections one has the greater the level of trust, as people gain knowledge about others in their community. Nevertheless, even for Hardin, to go from this kind of micro-level trust of known others to a broader sense of thin or generalized trust is fraught with problems, and, if it occurs, it happens on a very incremental basis. 'Trust is inherently a micro-level phenomenon . . . Trust and trustworthiness may permeate the social structure, but they do so bit by bit' (Hardin, 2002, p. 200). Hardin's account provides a philosophical, if limited and incremental, foundation for Putnam's close correlation, even causal relationship, between participation and trust.

Uslaner (2002) critiques both Putnam and Hardin, arguing that individual experience is largely irrelevant in understanding the particular type of trust at the heart of most social capital theories. Uslaner's argument turns on the idea that 'thin trust' is, by definition, a form of trust in people whom we *do not know*, and therefore cannot be derived from experience with known others. 'Presuming that strangers are trustworthy can't be based on evidence' (2002, p. 2). Uslaner argues that it matters little whether or not you join one group or many for this kind of trust, since we cannot extrapolate our tendency to trust strangers from our tendency to trust people we know; nor is it clear that we can extrapolate a tendency to trust people who are *not like us* from a tendency to trust people who are like us (which is generally the case with civic associations). Finally, Uslaner argues that we are unlikely to change our view of whether we trust people *in general* from any *individual* experience that we may have;[6] only a collective experience will affect our trust in strangers. If aggregate individual experiences have little impact on thin or civic trust then the close connection that Putnam makes between civic participation and

---

[6] Thus, if somebody acts in bad faith towards you as an individual, it is unlikely that you will change your generalized sense of trust towards most people but, rather, that you will change your sense of trust towards that individual.

civic trust is undermined, and the search to increase trust in the future through civic associations will be in vain.

Finally, empirical studies suggest that the trust/participation relationship may work in the opposite direction from the one suggested by Putnam – that is, *from* trust *to* participation. In a study of group members in Sweden, Germany and the United States, Dietlind Stolle concludes that the causal direction is from trust to group membership rather than the other way around (Stolle, 1998, 2001). Uslaner, using a simultaneous equation model, attempts to isolate the causal direction in the American data, and concludes – like Stolle – that trusting people tend to join organizations in the United States, but that 'civic engagement *does not* lead to greater trust. Simply put, group membership has *no effect on trust*' (2002, p. 128). This is critical, because it suggests that the focus should be on trust rather than, as most social capital theorists have argued, participation. Like Stolle and Uslaner, I would argue that we need to separate these two phenomena and attempt to understand what may be causing the decline or gap in trust as the priority of analysis, not the 'decline', or what more accurately be described as changes, in participation.

If an aggregate decline in the civic participation of individuals is not at the root of the decline in trust over time, then what is, and how do we explain *group* patterns in relation to the gap in trust? Uslaner provides a useful starting point for addressing both questions. He suggests that trust towards others is a *moral* disposition shaped by early family socialization and mediated by significant *collective* experiences. Uslaner concludes from his analysis of the data that civic trust is stable within individuals across a lifetime, largely reflecting the attitudes that their parents had, as they were growing up, towards their individual development and the future of the world. The critical correlative factor, for Uslaner, is optimism; and optimism in turn is related to levels of economic equality in society. As Uslaner concludes:

There is strong evidence that optimism leads to greater trust and that *both* depend upon economic equality. This finding eludes individual-level analysis, since there is no direct way to measure inequality at the individual level. *The distribution of income is the key to why trust has declined in the United States.* (2002, p. 189)

The growth of economic inequality in recent history, as Uslaner suggests, explains (in part) the decline in civic trust. It also helps to explain the *gap* in civic trust, identified above, between the economically marginalized and privileged. As Wuthnow concludes, '[Trust] is much more a function of socioeconomic privilege than it is of involvement in associations; indeed its apparent relationship with the latter appears to be a spurious function of its relationship with the former' (2002a, p. 86). If this is true, then the normative prescriptions implicit within Putnam's social capital theory for building civic trust in the future, namely resisting technology and engaging in civic activity, will not work. This is particularly true for the marginalized in society. As Wuthnow says, 'These conclusions . . . contradict the conventional view that social capital is a resource that the marginalized may be able to use even if they do not have other resources. If the hope is that associational memberships are enough to build trust despite an absence of other socioeconomic resources, however, that hope appears to be ill founded' (2002a, p. 86).

Ultimately, therefore, the central (taken as either a causal or a strong correlative) link between civic participation and civic trust simply does not hold up under closer scrutiny, for a number of reasons, as demonstrated above. First, cross-national data contradicts such a correlation. Secondly, even within the American context, the specific kind of trust required by social capital theory, namely 'thin' trust, is not something that is affected by aggregate individual experience but, rather, by larger social collective experiences that are clearly shaped by both space and time (that is, trust is differentiated across both generations *and between groups*). Perhaps most importantly, the theory of civic trust as an instrumental good (and the reliance on civic participation underlying it) simply does not provide us with any insights into the *gap* in civic trust between those who are privileged and those who are marginalized in society, by either class, race or gender.

This analysis of the relationship between trust and participation raises two broad concerns. The first is that conflating two very distinct issues (participation and trust) into one 'coherent syndrome' where participation seems to be the independent variable prevents us from considering the specific and *independent* causes for the decline (or gap) in trust as opposed to whatever changes have occurred with respect to civic participation. In the last section of this chapter we will take up this challenge directly by considering the root causes for both the decline and the gap in civic trust independently of participation. The second issue raised by this analysis is that, by making civic trust and participation (that is, community building) an essentially instrumental end to serve 'self-interest rightly understood' (Putnam, 2000, p. 135), the *nature* of the relations within the community (because it is not an end in and of itself) is of little concern. Put another way, what really matters in this functional or instrumental account of 'social capital' is the *amount* rather than the *kind* of participation; and a trusting community is thought to arise simply from increased participation without changing the nature of the community itself, when in reality a community 'of joiners' is quite different in character from a community of trusters, as we shall explore in detail below.

Civic trust, shared norms and civic unity

The second normative dimension to civic trust in social capital theory goes beyond individual participation and interests to the broader goal of social cohesion and/or civic unity. The World Bank refers to the cohesive role of social capital in the following terms: 'Social capital is . . . the glue that holds [society] together.' *Bowling Alone* moves past a neo-Tocquevillean concern with participation and 'joining' to embrace a neo-republican belief in cohesion and civic unity in which not only are disparate parts to be held together but difference is in some fundamental sense to be transcended. Like the more liberal thread of Tocqueville in Putnam's work, this emphasis on unity has a long legacy in the history of American ideas. Thus, the first motto of the United States, '*E pluribus unum*' ('From many come one'), is a succinct way of expressing Putnam's belief in 'coming together' as one. It is this transcendent aspect of Putnam's understanding of the 'social' in social capital theory that transforms what might have been a neo-Tocquevillean theory of participation and networks into a neo-republican vision of civic virtue and unity.[7] I explore Putnam's explicit call to America to 'come together' and its deployment by the present Bush administration in the following two chapters, but in this chapter I concentrate on the ways in which this idea of civic unity is embedded in the roles that both 'shared norms' and 'trust' play in a functional social capital theory, such as Putnam's.

The role of 'shared norms' has been somewhat overlooked in Putnam's theory, for a number of reasons. First, unlike 'trust' or 'participation', this aspect of social capital cannot be measured; as such, it has less interest to empirical social scientists. Secondly, because both norms and trust, within a functional model of social capital, are essentially just the vehicle or means by which to turn participation and networks into larger ends, their substantive content is of less importance than the degree to which they serve this larger purpose. Thirdly, shared 'norms' in *Bowling Alone* appear to be largely procedural rather than substantive, and seem just naturally to 'arise' from the process of making connections rather than being the result of cultural constructions imbued with power. In chapter 1, Putnam defines social capital as the 'connections among individuals . . . *and the norms of reciprocity and trustworthiness that arise from them*' (2000, p. 19, emphasis added). For the reader, the 'shared norms'

[7] There is a long debate within the history of American ideas as to whether the American state is based more in Lockean or liberal ideals (Becker, Hartz) or neoclassical republicanism (Pocock, Bailyn). The latter emphasize the centrality of civic virtue to American citizenship and the 'one nation under God' ethos rather than the more individualistic and conflictual rights-based liberal perspective.

of social capital seem to be the procedural ('reciprocity' and 'trustworthiness') and emerge naturally out of 'connectedness'. As I shall argue, however, embedded within Putnam's social capital theory are a number of cultural norms that are both substantive and also represent the socially constructed majority views in a given society, and not simply the 'natural' consequences of social connections.

It is worth noting that, while Putnam avoids any explicit substantive norms in his book, most scholars and institutions that utilize a functional definition of social capital (linking participation and trust to cooperation) are explicit in their recognition of the need for substantive shared norms to social capitalization as well as the sanctions that might be required to ensure that people conform. Consider the OECD definition of social capital: '[N]etworks together with shared *norms, values and understandings* that facilitate co-operation within or among groups' (OECD, 2001, emphasis added). This definition confirms that it is not just a norm such as reciprocity that is required but shared 'values and understandings' if trust is to arise, cooperation to follow and social capital to work in the way that Putnam envisages. A discussion paper prepared by the UK government defines *social* norms as 'the informal and formal "rules" that guide how network members behave to each other' along with 'sanctions', which are 'processes that help to ensure that network members keep to the rules' (Aldridge et al., 2002, p. 11). James Coleman also argues that sanctions are required to ensure conformity, referring to socially capitalized communities as ones that have 'social structures that make possible social norms and the sanctions that enforce them' (Coleman, 1988, p. 116). Rosalyn Harper, of the British Office for National Statistics, provides examples of both norms and sanctions in an OECD conference paper: '[T]he role of sanctions in underpinning norms is important. Examples of how these manifest themselves are: not parking in a disabled parking space at a supermarket; giving up your seat for an elderly person; tolerance of people of a different race, religious group or sexual orientation; looking after each other's house when neighbours are absent; and doing voluntary work' (Harper, 2002, p. 3).

Thus, as the OECD and Harper argue, 'shared norms' are not simply the procedural norms that 'attend' social capital theory *but also* the embedded cultural norms of the 'majority' in any particular society, underpinning the transformation in Putnam's theory from a 'community of joiners' in the Tocquevillean sense to a community of trusters. It is these latter norms (those of the majority) that play such an important but hidden role in the norm of 'trustworthiness' in America – one that I wish to make explicit. Ultimately, it is assumed in social capital theory that whatever general values and understandings a majority share in a liberal democracy such as the United States must be good for all, and that the sanctioning of those who do not conform is a legitimate price to pay in order to benefit from the more connected and trusting community. Taken together, however, the functional need for shared norms and sanctions to ensure conformity points towards a potentially coercive aspect of social capital theory in which the norms of the majority are enforced by the weight of civic society. As John Stuart Mill and Alexis de Tocqueville both observed, it is often the opinion of the majority backed by civic society that represents the greatest threat both to minority rights and individual dissent in a liberal democracy rooted in the will of the majority.

Ultimately, social capitalization in Putnam's theory is rooted in the transformative power of 'trust' underpinned by three broad majority norms: cultural homogeneity, Protestant Christianity, and the values of the 'broad silent middle'. While each has deep roots, more recently they have been challenged within the so-called 'cultural wars' by both secular and postmodern forces. Let us consider each of these aspects of a trusting, and socially capitalized, America in turn.

'E pluribus unum': *civic trust and cultural homogeneity*   As discussed earlier, the first motto of the United States was 'From many come one', the principle that America was a 'melting pot' where people were to adopt the ways of the 'New World' and leave behind the traditions of the Old. This is an early version of 'cultural homogeneity', and it has deep roots in American culture. Putnam does not argue that American communities should be culturally homogeneous; indeed, he states on a number of occasions that he believes in cultural diversity, but the functional nature of his social capital model requires 'trust' in order to facilitate cooperation and this pushes his analysis inexorably, if unwillingly, towards cultural homogeneity. The most trusting communities in America are those in which people are the most homogeneous; the most distrustful communities are those in which people are diverse (either culturally or socially). Empirical findings provide the evidence, as Putnam concludes, in his survey of communities across America in 2000:

Our survey results . . . make clear the serious challenges of building social capital in a large, ethnically diverse community. The more diverse a community in our study, the less likely its residents are *to trust other people*. It is perhaps not surprising, given the inevitable ethnic tensions associated with rapid change, that interracial trust is substantially lower in ethnically diverse communities, but the pattern we find is much broader.[8]

---

[8] Benchmark Survey: see www.ksg.harvard.edu/saguaro/communitysurvey/results4.html; accessed 12 February 2003.

Moreover, as Uslaner has argued at the level of the individual, while trusting people in America tend to be more tolerant of cultural minorities as individuals, they also exhibit a 'unitary temperament' towards the community as a whole; that is, underlying their trusting and tolerant attitudes is a fundamental belief in the need to share a *common culture* (Uslaner, 2002, p. 197). Trusting people therefore are 'especially likely to say that ethnic politicians should *not* serve their own communities . . . [and] are wary of the claim that high school and college students spend too much time reading classic literature' (p. 197). Trusting individuals therefore are tolerant of difference so long as those differences fall within the dominant understanding of community values and do not seek to differentiate a particular group as different from the whole. Uslaner concludes:

Trusters walk a fine line between empowering minorities and telling them how their politicians should conduct themselves and what the curriculum in their schools should be. This tension is the 'price' of a common vision underlying the culture. (p. 197)

The trade-off here is profound for those groups of cultural minorities who are not wanting inclusion in the existing community under its current norms, but wish to challenge the norms themselves or preserve their cultural difference. The push towards a more trusting society may have the negative impact of requiring cultural minorities to sign on to a particular set of dominant norms (those represented by 'classic Western literature', or 'non-ethnic' values, in Uslaner's study) in order to be included in the larger, socially capitalized community.

Putnam does speak to the negative implications of diversity in relation to 'bonding' social capital at the conclusion of his chapter on the 'dark side of social capital' (Putnam, 2000, pp. 361–3). Here he uses school integration as an example for examining the 'trade-offs between bridging and bonding social capital' with respect to diversity (p. 362). He suggests that the proponents of integration were arguing for diversity through the mechanism of 'bridging' capital, while the opponents of integration were defending bonding capital including 'friendship, habits of cooperation, solidarity' in the existing segregated schools. The desegregated school and its community would be less trusting, the segregated community would be more trusting. Putnam concludes that 'the deepest tragedy of the busing controversy is that both sides were probably right' (p. 362). Putnam's use of the opponents of desegregation as his example of bonding capital, solidarity and trust raises questions as to what the implications are for cultural minorities in highly trusting, socially bonded communities (given that they can be rooted in unjust cultural norms as held by the white majority in those communities at the time). In the case of desegregation, the question should not be whether it increases or decreases social capital but, rather, for all its divisive force, whether it helped to create a more *just* society for all.

'*In God we trust*':[9] *civic trust and the Protestant Church*   The second substantive cultural norm underpinning 'trust' in Putnam's social capital thesis in America is the Protestant Church. Empirically, as Inglehart makes clear, trust is highly correlated in cross-national comparisons with Protestantism. Indeed, he concludes that it may be Protestantism that underpins civic trust as much as economic development. 'The results of this analysis suggest that a given society's religious heritage may be fully as important as its level of economic development in shaping interpersonal trust' (Inglehart, 1999, p. 96). Francis Fukuyama is explicit in his endorsement of this normative thrust in a recent article on the role of social capital in the developing world.

Religion continues to be a factor in economic development. One of the most important and underrated cultural revolutions going on in the world today is the conversion of Catholics to Protestantism by (largely) American evangelicals and Mormons. This process, which has now been under empirical observation for nearly two generations, has produced social effects in the poor communities where it has occurred not unlike those ascribed to Puritanism by Weber: converts to Protestantism find their incomes, education levels, hygiene and social networks expanding . . . [A] potential external source of social capital that may be more effective in promoting civil society . . . is religion. (Fukuyama, 2001, pp. 17, 19)

While there may be economic pay-offs with respect to this global process of conversion, the question should also be: what are the costs with respect to cultural integrity and diversity?[10] Putnam in the final chapter of *Bowling Alone* endorses the idea of a 'great re-awakening' of the Church. Unlike Fukuyama, Putnam adds the caveat that such a renewal must be 'tolerant of the faiths and practices of other Americans', but it is unclear whether such a religion-based 'revival' *can* embrace cultural diversity and tolerance in the way that Putnam suggests, particularly given the demographic data on the fastest-growing (evangelical) Churches, where adherents tend to be less tolerant of diversity. What are the implications for gay

---

[9] 'In God we trust' is the second motto of the United States, replacing 'E *pluribus unum*' in 1957 at the height of the McCarthy era, when atheism and communism were seen as synonymous and needed to be distinguished from the United States of America, which had both a liberal constitution and a belief in God.

[10] At least one scholar has argued that the numbers of new Christians in both Africa and Latin America is growing at such a rate that there is already a shift in power, which will increasingly intensify, away from a Euro–American-centred Church to a Church of the 'south' (Jenkins, 2002).

and lesbian Americans, or equality-seeking women, or religious minorities in some of these 'faith-based communities'? This important question will be explored in more detail in the next chapter, when we look at the link between social cohesion, religion and community in present-day America.

Civic trust, civic unity and the middle class   The final cultural norm underpinning a trusting community in America is middle-class values, particularly at this historical juncture, when these values are seen to be silenced by the 'shrill' and uncompromising demands of the 'cultural margins'. Civic trust is difficult to cultivate, the argument goes, when there are deep divisions within American society fostered by both sides of the so-called 'cultural wars'. On the one hand, you have the traditionalist or orthodox religious right, who see the world in black and white terms based on traditional values; on the other, you have liberal and postmodern activists who seek radical changes on any number of cultural/lifestyle issues. Debate rages on everything from gay/lesbian rights to abortion and multiculturalism in public education. What social capital theorists believe is missing from this debate is the cohesion brought by the (currently silent) majority in the middle. Thus, the final report of Putnam's Saguaro Seminar on Civic Engagement in America, based at Harvard University, entitled *Better Together*, states: 'Americans are deeply divided over cultural values . . . These debates are often shrill and unyielding, with each side vilifying the other and no obvious "moderate middle" to broker civility or compromise.'[11] The solution, it is argued, is to find the placid socially cohesive centre. 'We further endorse using public policy . . . to encourage the revival of cross-class federated voluntary organizations, which represent the moderate middle Americans who have lately been AWOL from American political activism. These organizations represent an important forum for furthering our "Bridging" principle.'[12] Theda Skocpol (2000) has similarly called this phenomenon of cultural politics in social policy the 'missing middle', or, as Alan Wolfe claims, a middle class that has dropped out of moral debates (Wolfe, 1998). Thus, underpinning civic trust and social capital theory more broadly is the appeal to middle-class majoritarian values to transcend and supplant the demands being made at the cultural margins.

---

[11] See the first *Better Together* report, produced in 2001, available at www.bettertogether.org/pdfs/Religion.pdf (accessed 21 August 2002), chapter 5, 'Religion and social capital', p. 4.

[12] 2001 *Better Together* report, available at www.bettertogether.org/pdfs/Politics.pdf (accessed 21 August 2002), chapter 4, 'Politics and social capital', p. 9. See also Skocpol (2000) and Fiorina (1999).

Consequently, at the heart of community revival, as expressed in the subtitle of *Bowling Alone*, as well as in the title *Better Together* (a book of this name was published by Putnam and Lewis Feldstein in 2003), is a particular set of shared cultural norms around which citizens can develop trust for one another and unite ('the glue' that will hold American society together): the values of the silent middle class and the Christian Church, at the expense of the cultural margins and with a general emphasis on sameness rather than difference. These are the culturally embedded 'shared norms' of Putnam's social capital theory in America, and they are constitutive of the link between participation and trust in this model. This vision has empirical backing, as cross-national findings tend to support the idea that the more homogeneous, Protestant and middle-class a society is the more likely it is to be trusting and therefore socially capitalized. *Thus, if one wished to construct the most trusting hypothetical community in America, it would be a culturally homogeneous one, with a reawakened Protestant Church and dominated by a strong, middle-class set of values.* Multiculturalism and diversity ultimately become 'challenges' to be managed, overcome or transcended in the search for a common centre that will yield the necessary lubrication for cooperation between individuals and the unity of all. What social capital theorists fail to do in this push towards a more trusting society of shared norms is to acknowledge fully what the cultural norms underpinning the model itself achieve, or that a civically united society will come at the expense of cultural diversity.

Civic trust versus civic distrust: normative dimensions

Social capital theory assumes, by and large, that trust is a good thing and that distrust is bad. This is not surprising, given the dual role it plays – as described above. Trust is good because it serves both self-interest and the ideal of civic unity. Putnam admits, however, that to trust others is dependent upon the idea of trustworthiness. 'Social trust is a valuable community asset if – but only if – it is warranted' (2000, p. 135). He goes on to point out that trustworthiness rather than trust is key, but the assumption underlying social capital theory is that untrustworthiness is to be found in specific individuals or organizations, such as the Mafia or KKK, rather than society as a whole. Fukuyama takes up this theme, arguing that the goal of social capital theory should be to maximize the level of cohesion within an organization, while minimizing the distrust that such a collective entity might create for outsiders. Fukuyama comments:

It is clear that cohesiveness varies across groups and is a critical qualitative measure of social capital . . . [equally] a single group's social capital needs to be qualified by the external enmity it produces . . . Ideally one would like to maximize cohesiveness and minimize the radius of distrust . . . A society made up of Ku Klux Klan, the Nation of Islam, the Michigan Militia and various self-regarding ethnic and religious organizations may score high in terms of average group size, numbers of groups and cohesiveness, yet overall it would be hard to say that such a society had a large stock of social capital. (Fukuyama, 2001, pp. 13, 14, 15)

Thus it is particular discrete groups that create a 'radius of distrust' for 'the surrounding society' that are bad, from the perspective of social capital theory (p. 14). Even political commentators who are attempting to bring a more critical perspective to the analysis of trust (such as Simone Chambers and Jeffrey Kopstein, 2001) tend to focus on specific kinds of groups rather than the community itself (from the perspective of certain minority groups) as 'bad' or untrustworthy.

There seems to be no room in these analyses for the idea that civic society itself, rather than specific organizations within it, might be 'bad' or not worthy of trust from the perspective of marginalized groups of Americans – and, as such, a legitimate source of *distrust*. In this respect it limits the analysis of trust and, more importantly, *distrust* with respect to a group such as African-Americans. If, as Putnam himself points out, trust is inappropriate in a situation of untrustworthiness, the question must be: is American society worthy of the trust of African-Americans? Eighty-five per cent of African-Americans seem to think the answer is 'no'. As Orlando Patterson has argued, distrust is the natural effect of the deep structural forces of racial exclusion and discrimination. Moreover, it limits the scope of possible solutions to the problem. While social capital theory is able to make the case that the elimination of the KKK would contribute to trust amongst African-Americans (undoubtedly this is true), it is unable theoretically to take the next step and argue that the elimination of systemic forms of discrimination in society as a whole may be the real answer to addressing growing levels of distrust amongst this particular group of Americans. Moreover, generalized distrust (assumed to be universally bad) may not just be an appropriate response, it may even be a *constructive* response, to the extent that it acts as a positive force or catalyst for political action that brings about changes either to the existing (unjust) shared norms of society (civil rights movement versus Jim Crow laws) or to the economic and social conditions that give rise to the distrust in the first place.

The idea that distrust may be positive is not new; indeed, it has been a central principle in democratic theory back to the ancient Greeks. The catch is that in previous literature it is assumed that distrust is positive only in relation to the state (and not civil society). Demosthenes comments: 'There is one safeguard known generally to the wise, which is an advantage and security to all, but especially to democracies as against despots. What is it? Distrust' (Demosthenes, *Philippie 2*, sect. 24; cited in Hart, 1978, p. xi). Vivien Hart takes up the paradox suggested by Demosthenes and applies it to present-day America and Britain to challenge the popular idea that distrust is a negative force within democracy because it undermines the legitimacy of democratic institutions. Hart concludes, on the contrary, that *political* distrust is 'democratic, thoughtful, potentially constructive and threatening only to vested interests' (p. xii). The reason why distrust is seen so negatively, she argues, is because of the perspective of those analysing distrust and the failure to see it in light of historical circumstances:

> The misinterpretation of the distrustful as anti-democratic has arisen both because of the political values and preferences of analysts and because of inadequacies in methodology and evidence. In particular, current events have generally been treated in isolation from history. (p. xii)

Hart's contention is that distrust may lead to a more radical reconfiguration of the democratic state, as evidenced in American history. Hart's analysis deals with *political* distrust – that is, a lack of trust in government and political authorities; but is her analysis applicable to social or civic distrust? I would argue that, in the same way that political distrust is a threat to vested political interests, so too it is that social or civic distrust (particularly amongst those who are marginalized in society) may equally be a threat to vested social, cultural or economic interests in American society.[13] Moreover, like political distrust, both the decline and the gap in civic trust must be seen in light of the broad social, economic and political circumstances – in short, the historical context – whence it emerged. In the next section I want to suggest what some of those broad causal forces might be; and, moreover, to argue that, in some ways at least, distrust is both an appropriate response as well as a positive force for change.

In arguing that there may be a positive side to both the gap and the decline in civic trust, I do not want to suggest that the story of either of them is wholly positive for those groups experiencing greater levels of distrust. Indeed, to the extent that either the gap or the decline in trust is seen as an appropriate response to untrustworthy conditions in society, the positive aspect of distrust is largely limited to the notion that it would

---

[13] Indeed, the increasing levels of social distrust in society may explain why forms of political participation have moved towards more radical kinds of engagement, as Pippa Norris's work on the rising levels of boycotts, petitions and protests might suggest (Norris, 2002).

be even worse if African-Americans were treated unjustly and yet still expressed trust in an unjust and therefore untrustworthy society. Nevertheless, the underlying causes for the distrust (discrimination, inequality, racism) are wholly negative, and need to be addressed. The gap in distrust should be seen, in other words, as a symptom of a much deeper illness in the body polity rather than the problem itself.

Moreover, there may be very real and dire consequences of deep distrust. A specific example that can be used to illustrate this point is the impact that distrust has had on African-Americans seeking medical help. In an article entitled 'Distrust may lead blacks to be wary of AIDS vaccine testing', researchers report their discovery that African-Americans are generally 'suspicious of the health care system . . . doctors and scientists . . . and the reason can be summarized in one word: Tuskagee'. The Tuskagee Syphilis Study, conducted by the Tuskagee Institute between 1932 and 1972, withheld medical treatment from poor black men in Macon County, Alabama, for experimental purposes; 128 men died of syphilis as a result, when they could have been cured by penicillin. The damage incurred and the distrust sown by that medical study remains amongst the African-American community. As J. Lawrence Miller, executive director of the Black Education AIDS Project in Baltimore, comments, 'That distrust has become cultural.' This example provides an historical understanding as to why the level of distrust amongst African-Americans might be so high (in this case with respect to the American medical community); at the same time, it also suggests that such high levels of distrust hurt the African-American community itself, by adding an obstacle in the struggle to tackle AIDS through the development of a dependable vaccine. This is but one example of how distrust, in a myriad of ways, may have a potentially negative impact on the historically marginalized groups themselves in their contemporary lives.[14]

Ultimately, what I have been arguing in this section is that the normative story with respect to civic distrust must go beyond the social capital thesis of trust (as the largely positive product of civic participation, serving as a functional mechanism for social cooperation between individuals and as the civic glue of revived communities) to examine the profound cleavages in trust that occur between *groups* in American society as well as the social, cultural and economic factors that might have led to both the decline and the gap in trust over the last forty years. Perhaps, more than anything else, civic or social trust *must be treated as an independent variable*. To the extent that it is extricated from civic participation and the

---

[14] All references in this paragraph are taken from *Aids Weekly*, 17 March 2003, available at www.News.Rx.com. See also Jones (1992).

overarching social capital narrative, the closer we will get to the specific reasons underlying the patterns discussed above. In the next section, we turn to address these questions in more detail, developing in the process an alternative explanation (to the one provided by social capital theory) for both the decline and the gap in civic trust.

An alternative causal theory for the decline and the gap in civic trust

With regard to the underlying causes for the decline in civic trust, Putnam concludes that, like civic participation, 'generational succession explains most of the decline in social trust' (2000, p. 141). Generational change, as discussed in the previous chapter, ultimately rests on the dual impact of the pro-civic influence of the Second World War and the anti-civic effect of television. No doubt both these factors have contributed to the decline in civic trust, but, taken together, do they explain 'most' of it, as Putnam claims? And can television explain the *gap* in civic trust? In this section, we are looking for the answer to the question Putnam himself poses with respect to a generational decline in civic trust: 'What force could have affected Americans who came of age after World War II so differently from their parents and even from their older brothers and sisters?' (p. 266). We are also attempting to answer another question that is not posed by Putnam, but might have been by Wuthnow or Patterson, with regard to the *gap* in trust: 'What force could have affected marginalized Americans that would cause them to be so different, with regard to trust, from their more privileged counterparts?'

In searching for answers in relation to both dimensions of trust, the question that scholars must really ask themselves is: what is it in American life over the last four decades that has left Americans, and particular groups of Americans more than others, feeling so profoundly *betrayed*? Betrayal, after all, is at the heart of distrust. If we think about trust in this way, it puts a whole new light on Putnam's generational explanation. The pro-civic side of the Second World War analysis still resonates in terms of a cohort that, far from feeling betrayed by its leaders, believes America has fulfilled an important moral mission. But the decline in trust amongst the younger generation is more difficult to explain: one would be hard-pressed to make the argument that *television* has been the source of such a profound sense of betrayal. Rather, it may make more sense to see the increase in television watching (to the extent that it correlates with a decline in trust) as an *effect* of a generation who want to tune out *because* they feel betrayed, distrustful and therefore disengaged. In other words, if there are alternative causes for the patterns of distrust, it may mean, as some have argued, that the causal relations described in social capital theory are exactly the wrong way around, and the so-called 'causes' of the changing patterns in trust are actually the 'effects', thus putting television at the end of the causal chain rather than at the beginning.

I would like to suggest an alternative causal analysis rooted in a search for historical and collective feelings of betrayal. I begin with the idea that trust is not simply an instrumental tool of social cooperation in a world populated by self-interest individuals or civic associations but, rather, like Uslaner, I argue that it is the product of specific underlying *collective* experiences. It is these broad cultural, social and economic experiences that help us to explain the lack of trust amongst younger generations of Americans. As Sylvain Cote and Tom Healy of the OECD comment:

Although Putnam directs our attention toward succeeding generations, he gives short shrift to the cultural splits between older and younger Americans that occurred in the 1960s and 1970s. Putnam does not view a 'sixties and seventies period effect' as an important cause of declining civic engagement, on the grounds that everyone would have dropped out in equal numbers. But ever since the work of Karl Mannheim, historical social scientists have hypothesized that epochal watershed have their biggest influence on the outlooks of young adults. (OECD, 2001, p. 41)

I argue that there are three broad historical developments that explain the *decline* (particularly amongst a younger generation of Americans) as well as the *gap* in civic trust (between privileged and marginalized Americans). They are: economic turmoil and inequality, brought on by both globalization and economic changes in the period from the 1970s to the 1990s; crises in political leadership in America, crystallized in the events surrounding the Vietnam War and Watergate but made worse by the ever-brightening light of a rapidly emerging mass media during this same time-frame; and the rising expectation and dashed hopes of cultural and racial politics through the 1960s and subsequently. In each case there is a sense of historical betrayal or broken promises, for all but particularly amongst those who bore the brunt of both the hopes and the disappointments of these post-war years. Thus, the promise of financial prosperity for all in the economic euphoria of the era after the Second World War was lost in the economic turbulence and growing inequalities of the 1980s and 1990s; the post-war belief in the integrity of American political leadership was severely tested by both Watergate and Vietnam; and the promise of racial and gender equality in the civil rights era of the 1970s failed to materialize into the dream of full equality. In each case, these events have left Americans (particularly the young and the marginalized) with a profound sense of raised and dashed hope. Put simply, America, over the last four decades, has (for a variety of different historical reasons) felt betrayed by the failure to fulfil its own post-war promise in the political, economic and cultural realms. Let us consider each case in more detail.

Mediated political duplicity and civic trust

The sense of collective betrayal amongst American citizens over the last forty years with respect to political leadership can be traced to a couple of seminal historical events, namely the Vietnam War and Watergate. As Patterson comments of the latter:

> There is one powerful periodic political effect of the present era that cannot be overstated: the crisis of the presidency brought about by the disgrace and resignation of both the vice president and the president of the country. (Patterson, 1999, p. 178)

Everett Ladd concurs: 'In six national surveys taken from 1958 through 1972 . . . an average of 63% expressed trust. But in nine asking between 1974 and 1979, after Watergate and a host of other governmental problems, just 34% put themselves in the trusting camp' (Ladd, 1999, p. 96).[15]

Because of Watergate, people became less trustful of their leadership and American society as a whole. Wuthnow reports that Watergate has had a long-term impact on levels of trust in institutions. 'Nearly a decade later (in 1982), 66 percent still said that Watergate had reduced their confidence in the federal government' (2002a, p. 71). He goes on to suggest that some of the patterns of decline in political participation that Putnam records under generational change may also be the result of Watergate. 'Detailed analysis of the [political] activities suggests that a sharp decline may have occurred in the aftermath of Watergate' (p. 73).[16]

---

[15] While Ladd's analysis deals with trust in government as opposed to trust in others, as Putnam points out: '[A]cross individuals, across countries, and across time, social and political trust are, in fact, correlated, but social scientists are very far from agreement about why' (2000, p. 466). This correlation between political trust and social trust is particularly important for cultural minorities, as Patterson comments: 'Two trajectories can now be traced from this point. First, the greater generalized trust of the upper [socio-economic status] groups lead directly to greater political trust, while the opposite happens in the lower SES groups' (1999, p. 195). Uslaner argues that the correlation is not as strong as either Patterson or Putnam argue. Finally, it is worth noting that the seminal political events under consideration here (Watergate and Vietnam) have clearly had an impact on Americans' sense of trust not just in their government but in American society more broadly.

[16] Uslaner argues that, while the 'early boomers' may have initially been the most distrusting group at the time of Vietnam, they subsequently became the *most* trusting group in society, suggesting a different kind of generational analysis from the one Putnam provides and, perhaps more importantly, that any betrayal felt along generational lines is more easily surmounted over time than the gap along racial lines, particularly when the

The Vietnam War is a second source of the erosion of trust in institutions and American society alike during this period. As Patterson argues, Vietnam was as important to the patterns of trust during this period as Watergate. Moreover, both these collective experiences had a particular impact on those who were coming of age just as these events unfolded, providing some part of the explanation for the generational effects in trust. Patterson concludes that the persistent pattern of both political and civic distrust amongst the post-Second-World-War cohort is attributable to the combination of Watergate and Vietnam having a disproportionate and lasting effect on the generation coming of age during these events.

The defining events for the vast majority of this cohort were the Vietnam War and the Nixon–Agnew trauma. Any group of persons coming of voting age in the midst of such a national political scandal can be excused for being permanently turned off politics and distrustful of their fellow citizens. (Patterson, 1999, p. 184)

Beyond the events themselves, the changing nature of the media intensified the impact of both Watergate and the Vietnam War on average Americans' sense of their government and, as importantly, their country. With the advent of the nightly news, the competition for viewership and an increasing emphasis on political drama, coupled with the tendency to take a more aggressive role towards government officials, the media served to heighten the scepticism with respect not just to American politics but to society as a whole. Thus, the decline of citizens' sense of trust can be understood only in conjunction with the way in which the media conveyed these stories to Americans. Dan Rather expresses the critical change that occurred in the media (and the public) with respect to trust as a result of the Vietnam War in comparison to the Second World War. Given Putnam's emphasis on the Second World War as a 'civic ray' on that generation, the distinction that Rather draws between the media and the public during the Second World War versus Vietnam is critical:

The way the United States fought the Vietnam War and the way journalists covered it were light years apart from their counterparts in World War II . . . [A] core problem began with the belief held by some US political, diplomatic, and military leaders that they could effectively mislead journalists and, through them, the public about the reality of the war . . . Neither the very top political leaders nor their diplomatic and military chiefs in the Kennedy, Johnson and Nixon administrations believed they could afford to level with the public. When journalists went to Vietnam, they found a . . . quagmire, and . . . reported it . . . This led to an escalation of mistrust between experienced journalists and the country's leadership. (Rather, 2001, p. 68)

'American dream' (in economic terms) becomes a reality for many in this generation of Americans (2002, pp. 171–81). 'As their income matched their expectations, they regained faith in their fellow citizens' (p. 180).

The impact on the public was profound, but it took some time to develop. Rather comments: 'The public at home, understandably and admirably . . . wanted to believe their government . . . [But,] by the time of the Tet Offensive in 1968, the public's rising doubts about government propaganda overflowed into general mistrust' (p. 69). Thus, as the reality dawned on many Americans that their political leaders had misled them with respect to the reality of the war, their previous faith in government and the role of America in the world was replaced by a sense of betrayal and, ultimately, distrust.

The Vietnam War also helps to explain the *gap* in trust between African-Americans and white Americans, for the war effort had an important differential impact. As James Westheider (1997) makes clear in his aptly titled book *Fighting on Two Fronts*, African-American troops not only had to survive the war itself but also had to struggle against racial discrimination within their own units. One form of discrimination was the tendency to put black troops in combat units, resulting in much higher levels of injuries and deaths. As Westheider points out, one-third of the casualties in Vietnam before 1968 were African-Americans. Thus, the sense of betrayal and the resultant loss of trust were particularly acute in the African-American community, whose families paid a much greater proportionate price for the decisions made by political leaders in Washington.

This loss of trust by Americans should not, however, be seen as wholly negative when seen in light of Putnam's 'trustworthiness' requirement. While any betrayal of confidence is painful, the distrust amongst Americans was an entirely appropriate response to leaders who were misleading their citizens. Moreover, it can be argued that both Vietnam and Watergate served democracy. While domestic political scandals and engaging in mortal conflict are issues that still plague American governments, they are played out nowadays in a way that, arguably, makes political leaders more accountable to the people that have elected them. Finally, what is much less positive about this story of distrust is the contribution of Vietnam to the gap between black and whites in America in their sense of trust, particularly in government. For African-Americans, who bore a disproportionate brunt of the American government's decisions with regard to the Vietnam War, the sense of disillusionment and betrayal was, and is, all the stronger.

A second period of increased political distrust emerged in the 1990s when, after a period of renewed trust in government and society (with an average of 41 per cent of Americans expressing trust in government in the 1980s), the level fell even lower than after Watergate, to 27 per cent (Ladd, 1999, p. 96). Ladd suggests two possible reasons for this second decline, from the 1980s to the 1990s. The first was the change in the media and the emergence of a particular kind of public discourse: 'Call-in radio shows, candidates campaigning with increasingly negative advertising, and the advent of televised political shouting matches such as *Crossfire*' (p. 96), which, taken together, taught the consumers of the mass media, the public, to see politicians as either corrupt or inept. While a broad cross-section of Americans would be affected by the changing nature of the media and their tendency towards sensationalism and adversarial politics, the demographic that is of most interest to advertisers, and therefore the mass media serving them, is a younger cohort of consumers. Once again, therefore, the call-in radio show and televised 'shouting matches' may have had a differential impact on younger listeners and viewers, as they tended to be the targets of such programming. Thus, television may indeed have a role to play in the changing levels of trust in society, as Putnam has argued, but what Ladd is suggesting is that it is the content of television rather than the displacement effect that is the key to understanding this pattern.

A second factor in the 1990s, according to Ladd, was the rising level of concern amongst Americans with the actual performance of government in relation to two kinds of interlinked issues: 'special interest groups' and 'ballooning public debt'. Politicians were seen to be not only corrupt, since Watergate, and inept, as a result of the media, but in the 1980s and beyond they were also perceived to be abusing taxpayers' money at the behest of 'special interest' groups. As Ladd comments:

From the 1930s through the 1960s, Americans showed little concern about how the game of politics was being conducted . . . Since the 1960s, however, public frustrations have been building again. Many now believe that a new set of special interests is wielding excessive control over the political system. (p. 98)

What is interesting about this growing sense of disillusionment is that it originated amongst more traditional and conservative elements of American society, who argued that the cultural left was taking over the political agenda, and making increasing fiscal demands on the state along the way. This cultural backlash message fell on receptive ears amongst the general population when it was connected to the much-publicized problem of fiscal debts and deficits. Thus, populist economics in the form of fiscal restraint and cultural politics came together to form a powerful political current in the 1990s as the growing anger of the silent middle spilled over into a cultural backlash against the demands of so-called 'special interests'. This dynamic will be explored in more detail in the section on cultural warfare.

Economic turbulence and civic trust

A second important factor in the decline and the gap in trust in America has been the economic turbulence, the growth of unemployment and increasing economic inequality over the last thirty years. Lance Bennett, in the 1998 Ithiel de Sola Pool Lecture, argues that the reasons for the decline in both civic engagement and trust must be analysed from a broader perspective than Putnam allows in his social capital theory. Bennett concludes that television is not the prime suspect at all but should instead be seen as an effect (along with the decline of community) of two larger and interrelated societal forces, namely economic insecurity and 'lifestyle' politics (Bennett, 1998, pp. 749–53). Bennett puts particular emphasis on the former.

> What does appear to distress many Americans is their place in a new economy. Transformation of the work experience hit society about the same time that the television generation came of age, and seems a more likely explanation for a host of social and political changes than that confounded electronic box. (p. 750)

Many scholars have drawn this fundamental link between trust and economic factors in the United States and beyond (Offe, 1999; Inglehart, 1999; Wuthnow, 2002a; Uslaner, 2002; Hall, 1999). The underlying changes in the economy over the last three decades have included a shift towards service and technology jobs and away from manufacturing and resource-extraction industries; a shift away from full-time to part-time and contract work; and an increased number of women in the paid workforce. These changes have ultimately created a sense of employment insecurity and anxiety, particularly amongst blue-collar and lower-middle-class male workers (Bluestone and Rose, 1997). In essence, the 'postwar economic upswing came to an abrupt halt in 1973' (Patterson, 1999, p. 179). The downturn in economic growth was followed by oil crises, Third World debt crises, and deficit growth amongst industrialized countries, all of which contributed to the persistence of economic instability.

For Bennett, this creates a whole new perspective on both the 'civic generation' and the seemingly 'selfish' generation. While Wendy Rahn and John Transue have argued that the shift towards materialism, and in particular an emphasis on making money, in the post-war generation reflects the shift from a community-oriented generation to a 'me'-oriented age (Rahn and Transue, 1998),[17] the alternative explanation, according to Bennett, is that such material concerns represent 'a realistic response to

---

[17] Peter Hall also argues in connection with the United Kingdom that one of the important factors for the decline in social trust is a shift from an older to a younger generation with respect to 'other-regarding' and 'self-regarding' attitudes (1999).

an unpredictable economy defined by job and career instability' (Bennett, 1998, p. 751). Moreover, these economic changes have hit the younger generations harder, as younger 'cohorts felt the full impact of increased employment instability across their entire prime-age working years' (p. 753). Such anxieties about the future, as well as the sense that the rules of the economic game seem to have changed in the middle of play, have been important factors in seeding a sense of distrust in people, particularly blue-collar men, who have borne the brunt of the economic change in the industrial and resource-extraction industries – anxieties about the world around them and the forces at play, over which they seemingly have no control. The link between economic instability and civic trust is drawn by Patterson in his analysis of levels of civic trust in relation to economic changes: 'The swings in the percent of persons who trust others . . . almost exactly correspond to the erratic swings in the economy during this period' (Patterson, 1999, p. 180).

Adding to the economic turbulence is the increasing level of economic inequality. For Uslaner, the single most important aggregate variable in predicting civic trust in any society is the level of economic equality. Using comparative data, Uslaner demonstrates that those societies with greater levels of economic equality are more trusting. His thesis is that greater levels of inequality make people less optimistic about the future generally, and hence more distrustful. It is clear that economic inequality increased from the mid-1970s to the early 1990s in the United States. As Danziger and Weinberg comment:

Those in the middle of the income distribution as well as those at the bottom have fared relatively poorly over the past two decades. The income shares of the second and third quintiles were lower in the last few years than any other year in the post-World War II period. (Danziger and Weinberg, 1994, p. 24)

Thus, lower-middle-class Americans saw themselves falling behind, and feeling betrayed by an economic system that did not seem to reward those who followed the rules and worked hard. This sense of economic betrayal by virtue of growing levels of economic inequality was particularly strong amongst African-Americans and the young, and also amongst working-class men (Faludi, 1999). Once again the post-war promise of economic prosperity and equality had run up against the realities of, on the one hand, a growing inequality between those who were part of the information age and those who were not and, on the other hand, a persistent wage/employment gap between white and black, young and old. Thus, both the decline in trust (in terms of generational differences) and the gap in trust (between the economically privileged and disadvantaged) are, in part, explicable in terms of the increasing levels of economic inequality and insecurity, as many scholars have argued.

The role of economics, however, must be supplemented by the impact of other kinds of 'collective social experiences' that are also marked by inequality and marginalization and raised expectations and dashed hopes, namely the changes that have occurred over the last forty years with respect to cultural minorities and the response on both sides of the 'cultural divide' to such changes. We explore this aspect of American civic life and its impact on the gap and the decline in trust in the next section.

Culture wars and civic trust

Cultural conflict (in addition to economic and political turbulence) is the final contributory factor to both the decline and the gap in trust. There is a gap in trust in America between the culturally marginalized and the culturally privileged. Thus, higher levels of distrust amongst African-Americans cannot be attributed solely to lower levels of civic participation or economic inequality: we must also examine the issue of 'race'. There was an increase in levels of civic trust amongst African-Americans during the 1960s and 1970s on account of the hope (according to Uslaner) embodied in the struggle for civil rights, only to be followed by a sense of failure when these promises of racial equality were not fulfilled. As Patterson concludes in relation to his findings on race and trust, ultimately it is 'the distinctive historical experiences of Afro-Americans as descendants of a slave population . . . and their subjection to . . . segregation, racism and economic discrimination . . . [that] largely explain the extraordinarily low levels of trust among all classes of the group' (1999, p. 191). Alberto Alesina and Eliana Ferrara reinforce this link between racial marginalization and distrust through empirical analysis:

We find that the strongest factors associated with low trust are (i) a recent history of traumatic experience; (ii) belonging to a group that historically felt discriminated against, such as minorities (blacks in particular) and, to a lesser extent, women; (iii) being economically unsuccessful in terms of income and education; (iv) living in a racially mixed community and/or in one of a high degree of income disparity. (Alesina and Ferrara, 2002, p. 207)

What these findings suggest is that trust is clearly linked to the collective experiences of particular groups of people based on the extent to which they have experienced society-wide discrimination or marginalization. This makes sense intuitively, for, as Uslaner suggests, it is collective (as opposed to individual) experiences that determine our generalized view of society and, by extension, the 'generalized other' that constitutes

it. While Uslaner focuses on the loss of optimism that results from economic inequalities, one's sense of either optimism or faith – and the
corollary: a loss of faith, or betrayal – is linked to cultural attributes as
well as socio-economic status. Thus, for some groups of Americans, their
society appears to them (on the basis of their own cultural attributes) to
be fundamentally unfair and a source of their own collective sense of
betrayal.

While cultural marginalization and discrimination may, in part, explain
the gap in levels of trust between, for example, blacks and whites, does it
help to explain the decline? The answer is 'yes'. To understand why, it is
necessary to take a closer look at the emergence of the so-called cultural
wars, as well as the response to them. Over the last four decades American
society has experienced a cultural roller coaster, from the highs associated
with the civil rights movements and the victories won to the disillusionment, stemming from a collective sense of broken promises or lost hope
as racial or sexual inequalities persisted, on the part of those who sought
empowerment or equality, and a backlash against such demands on the
part of those more culturally traditional groups who saw their vision of
American society slipping away. While the civil rights movement brought
advances for women and cultural minorities (African-Americans, people
with disabilities, and gays and lesbians) there is still a sense amongst these
groups that the promises of the 1960s have never been entirely fulfilled,
and the optimism felt during that period has given way to cynicism about
the continuing levels of inequality in American society. Put simply, the
decline in civic trust is an effect of the profound cultural changes that
have occurred over the last forty years: from the 1960s, when politics
were transformed from a battle over ideas and ideologies into a struggle
over identity and lifestyle politics, to the backlash against such forces that
is being experienced now.

James Hunter and Todd Gitlin argue that, between the first and second
halves of the twentieth century, there was a profound change in American
society (Hunter, 1991, 1994; Gitlin, 1995). In *Culture Wars* (1991),
Hunter suggests that the basic cleavage in American society is between
those who believe that authority is located in a transcendent source outside society (orthodox) and those who believe that it is located in human
reason, science and contemporary culture (progressives) (see also Wuthnow, 1988). The idea that America is polarized into two warring camps of
orthodox versus progressive thinkers was taken up by the religious right in
the 1990s and the Republican Party, most notably at the 1992 national
convention, at which Pat Buchanan argued that there was a war going
on for the 'soul of America' (Wald, 1997, p. 1). A more recent version
of the culture war transforms Hunter's vision of a society split between

orthodox and progressives into a different kind of conflict. Underlying the 'progressive' side of Hunter's war, according to Gitlin (1995), are not just modern progressives but 'postmodern' identity-based cultural groups – feminists, African-American activists and a 'queer' movement – that constitute a more radical, postmodern challenge to American society than the more 'liberal' civil rights activists did four decades earlier.

Postmodern politics goes beyond seeking equality within the existing cultural and political norms to questioning the normative framework itself. As Gitlin comments: 'The virtue of Western civilization, the nature of merit and authority, the rules of reason, the proper constitution of canon and curriculum' are seen to be fundamentally 'sexist, racist' and homophobic from the perspective of these 'postmodern' cultural groups (1995, p. 1). The postmodern side of the 'culture wars' challenges not only the orthodox religious perspective but also the liberal/progressive side of American society. The more radical agenda emerged out of the ashes and unfulfilled promises of the 1960s civil rights movement. While different groups fought for, and won, the right for individuals not to be discriminated against on the basis of any particular personal attribute such as gender or race, the latter-day cultural politics goes beyond these demands for individual equality and inclusion within the community under its existing norms to demands for a broader recognition of the group's public and collective existence and a challenge to the norms themselves. Thus, the struggle amongst queer activists and theorists is not simply to ensure that gay men or lesbians have the right to engage in particular sexual acts in the privacy of their homes but to insist that the public existence of the queer community be recognized, embraced and celebrated. In the words of Shane Phelan, a 'queering of citizenship' is required rather than just the inclusion of sexual minorities into existing heterosexual norms (Phelan, 2001). This new kind of cultural warfare is deeply personal on both sides of the divide: for traditional, 'orthodox' Christian Americans the transcendent authority of God is under threat; for cultural minorities the recognition of their very identity, as gay or lesbian queer citizens, is at stake.

New divisions within civic society   What traditional American society had not bargained on was the impact on both political and civic life of including new groups in the body politic as the very nature and terms of the political dialogue changed.[18] Abortion, 'gay pride', 'black power' all became part of the political lexicon as women, homosexual men, lesbians

---

[18] For more on the importance of the presence of particular people in politics and the effect on the content of the debate, see Phillips (1995).

and African-Americans entered the political realm in greater numbers, reached critical mass and exerted their influence on the policy agenda. The introduction of such contentious issues increased incivility, for a number of reasons. First, issues such as abortion and gay pride hit at the heart of each group's sense of self on both sides of the cultural divide. Thus, in the case of abortion, both pro-choice women, who feel that the very integrity of their bodies is at stake, and 'orthodox' citizens (as Hunter calls them), who feel that the transcendent authority of God is being challenged, are equally, and *personally*, invested in the issue. The same is true of most of the current, salient political issues (which have largely arisen out of cultural politics), such as gay and lesbian rights, affirmative action, sexual harassment and language rights. As Bennett comments: 'It is not surprising that people get personal about issues that are increasingly close to home' (1998, p. 749). Incivility also results from the fact that such issues are often not 'amenable to compromise'. As such, cultural politics tends to involve zero-sum games, in which each side sees the outcome of any conflict as a win/lose proposition. Cultural wars are, consequently, deeply divisive in the communities concerned. Inglehart (1990) provides some specific examples of cultural issues, from his comparative studies, that create irreconcilable differences: affirmative action, abortion, and the rights of sexual minorities. Unlike the pre-war generation, which could often reach some consensus on issues such as national security and economic wealth distribution, these kinds of issues leave little room for compromise. It is for this reason, in part, that the idea so often proposed by contemporary scholars, including Putnam, that Americans need to find common ground and unity amongst so much difference is somewhat naïve and potentially dangerous. Where there is no common ground on an issue such as abortion, what does it mean to try and find commonality? There is, quite simply, *no* common answer. Unity often means that decisions are deferred on sensitive issues, in the interests of not creating divisions but at the expense of a particular minority. In the case of same-sex marriage, for example, the decision to postpone decisions and therefore make no changes to current practice in the interests of unity (either in the Church or amongst state actors) is to continue to deny the equality rights of a minority population based on their sexual orientation.

What we are witnessing at the beginning of the twenty-first century is the legacy of a whole range of cultural issues of this kind: emotive, inherently incommensurable, and linked to particular identities. The sense of betrayal when one side or the other wins in a given court case or piece of legislation is, necessarily, personal and strongly felt. This sense of betrayal has only grown since the 1960s, as the heady optimism of those early days (at least amongst those who were agitating for change) has given way to the real effects of inclusion, not only with regard to the contentious nature of the issues, as described above, but also with the sense that the pace of change has been (depending on one's perspective) either too slow or too quick. Thus, the cultural hangover of the 1960s has been far from pleasant for both sets of citizens across the cultural divide, however necessary it has been in terms of justice.

The implications of this cultural divide are still being felt in present-day American communities, and are reflected in the higher levels of distrust over the last forty years, as measured by Putnam in *Bowling Alone*. The sense of betrayal affects both sides of the cultural divide. Those who had traditionally held a dominant cultural – if not economic – sway, namely white, heterosexual Protestant men, have experienced an eroding sense of power, in relation to all these other groups making inroads and gaining the strength to challenge the status quo and the past norms of American society. When one couples this diminished feeling of power with the economic factors discussed above, namely the vagaries of a globalized market place that has displaced countless American male workers from traditional jobs in either manufacturing or resource-extraction industries, the overall sense of what is happening to American male citizens is well captured in the title of feminist Susan Faludi's book: *Stiffed: The Betrayal of the American Man* (Faludi, 1999). The political and civic response to this sense of economic betrayal is anger. And this resentment is reflected, politically, in the growth in male support for more conservative party options[19] and, in popular culture, by the growth of 'in-your-face' news radio programmes, from Rush Limbaugh to Howard Stern, increased calls to get 'tough on criminals' and the push towards re-establishing the dominant culture, through English-language ordinances, the inclusion of prayers and the Pledge of Allegiance in schools, and a return to 'traditional values'.

Bennett provides some interesting statistics on the breadth of these attitudes amongst American citizens, taken from a Roper survey of 1997:

The most popular solution to society's ills is to get even tougher on criminals, with 59% believing that this would 'help a lot' to improve the country. The second most popular remedy, which received a 52% endorsement, is for fathers to 'focus more on their families and less upon other things.' Next came teaching traditional values in public schools, a measure strongly favored by 51% of respondents . . . A majority of 53% of respondents felt that Americans have the essential obligation to 'speak and understand English.' (1998, p. 749)

---

[19] The 'gender gap' in voting is often attributed to women moving to the left on the political spectrum, towards the Democrats in the United States or the New Democratic Party in Canada; but other analyses have shown that the gap may also be the result of men moving to the right (towards the Republican Party in the US and the Reform/Alliance Party in Canada). See Steele (1998).

At the same time, it is not surprising that the other side of the cultural divide (particularly cultural minorities) exhibits ever-higher levels of distrust in the American community as it feels the sting of this anger, the resistance towards greater empowerment and the return to conventional beliefs or values. At the heart of these figures is a sense that the hopes promised by the protest movements of the 1960s and 1970s have been dashed, as cultural minorities still struggle to belong and flourish in American society. Lost hope and a sense of betrayal explain civic distrust and, in particular, the higher levels amongst ethnic minorities. Putnam's analysis, in the Community Benchmark survey of 2001, reinforces these findings in relation to Hispanics and black Americans.[20] On the specific question regarding social trust, 54 per cent of 'White Americans' agreed that most people could be trusted; only 27 per cent of blacks and 23 per cent of Hispanics concurred with this view.

The gap between whites and racial minorities on social trust is reinforced by the data of trust in authority figures. With regard to the police (who represent the face of authority within the community) the ethnic gap is almost exactly the same between blacks and whites on this indicator as the social trust findings, with 57 per cent of white Americans saying that they trust the police 'a lot', 27 per cent of blacks and 38 per cent of Hispanics. Within these figures is a critical clue to the levels of distrust and lack of reciprocity amongst cultural minorities. For African-Americans and Hispanic-Americans, the gains made through civil rights mean little when videotapes of white police officers beating up minority youths are shown at regular intervals on television news broadcasts, and then a group of their community 'peers' dismisses the charges in a court of law. This sense of betrayal is a continuum from community to state, brought home through the power of mass-market technology. Thus, television does indeed play a role in the growth of civic distrust, but with a different emphasis from that suggested by Putnam. For African-Americans, videotapes played in the mass media provide evidence, in stark and visceral terms, that despite the civil rights movement such actions by the state are still possible, and perhaps even inevitable, and in the end the community – as represented by a jury of one's 'peers' – will back these actions up. African-Americans watching such scenes experience the collective anger directed at them and respond to it with a lack of trust, in both their fellow citizens and the authorities who are supposed to protect all equally. Thus, while the civil rights movement brought hope to African-Americans (and other ethnic minorities) that, at last, they might

---

[20] The Social Capital Community Benchmark survey, available at www.bettertogether.org (see questions 6, 17, 21, 22, 23 and 28). The relevant figures: low involvement in electoral politics stands at 30 per cent amongst white Americans, 45 per cent amongst black Americans and 69 per cent amongst Hispanic-Americans.

be full and equal participants, it is the betrayal represented in the loss of this hope (in light of how racism and prejudice continues to exert itself) that creates the mistrust endemic to these minority communities.

Resurgence of the middle: pushing back   Rather than addressing the questions raised by the inclusion of a variety of actors in the political realm (and the incommensurable policy issues that come with them), there is an emerging trend amongst some prominent American academics to dismiss divisive cultural politics in America as a game that has gone too far with very little at stake: a lot of sound and fury created by the overly strident and 'shrill' nature of what are perceived to be the margins of American society. There is a general call to find unity in the middle amongst the clatter of diversity.[21] What is desperately needed is for the broad, unified middle of America to reassert itself against these margins.[22] Todd Gitlin certainly makes this case, appealing on behalf of the future of the progressive left in America that '[t]he commons is needed . . . Democracy is more than a license to celebrate differences . . . The dialogue today is inflamed and incoherent because the symbolic stakes are overloaded on every side. There is a lot of fantasy in circulation' (Gitlin, 1995, p. 236).

This view, as discussed earlier, in the section on norms and trust, tends to be shared by those academics concerned with social capital and civil society as well. The report of Putnam's Saguaro Seminar on Civic Engagement, as alluded to earlier, calls for a resurgence of the common middle at the expense of the cultural margins.[23] In all these cases, it is the metaphor of 'bridging' between different sides, by asserting the commonality of both, that is often deployed. Gitlin concludes his book: 'Enough bunkers! Enough of the perfection of differences! We ought to be building bridges' (1995, p. 237). The *Better Together* report makes explicit the need to revive the silent majority, the middle class of Americans, in this 'bridging' activity.[24] By describing the 'bridge' between the different sides of the current debates over cultural justice as the search for a common middle, these scholars are underestimating the substantive and incommensurable nature of the questions of justice at stake at present (by overemphasizing the merely rhetorical or symbolic importance of these divides in current

---

[21] Included within this number would be not only the book resulting from the Saguaro Seminar (Putnam and Feldstein, 2003) *Better Together* but also Rorty (1999), Schlesinger (1998), Miller (1998) and Skocpol (2000).
[22] The term 'middle' has various meanings depending on one's political perspective.
[23] 2001 *Better Together* report, available at www.bettertogether.org/pdfs/Religion.pdf (accessed 21 August 2002), chapter 5, 'Religion and social capital', p. 4.
[24] 2001 *Better Together* report, available at www.bettertogether.org/pdfs/Politics.pdf (accessed 21 August 2002), chapter 4, 'Politics and social capital', p. 9. See also Skocpol (2000) and Fiorina (1999).

politics) and failing to take into account the historical lessons learned by previous attempts at civic unity through an appeal to the central norms of American citizenship.

The first chapter in this book laid out the deep historical wrongs (ranging from exclusion and assimilation to eradication) that have been committed in defence of an overarching set of American civic norms against particular groups of marginalized American citizens, based on both gender and cultural characteristics. This history helps to explain the anger felt by these groups, who have fought and are still fighting to enter the public realm with their identity intact. It also provides us with some important warnings about the dangers inherent in imposing a shared middle at the expense of the margins in contemporary debates. The real question, today, is whether the middle ground is indeed the 'golden mean' suggested by latter-day Aristotelians or, alternatively, nothing more than a way of circumscribing the debate. At many stages in American political history the search for justice has required extreme forms of political activity at the margins: from the suffragettes fighting for the vote, to Martin Luther King's civil disobedience, to the activities of more recent years by some advocates for either Americans with disabilities or gays and lesbians. What needs to be recognized by those scholars who seek now simply to assert a common middle against the noisy margins is that dissonance, pulling apart and profound conflict have always been, and may once again turn out to be, the very stuff upon which justice is achieved. This is not to say that all the rhetoric, tactics, distrust and incivility created by cultural politics are positive developments in and of themselves; rather, I am arguing that they may be the inevitable precursors and by-products of a profoundly important, substantive and continuing debate about justice and diversity that has been occurring in the United States over the last four decades, up to and including today.

Conclusions

This analysis of the underlying cultural, political and economic causes of both the decreasing level of trust in American society and the widening gap in trust between groups of Americans contains a number of important insights concerning future directions for the study of trust within American communities. The first is that civic trust must be addressed independently of civic activity, rather than assuming, as Putnam does, that either they are simply two parts of one 'coherent syndrome' or that one causes the other. The implication in Putnam's work seems to be that, if communities become more socially connected, trust and reciprocity will surely follow. My analysis of the underlying causes of distrust in

America suggests that civic engagement will not, in and of itself, lead to any changes, if, in fact, there are deeper societal forces at play. Moreover, like the changes in civic engagement, the decline in trust is not a wholly negative development: it should be seen, to some extent, as part of the inevitable consequences of the positive evolution towards an increasingly just society. It may be that Americans were more trusting of and less angry with one other before the advent of cultural politics and the openly divisive debates over gay rights, abortion policies and racial politics, but such divisions will have been not just inevitable but worthwhile, from a normative perspective, if the outcome is greater justice for all groups in American politics, along with the messy, contentious, identity-driven issues that accompany their entry. Ultimately, the decline and the gap in trust should be seen, at one and the same time, as a negative outcome of economic instability and inequality, political crises and the power of the media and cultural warfare, *and*, equally, a potentially positive influence on (as well as a by-product of) the social forces for inclusive justice at work from the 1960s to the present day. As such, the changing dimensions of trust constitute both a negative and a positive reflection on American society.

How, then, do we address the decline in trust or the gap in trust if not through a renewed appeal to civic participation and social connectedness or a common set of values? There are a number of possibilities that might be explored. To begin with Putnam's own conclusions: he is correct to look at the impact of television (particularly its content), but talk radio should also be included in this analysis of the media on levels of distrust and incivility. To this end, the American public and those in the media need to have a long, hard look at the implications of both the time spent watching television and its content, either seen or heard on both kinds of media, for their impact on the overall levels of violence, incivility and distrust among the American public, and more particularly among children and youths. Television, however, should not be seen as wholly negative in this regard, even if it does sow the seeds of distrust. It is a positive development on the part of the mass media that they can provide coverage of events that should instil distrust, from major events such as the Watergate hearings to hand-held videotapes of police actions against racial minorities. Television may contribute to civic distrust in these instances, but it also contributes to the broader cause of democracy and justice by bringing to light the sometimes ugly realities of American society.

More importantly, economic instability and inequality (which have been partially responsible for both the decline and the gap in trust) must be addressed, as Uslaner suggests, by state initiatives directed at bridging the gap between those who have been left behind in the old economy with the demands of the new. Certainly, this is the case in Scandinavian countries, where the levels of trust are highest. Thus, the general trend of neo-liberal and 'third way' governments in the United Kingdom, Canada and the United States to move away from redistributive policies towards a smaller welfare state may be politically and fiscally expedient, but it may also carry a price in terms of economic marginalization, inequality and rising levels of distrust in society. Social democratic solutions will go only so far in liberal societies such as the United States, but education, in any case, continues to be a critical element in overcoming such disparity. The solutions to the issue of economic inequality are complex and multifaceted and beyond the scope of this book. The point is that what this analysis suggests is that, if you want to address the *gap* in trust as well as the decline, it is necessary to go beyond civic organizations and their memberships to the economic context more broadly and address the twin problem of economic displacement and inequality directly through the power of the state and courts. Finally, given that it is both economic inequality and cultural misrecognition that lies at the heart of the gap in trust, it is necessary to engage in the question of cultural politics directly. Nancy Fraser has provided one model of how the twin questions of economics and culture may be addressed (see Fraser, 1998), and this could be a good place to begin the analysis.

What is clear, with regard to cultural politics, is the inevitability that higher levels of distrust will continue in the foreseeable future amongst cultural minorities. It may even be that this focus on generalized *trust*, in an increasingly diverse society, is entirely wrong-headed. In a fascinating analysis, Marc Hooghe has suggested that the idea of trust itself, from a multicultural perspective, should be replaced by a new focus on reciprocity. Precisely because trust seems to flourish only in 'predictable, homogenous and closed settings . . . for contemporary societies, the maintenance of high trust levels will become increasingly problematic' (Hooghe, 2002, p. 11). As both Hooghe and Diego Gambetta argue, 'We should set our sights on cooperation rather than trust' (Gambetta, 1988, p. 229; Hooghe, 2002, p. 14). Reciprocity, for Hooghe, is a 'starting mechanism' between deeply divided populations. Rather than assuming that one can construct either a culturally homogeneous population or assert some kind of shared consensus upon which trust may be built, one can begin instead with the idea of mutual respect, through limited reciprocal negotiations (that is, a thinner sense of community), but one that is more inclusive and democratic. In essence, in deeply cleaved societies, rather than forcing cohesion through the revival of a middle class or the Protestant Church, it might be preferable to replace the substantive norm of trust, and the associated ideas of cohesion that accompany it, with the more procedural norm of reciprocity.

Ultimately, the underlying argument in this chapter is that trust and shared norms need to be conceptualized in a wholly different way from how they are currently understood in social capital theory. The social capital argument suggests that only the decline matters (and the gap is barely mentioned), and the decline matters only because of its functional role in creating cooperation between individuals. My argument has been that both the decline *and the gap* matter because of what they reflect about the broader collective historical forces of injustice and betrayal that underpin both dimensions of the trust question in American society. Moreover, to the extent that the goal of trust is embedded in a socially cohesive and even homogeneous community of shared cultural norms (one that tends to emphasize the middle at the expense of the margins, sameness over difference, and a socially engaged Protestant Church to anchor it), socially capitalized communities will develop at the expense of both cultural diversity and gender equality. If the trade-off is between justice for cultural minorities and women versus an increase in the overall level of trust in society, this chapter has endeavoured to show that such a trade-off is neither desirable in the short term nor tenable – given the forces at work in society at present – in the long term.

6   Beyond *Bowling Alone*: social capital in twenty-first-century America

In the years since *Bowling Alone* was published there have been a number of further developments that shed new light on the preceding analysis, including new research data by Robert Putnam into social capital accumulation in specific communities in America, as well as the impact of larger world events – particularly 9/11 – on the conceptualization of social capital by both academics and politicians in the United States. In 2000, after the publication of *Bowling Alone*, Robert Putnam and a group of academics, politicians and local community activists created the Saguaro Seminar for Civic Engagement in America, at the Kennedy School of Government at Harvard University. Its purpose was twofold: to do further, detailed, local research into the nature of the problem across the country (the Social Capital Community Benchmark surveys) and to create an advocacy movement dedicated to rebuilding social capital in local American communities. The Saguaro Seminar ultimately produced a report entitled *Better Together* in 2001, and a book by the same title was published in 2003. This dual focus (on research and advocacy) reflects a development in both the empirical dimension (represented by the data) and the normative dimension (represented by the advocacy) of the social capital story. Often the research results bleed into the advocacy work, and vice versa, as we shall explore. This chapter will analyse these developments as well as the ways in which President George W. Bush's domestic policies have been shaped by the idea of social capital, and most particularly by the link between the revival of American community and the Church (through the faith-based community initiatives), on the one hand, and patriotism in the wake of 9/11 (through the USA Freedom Corps), on the other. Both theory and policy are troubling, as shall be discussed, given a general tendency to mix Church and government, as well as civil society and national interests, all in the name of 'reviving' community.

Spiritual capital: Christianity as the engine for civic revival?

In March 2001 the Saguaro Seminar published the Social Capital Community Benchmark survey. This study surveyed 30,000 Americans in forty local communities spanning twenty-nine states on their attitudes to a variety of questions that tried to provide a snapshot of the degree of civic engagement in America at that time. The first major finding of the Benchmark survey was that religious involvement is among the 'strongest predictors' of civic engagement. Putnam moves from the empirical to the prescriptive in his summary of the research, arguing that the Church not only is but also *should be* central to American social capital in the future. 'Religious communities embody one of the most important sources of social capital . . . Our survey shows that faith-based communities have some matchless strengths as sources of civic engagement.'[1] Some local communities involved in the study have taken such recommendations to heart. 'Our religious connection has all sorts of potential for doing good. Right now it tends to be used within groups, instead of across groups. *Churches need to spill over into the world and do these things*' (Kemp, 2001, emphasis added). At the same time, the survey found that religious involvement was also associated with higher levels of intolerance, in terms of, for example, 'banning unpopular books from libraries, antipathy to equal rights for immigrants, lower levels of support for racial intermarriage and lower levels of friendships with gays'.[2] In addition, 'religious involvement is linked to greater support for needy individuals, but is not necessarily associated with greater support for social justice'.[3]

Proposing a central role for the Church in the future of American social capital grows out of the proposals made at the conclusion of *Bowling Alone*, as discussed in the previous chapter. In the 'Agenda' for the future, Putnam sees the revival of religion as an almost undiluted good in his search for a renewed community (2000, pp. 409–10). Thus, he refers in his closing chapter to three previous awakenings in *Christianity* in America as all largely positive forces for social capital building, and asks: 'Are the ingredients [there] in America at the beginning of the twenty-first century for another Great Awakening?' (p. 409). Putnam suggests that Churches use the social projects of bygone eras as their models for today. 'In addition, some of the innovations of the Gilded Age and Progressive Era, like the settlement house and the Chautauqua movement, though not narrowly religious, could inspire twenty-first century

---

[1] See www.cfsv.org/communitysurvey/results2.html; accessed 28 June 2002.
[2] See www.cfsv.org/communitysurvey/results_pr.html; accessed 28 June 2002.
[3] See www.cfsv.org/communitysurvey/results2.html; accessed 28 June 2002.

equivalents.' The qualifier 'though not narrowly religious' is explained in a footnote, where Call to Renewal, 'an evangelical coalition spanning the political spectrum from ultra-liberal to ultra-conservative' (p. 502), is given as a contemporary model. There are a couple of difficulties with using such an organization as the model for future *faith-based* community building. The first is to recognize that this coalition is not a *broad* religious (meaning inter-faith) group but a Christian coalition: while its political perspective may be broad, its religious parameters are limited to one faith. Secondly, while overcoming poverty, as stipulated in its motto 'People of faith overcoming poverty',[4] speaks to the issue of social justice, other more divisive justice concerns – in particular the claims for recognition based on identity – are not addressed. The analysis of the Progressive Era in chapter 2 has demonstrated that an emphasis on the 'social gospel' without due respect for cultural diversity can, potentially, have a profoundly negative impact on indigenous Americans, non-Protestant immigrants, and gays and lesbians. Thus, questions must be raised as to whether such historical projects alluded to by Putnam as models really are appropriate to a culturally diverse American community of the future.

There is an important point to be made about 'faith'-based renewal that emerges from *Bowling Alone*, and continues through both the theory and practice of 'faith-based' community building, that needs to be explicitly addressed, namely the extent to which the language of 'faith-based' initiatives is somewhat disingenuous when what is really meant is Christianity. The question of what is meant by 'faith', of course, is critical to non-Christian religious minorities in the United States. 'Faith-based' suggests diversity and plurality, but while the language implies inclusivity and respect for difference it seems clear that Christianity is the operative norm. Thus, there is a sense one gets in *Bowling Alone* that Putnam, in his choice of language, sees Christianity as the overarching paradigm within which 'others' are to be accommodated or tolerated. In the concluding chapter, Putnam begins the section on the importance of religion to social capital building by stating: 'Faith-based communities remain such a crucial reservoir of social capital in America,' suggesting an inclusive view of religion, but by the end of the paragraph his focus is clearly on the Christian faith. 'I challenge America's *clergy*, lay leaders, *theologians* and ordinary worshipers: Let *us* spur a [great awakening] . . . while at the same time becoming more *tolerant* of the faiths and practices of *other* Americans' (p. 409, emphasis added). It is clear from this statement who the 'us' and 'them' of the American religious community continue to be.[5]

[4] See www.calltorenewal.com.
[5] It could be argued, of course, that the reason why the Church is so central to Putnam's analysis is simply because Americans genuinely *are* overwhelmingly Christian in their

The centrality of the Christian Church, and its seemingly universal nature, is reinforced in the chapter on religious participation when, in a startling footnote, Putnam states: 'For simplicity's sake I use the term *church* here to refer to all religious institutions of whatever faith, including mosques, temples and synagogues' (p. 65). The first point to be made is that there are religions beyond those designated by the buildings listed. Secondly, the role that the building or congregation (the church) plays in the Christian religion may be quite different in other religions, where ceremonial practice may be more focused in the family home and less in the institution. Thirdly, such an analysis ignores the specific characteristics of Christianity that have played such an important role in American history. The Church is uniquely dedicated to conversion and proselytizing. Depending on your religious viewpoint, this may be a positive or negative aspect of the Christian Church.

While there have been many positive outcomes of the Christian Church's engagement in the political and social life of America (particularly in relation to the poor) there is also a profoundly negative side to this story with respect to women and cultural minorities (one that stretches from the Trials at Salem to the cultural assimilation of Native Americans and non-Protestant immigrants in the Progressive Era, to the McCarthy era's use of Christianity as a weapon in his witch-hunt for 'godless Communists', to the current opposition of many Churches to same-sex marriage). This history, and the role of power over others within it, must be acknowledged by both American society at large and the Churches themselves if future community building is to be cognizant of the mistakes of the past, respectful of a multicultural present, and building towards a genuinely inclusive future. Recognizing this *particular* history in relation to other religious histories means that one uses 'Church' to mean 'Church' and not to subsume all other forms of religion or faith (be they monotheistic or polytheistic) under a single label.

The role of the Church in America

What are we to make of this call for the Church to play a central role in community building? The first point is that the Church and its community involvement constitute a fact of life in the United States. This

---

religious affiliation. It is a critical point, and I will address this question fully in the next section, when we consider Christian religiosity in America. My concern with making 'Christianity' the working definition of all 'faiths' is the failure to analyse the specific characteristics of *Christianity*, and more specifically Protestant Christianity, as opposed to other religions in both historical and contemporary terms, as well as the tendency to make non-Christians 'others' in relation to a generalized norm of 'American' society.

growing reality is in some sense unique amongst industrialized nations; as Kenneth Wald and others have argued, America is 'exceptional' in its rising popular adherence to the Christian religion (Wald, 1997; Bradley et al., 1992). Moreover, the American Church has a history of active engagement in community affairs, although, since the Second World War, there is evidence that this involvement in social issues has given way either to political advocacy and party politics, in the case of the Christian right, or to a more individualized and 'therapy'-driven spirituality, in the case of many Americans who have joined the Church (Bellah, 1985; Wuthnow, 1998). Nevertheless, because Putnam has called on the Church to play a central role in community building (a suggestion that has been used by President Bush as a theoretical underpinning for his 'faith-based initiatives'), it is important to analyse the extent to which the Church is a positive or negative force in the building of an inclusive and, equally, socially robust community in the context of an increasingly diverse society.

Wald, in his influential book *Religion and Politics in the United States*, provides a good case both for and against religious influence in American political life generally (1997, pp. 319–45). His arguments are focused on religion's influence on organized politics as opposed to community service and organization, but let us look at his general themes before we consider the extent to which they are relevant to social connectedness in the community. Ultimately, he argues that religion has a mixed influence. On the negative side, religion and state politics can lead to extremism, polarization and even violence, in part because religion may not lend itself to compromise on strongly held views (such as abortion in America). Wald points to examples around the world, including Northern Ireland, India and Bosnia, where religion has played an important role in creating intense and violent clashes between different political sides. He also points to the worrying correlation between intolerance and people with a religious affiliation (a topic to which we will return shortly).

On the positive side, he suggests that religion in America has been politically pluralistic, meaning that it has tended to support a diversity of political views on any given issue (a point Putnam makes as well). Secondly, Christianity has tended to inject a moral dimension into politics, pushing nation states to recognize that their decisions are not simply about balancing different interests but 'inescapably involve and reflect values' (p. 337). Wald concludes that the preferred role of religious institutions in relation to the political realm is that of moral gadfly: 'Religious institutions have a responsibility to remind the state of its ethical obligations . . . I am more comfortable when churches challenge the government than when they vest the state with a holy aura' (p. xiv). Thus, religious institutions, it is argued, are important counterweights to the potential abuse of power by the state. There are numerous examples of totalitarian regimes around the world in which the Church has played an important role in resisting the oppressive use of power against citizens, and in defence of human rights. In the American context, Churches have been central in offering resistance to the practices of a potentially unjust state or law, most particularly in the civil rights movement (Wald, p. 338; Neuhaus, 1984).

Political science scholarship, including the work of Wald, has tended to focus on the impact of religion on the *state*, particularly the influence of the 'religious right'. The question that we are concerned with here, however, is the Church's role with respect to the *community*, or civic society, as opposed to the state. Unlike the state, the community (as understood by social capital, communitarian and 'third way' theories) is non-hierarchical and non-coercive; associations are voluntary and the rules governing involvement are unwritten mores and practices rather than written rules and laws with checks and balances. Religion, in this context, has a very different role from that envisaged by Wald. At the political level there is an inbuilt set of legal and constitutional checks backed by the power of a sovereign and largely secular state. Thus, while the Church may be seen, in the American context, as a moral check on the state, so too the state is the check on the power of the Church by way of the Jeffersonian wall of separation between these two distinct realms. The community has no such commensurate counterweight to the power of the Church. Thus, as the community becomes the *preferred* ethical and analytical focus of contemporary political theory (over the state), and the Church is increasingly called on to be the vehicle through which citizens, particularly vulnerable citizens, are provided social services, this balance of powers between the secular public sphere and religious private sphere may be reconfigured, with the Church potentially playing a pivotal role (within social capital theory) in defining the membership, boundaries, values and norms of this newly revived community.

Christianity, women and cultural minorities

The impact of the Church with respect to women and cultural minorities is also a very complicated but important story. Several studies have pointed to the significance of the Church for women and the building of social capital. Thus, American women are more likely to be involved in religious institutions, and civic participation by women is more likely to be linked to religion than that of men (Burns et al., 2001, pp. 89–91, 234–8).

Some scholars have argued more broadly that the importance of religion to women, particularly in rural communities, needs to be acknowledged by feminist scholarship, which has a tendency to dismiss the Church as anti-feminist (O'Neill, 2006; Everitt, 2006). African-American women in particular have had a long and profound relationship with the Christian Church (Ross, 2003). Other scholars, however, point to the negative role that the Church has played with regard to women's concerns on a number of different equity issues, most notably reproductive choice (Martin, 1996; Howland and Buergenthal, 2001). Thus, the relationship between women, community and Church is 'a complex and ambiguous one' (Burns et al., 2001, p. 89).

Putnam also points to the important link between the Church and social capital building for African-Americans. 'Faith-based organizations are particularly central to social capital and civic engagement in the African-American community' (Putnam, 2000, p. 68). This is recon-firmed in the 2000 Benchmark survey. The historical roots of this rela-tionship date from the abolition of slavery through to the civil rights movement and beyond (p. 68). The power of the Church to make these changes, as Wald would argue, was rooted in its moral claims to uphold the dignity of all human beings. There is no question, therefore, that the Church has played a central role in the progressive emancipation of African-Americans, but religion should not be limited to a discussion of Christianity in relation to African-Americans, for the connection between black America and Christianity has lived alongside a very strong political link (albeit involving fewer people) to the Islamic faith.

In black America, Islam has long represented a form of resistance to white European ways and Christianity. As Richard Brent Turner argues about the early black Muslims: 'Writing in Arabic, fasting, wearing Muslim clothing and reciting and reflecting on the Quran were the keys to an inner struggle of liberation against Christian tyranny' (Turner, 1997, p. 25). The link between black politics and Islam continued in the latter half of the twentieth century, through the civil rights period and after, as represented by such figures as Malcolm X, Mohammed Ali and Louis Farrakhan, and through groups such as the Nation of Islam.[6] This history needs to be recognized, in and of itself, but also because the extent to which Christianity and the projects it supports are seen as vehi-cles for either equality or subordination for African-Americans depends upon the religious identity and perspective of various groups within a *diverse* religious community. Finally, the historical link between Islam and

---

[6] Malcolm X, in particular, argued that Islam provided a 'more authentic identity' for black Americans since the link to Africa, as opposed to Europe, was closer.

African-Americans is under a particular strain in the contemporary context as a result of 9/11 and the backlash against Islam, felt in America and beyond.

The intersection between ethnicity and religion is important not only to African-Americans but to other ethnic minorities as well. In a recent collection of articles on faith communities amongst Asian Americans, Pyong Gap Min and Jung Ha Kim argue that religion plays a very important role in the Asian-American community to 'preserve their cultural traditions and ethnic identity' (Min and Kim, 2002, p. 16). There is a diversity of religions amongst Asian-Americans, including Christianity, Buddhism, Islam, Hinduism and Sikhism. One important point made by Min and Kim is that many of the religions practised by Asian-Americans do not have the same institutional focus that Western religions do. In particular, 'Hindus, Muslims and Buddhists – mostly Asian immigrants – usually practice through family rituals and/or small group prayer meetings without regularly participating in a religious congregation' (p. 17). This is important, not just in terms of how one measures religiosity amongst this group of religious Americans, but also because it means that there is not the same centralizing focus to religion that a Church might have, and one must be careful about making the assumption that 'faith-based' initiatives can work in the same way with different religions. The religious diversity of Asian-Americans is, nonetheless, shaped by American culture. For example, amongst Chinese in Taiwan, Hong Kong and mainland China, Buddhism is the majority religion amongst those who have a faith, while Christianity represents only one in five adherents. In America, on the other hand, Christianity is the largest religion (one-third), Buddhism the second largest (one-quarter), with close to a half of Asian-Americans claiming no religious affiliation at all (Yang, 2002, p. 71).

Christianity may be the largest religious affiliation for Asian-Americans but the link between religion and ethnicity changed over the course of the twentieth century. For example, while, initially, Chinese Churches were missions of American denominations, since the 1950s there has been an increasing growth in 'Asian Churches', independent of the mainstream American denominations. As such, the Church represents less a form of assimilation than a force for reinforcing a particular ethnic identity; or, to put it another way, these Churches represent (in relation to ethnicity) a form of bonding rather than bridging capital vis-à-vis the larger American culture (Yang, 2002). However, they also represent a form of bridging capital in terms of the Asian community. As Russell Jeung suggests, the transition during the second half of the twentieth century was from specific Chinese or Japanese Churches to 'pan-Asian' congregations. This continued link between ethnicity and religion several generations after

Asian immigrants first arrived in the United States contradicts the general expectation that, over time, Churches will tend to become 'deethnicized' as they adapt to generational differences (Mullins, 1987). 'Contrary to expectations . . . Chinese and Japanese American Churches are not dying out or becoming open to all but are adapting by becoming Asian American' (Jeung, 2002, p. 218). While Churches are important vehicles through which Asian-Americans express and reinforce their pan-ethnic identity, this varies with different denominations, as shall be discussed in the next section, in relation to the growth of the evangelical Church.

The growing evangelical Church

So far, we have been discussing the role of the Church in America in both abstract and historical terms. In this section, we will address perhaps the most important contemporary empirical dimension of the Church in America today, namely the growth of the evangelical[7] Church and the implications that this has for cultural minorities. Everett Ladd demonstrates that the top five Churches experiencing increases in membership between 1962 and 1995 were the Pentecostals (a 469 per cent rise), the Jehovah's Witnesses (286 per cent), the Adventists (132 per cent), the Mennonites (85 per cent) and the Baptists (73 per cent). Over the same time period the more traditional denominations, including the Presbyterians, Churches of Christ and Episcopalians, experienced decreases in membership (ranging from 4 per cent to 26 per cent) (Ladd, 1999, p. 47). Putnam acknowledges these changes in the configuration of Christianity in his chapter on religious participation, but the main concern with the growing numbers of evangelical Christians, from his point of view, is their failure to get *more* involved in community building, rather than the particular attributes the evangelical Church may bring to community building. 'It is that broader civic role that, with few exceptions, evangelical religion has not yet come to play in contemporary America . . . the new denominations have been directed inward rather than outward, thus limiting their otherwise salutary effects' (pp. 78–9).[8]

The evangelical Church is different from the more traditional Protestant congregations, and these differences are highly relevant to our consideration of the Church as a leading force in American civic renewal. The

---

[7] 'Evangelical' is taken to mean those people who follow a faith characterized by the need to be 'born again' as an adult and who believe in the fundamental authority of the Bible as the font of all truth (Guth et al., 1988).

[8] Putnam is not alone in this view of American Christianity as becoming too isolated and individualistic. Wuthnow has argued that, since the Second World War, Christianity has become little more than a 'therapeutic device' and highly individualized. Like Putnam, he calls on the Church to become more 'other oriented' (Wuthnow, 1999).

first is the degree of cohesion, as well as the strength of views, amongst evangelical Churches. After looking at a number of factors in trying to explain why some Churches are very cohesive in their views and others diverse, Wald, Dennis Owen and Samuel Hill Jr. conclude that 'the "strong religion" factor [is] the major predictor of attitudinal cohesion' (Wald et al., 1990, p. 210).[9] The evangelical nature of these Churches, with their central commitment to a singular received truth in the Bible, is the key predictor of moral (and political) cohesion amongst their members. It follows that, to the extent that the evangelical Church is the vehicle for community building, there will be much less room for diversity, either in opinion or lifestyle, for the members of such a Church.

The second issue is the degree to which 'strong religions' see their moral norms as true for all people, not just themselves. 'The fundamentalist style in religion aims to infuse the entire culture, all spheres of human existence, with the values and truth of the faith . . . This position legitimizes political action by conservative religious groups and simultaneously endows the political norms with a transcendent quality' (Wald et al., p. 211). Although Wald, Owen and Hill are principally concerned with the impact of religion on politics (meaning legislatures and policies), this conclusion has important implications for community building as well. Adherents to 'strong religion' believe that their religious norms are not limited in applicability to those who belong to the Church but govern the *community* as a whole, and every individual who lives in it, whether or not they realize it or agree with them. Put simply, while the first conclusion suggests that 'strong religions' value conformity in moral views *within* their own membership, the second conclusion suggests that a similar conformity is ultimately expected in the wider community as its members come to recognize the 'fundamental truth' of Christianity.

The strength of these moral views in community building is one important concern; intolerance is another. Studies carried out on attitudes towards cultural minorities have consistently shown that evangelical Christians are more intolerant than other Americans towards particular groups of American citizens, ranging from communists to homosexuals to atheists (Wald, 1997; Jelen, 1982; Wilcox and Jelen, 1990). Clyde Wilcox and Ted Jelen use data from the GSS to document the levels of intolerance amongst evangelical Christians towards specific cultural and political minorities, and hypothesize reasons for the elevated levels of hostility. According to Wilcox and Jelen, evangelicals, fundamentalists and Pentecostals all demonstrate significantly higher levels of intolerance, with the Pentecostals having the highest levels of all. The main

---

[9] They go on to say: 'Strong religion is characterized by a number of elements, including: intense faith, supernaturalism, strong commitment to the Church as a source of truth and community' (p. 210).

reason for this difference, according to Wilcox and Jelen, is religious doctrine (as opposed to demographic variables or religiosity). They suggest two important aspects of evangelical theology that might account for the higher levels of intolerance:

It may be that the commitment to an inerrant Bible, which characterizes evangelical doctrine, renders doctrinally conservative Christians skeptical about the benefits of free thought and expression. Conversely it may be the belief in a literal, interventionist Devil that generates intolerance. (Wilcox and Jelen, 1990, p. 43)[10]

Jelen ultimately argues, in research carried out specifically on supporters of the Christian right, that 'support is primarily driven by attitudes toward cultural and ascriptive minorities' (Jelen, 1993, p. 178). In addition to polling data, macro-political analyses have also demonstrated that those jurisdictions with a significant population of fundamentalists are more likely to produce legislation that restricts alternative lifestyles (Bolton and Ledbetter, 1983; Morgan and Meier, 1980).

The growth of the evangelical Church also has important implications with respect to women's equality and reproductive rights. Using the American National Election study, Wald finds that evangelical Protestants are the most likely of all religious groups to be opposed to women's rights and abortion under most circumstances (1997, pp. 185–6). Moreover, religiosity was correlated with a traditional view of women's role in the home, particularly amongst evangelical Christians. As Wald concludes: 'Greater involvement in the religious group promoted a more traditional understanding of women's role' (p. 186). Thus, the growth of the evangelical Church has a potentially negative impact on both cultural recognition and women's equality.

Beyond the academic findings, we can also consider the evidence of current evangelical Church *practice* with respect to women and cultural minorities. Recent statements by some American evangelical Churches suggest that the examination of the issues of race (particularly as it applies to the history of African-Americans) and gender are being given some serious consideration.[11] At the same time, the extent to which cultural diversity and respect may be reconciled within a transcendent singular truth continues to plague evangelical religious practice with regard to Native Americans, for example. The Pentecostal Church, the fastest-growing Church in America, continues to extol its 'Ministry to the

---

[10] See also Nunn et al. (1978).

[11] For example, the Pentecostal/Charismatic Churches of North America have released a 'Racial Reconciliation Manifesto'. The debate is robust and of enormous significance. Similarly, the Methodist Church has established general commissions on both race and women. See www.pcg.org (Pentecostals) and www.umc.org/faithinaction/racism (Methodists); accessed 2 July 2002.

American Indian'.[12] The Church claims that 'rituals and witchcraft are
a major part of many American Indians' lives', and, accordingly, established missions across the United States to convert 'Indians' to Christianity. Put simply, the policy of the Pentecostal Church continues to be
cultural assimilation with respect to the Native American. As a religious
organization, they have every right to hold this particular belief; but to
ask them, as social capital theory and practice does, to go beyond their
religious community and play a key role in building a 'network' or trust
in the larger community is not only wrong with respect to Native Americans but will probably have the opposite effect, namely increasing levels
of 'distrust' amongst cultural minorities in the community.

Other minorities face similar kinds of pressure to assimilate in relation
to the evangelical Church. For example, in a study of forty-four 'pan-
Asian' congregations in the San Francisco Bay area, Russell Jeung found
a significant difference between evangelical and 'mainline' Churches. The
mainline Churches, 'following a politics of identity model . . . , acknowledged the historical, racialized experiences of this group as the primary
bond of pan-ethnic identity and solidarity . . . Mainline liberals thus
see Asian Americans as a marginalized group in need of empowerment'
(Jeung, 2002, p. 225). Evangelicals, on the other hand, focused on assim-
ilating Asian-Americans into the dominant evangelical culture.

> Asian American evangelicals adopt the identities and practices that assimilate
> them into the broader evangelical world and discourage them from maintaining
> certain traditional ways. One's Asian American background is more of a nega-
> tive past from which one has to be healed and a culture that needs to be trans-
> formed . . . How to build an Asian American expression of faith, then, becomes
> problematic when Asian Americans have become acculturated into a very Amer-
> ican evangelical subculture. (Jeung, 2002, p. 239)

Thus, ethnic diversity, to the evangelical Churches, is more likely to be
seen as a problem to be transcended by a 'universal' truth than a wider
manifestation of a culturally differentiated belief system to be embraced.
Jeung's distinction between these two approaches is critical in relation
to ethnic minorities, because it makes clear that the issue of embracing
ethnic diversity within a Church or a community as a whole is not simply
a matter of the *number* of individuals from a particular cultural minority
in a congregation but how cultural difference is perceived by the Church
itself: is it something that should be celebrated or transcended? This focus
on the Asian-American Church is important, because, as was suggested
earlier, Asian-Americans (particularly within mainline Churches) have
become *more* connected to their ethnic identity rather than less with each
passing generation. As such, they are resisting assimilation by finding

---

[12] See www.pcg.org.im/index2.html; accessed 2 June 2002.

congregations that recognize and celebrate this sense of ethnic difference from mainstream culture.

The issue of cultural diversity within the evangelical Church is not limited to ethnicity. The leadership of the Methodist, Pentecostal, Catholic and Mormon Churches (the four that have grown the most in absolute numbers) continues to be intolerant of gay men and lesbians. John Green concludes, in an analysis of the opposition to gay rights in America, that 'organized religion is the most potent source of opposition', particularly the evangelical wing of the Church (Green, 2000, p. 122; see also Herman, 2000). In November 2001 the top court in the United Methodist Church ruled that practising gays could not be in the ministry, concluding that 'homosexual practices are incompatible with Christian teaching' (Culver, 2001). The Mormon Church was very supportive of the Boy Scouts' decision to exclude gays from their organization. Indeed, the Mormon Church 'told the Supreme Court . . . they would withdraw from the Boy Scouts and "the Scouting Movement as presently constituted would cease to exist" if Scouts were forced to accept openly gay leaders' (Burgess, 2001). The other two major supporters of the Boy Scouts' policy were the Catholic Church and the Methodist Church.

There has been an interesting development in relationship to homosexuality within the broader Christian Church in America that provides some insight into the profound problems (and dangerous trade-offs) involved in reconciling diversity with unity. The National Council of Churches has been exploring the idea of a broader Christian unity by bringing together mainline Protestant Churches with Roman Catholics and evangelical Christians. While the latter two groups have been described as 'suspicious of the liberal-leaning National Council of Churches', the former has 'felt their influence to be diminished by the growing clout of Catholics and evangelicals' (Eckstrom, 2002). In seeking to build this larger religious community, the trade-offs between the goal of solidarity or unity and the need to recognize diversity became apparent: the latter has been deferred in favour of the former.

One of the most hotly contested issues between the NCC and the Catholic and evangelical Churches is homosexuality. In the past the NCC has recognized the concerns of gay and lesbian Christians, and taken positions to protect them from measures that might be discriminatory. In order to unite with the Catholic and evangelical Churches, however, the NCC has begun to back-pedal on the question of inclusion and recognition. At first, the issue divided the NCC from other Church groups so much that a 'planned statement on marriage involving the NCC, the Southern Baptist Convention, Catholic bishops and the National Association of Evangelicals was shelved when Edgar [Bob Edgar, NCC general secretary] withdrew his support *for fear that it could be used against gays and lesbians*' (Eckstrom, 2002, emphasis added). Dissent was in the open at this point, but by 2002, at a meeting held in Harrisburg, Pennsylvania, the NCC chose not to discuss the issue at all, in the interests of the unity of the organization. 'This time [Edgar] said, the groups are focusing on areas of agreement, not disagreement' (Eckstrom). This change in emphasis may seem at first insignificant, but at its heart is a key issue: the degree to which 'overcoming differences' and pulling together, whether it be the Christian Church or the American community, entails setting aside issues that are divisive in order to maintain unity.

The NCC is not the only organization to choose unity over dissent; the Presbyterian Church in June 2002 also 'sidestepped the debate on homosexuality' at its general assembly meeting by putting the decision off for another year. As one Presbyterian minister commented, 'This is a conciliatory assembly. We are trying to get on with the business of being the Church' (Rodgers-Melnick, 2002). The evangelical coalition Call to Renewal, cited by Putnam in his final chapter as a model for the future, uses similar language: 'Call to Renewal will stay focused on its priority issues [race and poverty] rather than being drawn into debates over . . . social issues.'[13] By putting the goal of unity ahead of diversity, these organizations are exacting a very high price indeed from certain quarters of the American community. Ultimately, if the exclusion of gays and lesbians is the price to be paid in order to create a shared community, one must surely question whether social solidarity and a 'coming together' under the auspices of a broader Church is worth the price of admission.

Thus, for Asian-Americans as well as gays and lesbians, the issue at stake with respect to the evangelical Church is one of authenticity: the need to be true to one's fundamental identity and to resist those institutions in society that fail to recognize and embrace those differences. Canadian political philosopher Charles Taylor provides some important philosophical insight into this question in his basic distinction between the politics of equal dignity (unity based on sameness) and the politics of difference (the recognition of diversity).

With the politics of equal dignity, what is established is meant to be universally the same, an identical basket of rights and immunities; with the politics of difference, what we are asked to recognize is the unique identity of this individual or group, their distinctness from everyone else. The idea is that it is precisely this distinctness that has been ignored, glossed over, assimilated to a dominant or majority identity. And this assimilation is the cardinal sin against the ideal of authenticity. (Taylor, 1994, p. 38)

---

[13] See www.calltorenewal.com; accessed 2 July 2002.

There are, of course, some very good reasons to support the difference-blind principle of 'equal dignity', particularly in the American context, where women and African-Americans were long treated as second-class citizens, precisely because of a sexual or racial difference. Taylor's point is that if you use this same, universal principle with regard to members of cultural groups who wish to be recognized as different from the dominant cultural norms, such as Native Americans, or to try to assimilate those who are different into an existing set of norms (such as gays or lesbians) you will commit a different kind of ethical 'sin'. In the case of the members of the Asian-American Church, who may wish, through the membership of their Churches, to retain a distinct ethnic identity, glossing over or attempting to transcend such ethnic differences is, again, a failure – what Taylor calls 'misrecognition' to recognize them as they see themselves.

Cultural diversity versus social capital: is bridging capital the answer?

These concerns over women and cultural minorities in a Church-led renewal are compounded by a second major conclusion in the Social Capital Community Benchmark survey regarding social capital building in multicultural communities. After looking at levels of social cohesion in selected urban and rural communities, it emerged that 'inequality and ethnic diversity are inversely related to social capital'.[14] Essentially, the more diverse (both economically and culturally) a community is the less likely the residents are to trust other people (as discussed in chapter 5), to connect with them and to participate in community affairs or politics. Putnam states in an interview about this survey: 'The bottom line is that there are special challenges that are posed to building social capital by ethnic diversity' (Delacourt, 2001). Putnam concludes that the problem is largely one of access: 'Americans lacking access to financial and human capital also lack access to social connections.' The solution would appear to be a simple matter of distribution through 'bridging' capital. 'Quite apart from increasing the level of civic engagement in American communities, we need to attend to its social distribution.'[15] The problem, and therefore the solution, may be more involved and complicated than suggested by Putnam, however. Let us consider four specific problems with Putnam's suggested solution of simply increasing bridging

[14] Government of Canada, Policy Research Initiative, Luncheon Plenary: 'Social capital in the Canadian context' (Mel Cappe, Clerk of the Privy Council, John Helliwell, University of British Columbia, and Robert Putnam, Harvard University), 7 December 2001. See http://policyresearch.gc.ca; accessed 27 June 2002.
[15] See www.cfsv.org/communitysurvey/results3.html; accessed 28 June 2002.

capital. If bridging capital is so important, why is it not measured? What is the difference between bridging and bonding capital? Is bridging capital appropriate to all minorities? And, finally, is it strong enough?

If bridging capital is so important to social capital theory with respect to diverse communities, then more emphasis needs to be placed on its measurement. Putnam admits that '[i]n our empirical account of recent social trends in this book . . . this distinction [between bonding and bridging social capital] will be less prominent than I would prefer' (2000, p. 24). If bridging capital is to be real, not only those studying civic society but associations and organizations as well need to measure and routinely provide numbers with respect to the diversity of membership (percentages of members who belong to different cultural groups or genders).[16] If such data were available, it would be possible to measure the degree to which any organization provided a bridging effect and whether this changed over time. Some examples of organizations that already provide such information, as discussed in the preceding analysis, include the Girl Scouts of America, the NCAA and the ABA, but these associations tend to be exceptions rather than the rule and, not surprisingly, their underlying philosophies are supportive of equity and diversity within their organizations. Social capital theorists should be at the forefront of this push towards a database by which one could measure the 'bridging' dimension of social capital in as many associations as possible.[17]

Even if the need to provide accounts for bridging capital were accepted in principle, a second problem that emerges is the extent to which it can be distinguished from bonding capital. While Putnam and the social capital literature generally assume that it is possible to distinguish between what are considered to be very different types of capital building, these distinctions may depend very much on one's perspective within the larger society. For example, the Boy Scouts of America may be seen as a mechanism of 'bridging capital' across racial boundaries, but with respect to sexual identities it is very much a form of bonding social capital. Similarly, with women's organizations, both dimensions are present to varying degrees. Indeed, for virtually any organization, the degree to which it

---

[16] Clearly, there are groups that are exclusive, and I am not suggesting that every association should be reflective of the general population, but for most associations there will be some level of diversity that is possible. Moreover, for the associations that Putnam is most interested in, namely the broad-based ones, this kind of information is both possible and necessary.

[17] Measuring difference is not without its problems, however. Indeed, one of the key issues here is how to define groups; which measurements are relevant and how to decide. There are also ethical questions to be addressed: for example, whether it is appropriate to ask members about their incomes when developing a picture of the diversity of an association's class membership.

represents a bonding form of social capital as opposed to a bridging form will depend very much on the way in which one defines group differences in society at large as well as within the organization itself.

Thirdly, if the ultimate ideal of bridging capital is the transcendence of different identities, as Putnam comments: 'To build bridging social capital requires that we transcend our social and political and professional identities' (p. 411); it may be singularly inappropriate to suggest 'bridging capital' as the solution for those cultural minorities that have experienced and resisted cultural assimilation. For Asian-American Churches, for example, the preference is to preserve their cultural identity. For indigenous Americans, the transcendent majority community is often *the problem* rather than the solution. Gay men and lesbians, who have faced the powerful force of 'shared' community norms, described by Adrienne Rich as 'compulsory heterosexuality', may also resist a common identity. Finally, for the Deaf community, which sees itself as a linguistic minority rather than individuals with disabilities, it is not 'inclusion' in the majority speaking community that is sought so much as institutions and communities that will respect and preserve its linguistic and cultural difference. As one Deaf scholar summarizes the distinction between the disability and Deaf perspective with respect to inclusion in mainstream education:

It is because disability advocates think of Deaf children as disabled that they want to close the special schools and absurdly plunge Deaf children into hearing classrooms in a totally exclusionary program called inclusion. (Lane, 1997, p. 164)

In all these cases, the notion of bridging capital, to the extent that it requires groups to 'transcend' their particular identity, represents a danger. Within political theory, these ethical demands on the part of groups for the preservation of group identities, as discussed previously, have been articulated either in the form of group rights (Kymlicka, 1995) or group recognition (Taylor, 1994).

The final problem with 'bridging capital' is whether it is a strong enough response with respect to some cultural minorities where it is appropriate to address the powerful forces of segregation and discrimination, in the past and present. At the conclusion of *Bowling Alone*, after a single sentence on sports, the entire section on bridging capital is devoted to the 'less exploited . . . arts and cultural activities' (p. 410). Given the long history of exclusion and the lower levels of trust amongst Hispanic- and African-Americans, one must ask whether choirs and theatre groups really are an adequate response to the profound and intractable problems of racial divisions in American communities today. Is it more appropriate to look to the state and the courts as the key actors in overcoming the racial divide? The question of educational policy in response to the gaps between different ethnic minorities is a critical consideration. Given the impact of Title IX on the exponential growth in women's athletics, is there a similar role to be played by either the courts or political bodies in the United States in removing long-standing and entrenched obstacles to racial, or more broadly cultural, minorities as well? The question of lack of trust and social connectedness of African-Americans towards the larger community is a deep and complicated historical problem. The solution is beyond the scope of the current study, but it is clear that it requires a multifaceted and complex set of solutions. To the extent that civic society should be involved in the solution (which is, after all, Putnam's main focus here) the analysis needs to go beyond a consideration of dance troupes and theatre clubs to every kind of activity and association, including those who advocate change.

There is a profound question at stake in this debate: whether or not bridging social capital, in contemporary America, is simply incommensurable with cultural diversity. Or, to put it another way, does social capitalization, particularly as it is rendered in a functionalist model of social capital, require at this point in history a push towards 'homogeneous communities', as suggested in chapter 5? Dora Costa and Matthew Kahn (2003) have concluded, after an examination of a variety of economic studies on this question, that the answer is 'yes'. Moreover, this conclusion seems, at first glance, to be the same as that of the Saguaro Seminar: 'Costa and Kahn [are] consistent with our initial analysis of our *Social Capital Community Benchmark Survey*.'[18]

A different perspective, rooted in the experience of Canadian multiculturalism, is provided by John Helliwell in a paper presented at an international conference recently, co-sponsored by the Canadian Privy Council Office and the OECD, on the subject of diversity and social capital building (see Helliwell, 2003). Helliwell concludes that bridging social capital and diversity are not necessarily incommensurable with respect to new immigrants as long as governments engage in an 'integrationist' and multicultural rather than 'assimilationist' immigration policy. Helliwell argues that Costa and Kahn's work is far too reliant on American studies and suggests that Canada's emphasis on multiculturalism rather than a 'melting pot' has led to higher levels of trust amongst Canadian immigrants than American immigrants, as well as doubling the likelihood that immigrants to Canada will naturalize (and join the national community). One conclusion that can be drawn from this analysis is that the clash between social capital and diversity is a product of 'governmental policy

---

[18] See www.ksg.harvard.edu/saguaro/socialcapitalresearch.htm; accessed January 2005.

rather than natural law'. For Helliwell, state immigration policies must
have a dual focus: economic integration combined with the protection
of cultural heritage.[19] There is certainly something to be said for this
argument advanced by Helliwell (and Irene Bloemraad) in their comparisons of Canadian and American immigration policies, that multiculturalism and the preservation of difference within a nation state may
create stronger levels of trust (amongst recently arrived immigrants) in
the society they have just entered, and it suggests a certain direction
for immigration policy (integrationist rather than assimilationist). What
remains unclear in Helliwell's analysis (a question that is relevant not
only for immigrants but also for Quebec, First Nations, the Deaf and
gay and lesbian citizens in Canada) is: where is the line that distinguishes
'integrationist' policies from 'assimilationist' ones? Is there the danger
that 'integration' continues to make unity a priority over difference and
continues to be what some have termed 'seductive integration' or 'soft
assimilation' (Day, 2000)?

In the final analysis, taking the issue of diversity seriously does not
simply mean paying attention to the 'distribution' of social capital via
bridging mechanisms but being aware of the nature of the connections,
or 'bridges', that are being built. And it will probably mean, in some cases,
using the metaphor of a 'bridge' within bridging capital in its more literal sense; not as a transcendent mechanism to overcome difference and
'bring two diverse identities together' but as a means by which people
can travel between different cultural places. Thus, to bridge difference
is *not* to 'bring' together two parts into one but to provide a mechanism by which those who wish to *move between* them can do so. The
bridge, in this use of the word, ultimately depends upon a spatial separation to retain any literal meaning. To express this same point using a
different metaphor, one might utilize the indigenous American two-row
wampum, first described in the agreement between the Iroquois and the
Europeans in seventeenth-century North America. The image is simply
that of two peoples (aboriginal and non-aboriginal) who share a river
but travel in two canoes, along parallel but different trajectories.[20] As
Mohawk scholar Taiaiake Alfred and political theorist Melissa Williams

---

[19] The differences between Canada and the United States with respect to multicultural
policies and various immigrant groups is analysed in a doctoral dissertation by Irene
Bloemraad, *From Foreigner to Full Citizen: The Political Incorporation of Immigrants and
Refugees in the United States and Canada*, under the supervision of Theda Skocpol at
Harvard University.
[20] There are several scholars (both aboriginal and non-aboriginal) who have used this
metaphor in their analyses of the relationship between Canada and the First Nations
people who reside within Canada: Williams (2002); Alfred (1999); Tully (1995); and
Mercredi and Turpel (1993).

conclude, the two-row wampum can represent 'respect for the autonomy and distinctive nature of each partner' (Williams, 2002; Alfred, 1999). It is this respect for difference, rather than a transcendent sameness, that may ultimately create a real basis of trust and connection amongst certain kinds of cultural groups in relation to the dominant cultural community.

The impact of 9/11: national interest and social capital

Any concerns regarding either the role of the Church or cultural diversity in building community have taken on new meaning in America since 11 September 2001. In an op-ed article in the *New York Times* about a month after 9/11, Putnam calls the terrorist attacks on the United States an important potential catalyst for social capital building. Using Pearl Harbor as his historical metaphor, he argues that such attacks against a people, while terrible in their own right, may also represent opportunities for new kinds of 'cooperation between the federal government and civic society', if young people are 'taught practical civic lessons', churches 'plan interfaith services over Thanksgiving weekend' and adults ensure the 'resurgence of community involvement' through an appeal to 'deeper community connections' (Putnam, 2001). While the desire to do something proactive and positive in response to such events is understandable, the specific linking of community building with American national interests should give pause for thought. As Putnam's own analysis shows (in the second wave of the Community Benchmark survey, in the autumn of 2001), 9/11 changed attitudes amongst the American public towards their country and their government. Americans have tended to 'rally round the flag', and engaged in a 'burst of enthusiasm for the federal government'.[21] Putnam sees the change in attitude as positive:

In the aftermath of September's tragedy a window of opportunity has opened for a sort of civic renewal that occurs only once or twice a century. And yet, though the crisis revealed and replenished the wells of solidarity in American communities, those wells so far remain untapped. (2001)

Putnam is tapping into a well of emotion that is driven not only by a nostalgic appeal to an old-time community but by a patriotic appeal to the defence of the nation. The potentially dark side of this patriotic civic engagement is the implicit notion of a civic solidarity built in opposition to a common enemy. Moreover, unlike the Second World War, the enemy that perpetrated 9/11 was not a foreign state across the ocean so much

---

[21] It should be noted that Putnam also finds that Americans tend to trust all other ethnic groups more – i.e. 'whites', blacks, Hispanics and Asian-Americans – with the notable exception of Arab-Americans (Putnam, 2002a).

as members of a network who lived within the very communities that were attacked. As such, the civic service expected of American citizens in light of 9/11 will involve vigilance against this internal threat to security. This creates a different kind of dynamic in the community, revolving around what Carl Schmitt once called the friend/enemy distinction that characterizes all politics.

As Cathy Young argues in an op-ed piece in the *Boston Globe*, in response to Putnam's article in the *New York Times*: 'War-inspired civic virtue also has its less attractive side. For one, what brings us together is not just love of our country but hatred and fear of the enemy . . . Could it be that what we gain in shared values, we may lose in pluralism and healthy dissent?' (Young, 2001). Moreover, history attests to the impact on specific ethnic minorities of solidarity built upon patriotic foundations at comparable historical junctures. John Sanbonmatsu writes in a letter to the editor of the *New York Times*:

Robert Putnam's case for cherishing World War II and our present crisis as boons to the American civic spirit would have been far more convincing had he acknowledged the violence, xenophobia and racism that typically attend such unifying moments . . . [T]he convivial spirit in America did not extend to all, particularly to the 100,000 Japanese-Americans herded into camps (including my own family). Today, of course, it is Arab-Americans who are bearing the brunt of the 'deeper community connections' that Mr. Putnam celebrates. (Sanbonmatsu, 2001)

Putnam's post-9/11 survey demonstrates that these concerns are well founded. In the autumn of 2001 the Saguaro Seminar conducted a follow-up interview with many of the same people who had been interviewed in the Social Capital Community Benchmark survey in 2000, in order to measure any changes in attitudes that had occurred as a result of 9/11. At first glance, the changes from one year to the next seemed to be positive in relation to multiculturalism. Putnam finds that, across most racial and class boundaries, people seemed to trust each other more than before 11 September (Putnam, 2002b). But this conclusion needs to be considered in light of two other findings.

The first, consistent with the worries of John Sanbonmatsu, is that Arab-Americans are being treated differently. Thus, Putnam found that the level of trust towards Arab-Americans as a whole was about 10 per cent less than for other ethnic minorities. This result needs to take into account the fact that similar attitudes would probably also be expressed towards Muslim-Americans. Moreover, there are other ethnic minorities who have also faced discrimination, most notably members of the 300,000-strong Sikh-American community, simply because their religious practice of wearing turbans has meant for some Americans that they have a similar appearance to Osama bin Laden.[22] Sikhs, along with people of Middle Eastern and Asian descent more broadly, were the subject of physical attacks, from Arizona to Montreal to Ireland, as part of the fallout from 9/11 (Rice, 2001; Haughey, 2001). Thus, although Putnam asked only about Arab-Americans, the community of possible people affected by such attitudes is probably larger than the data for this particular question might suggest.

While Putnam is buoyed by the survey results suggesting that all other ethnic groups are seen in a more positive light, previous literature on intolerance in America suggests that a focus on one specific group is dangerous, particularly in a period of national insecurity, as the larger community's anxieties coalesce around a singular cultural target. In an influential analysis, John Sullivan, James Pierson and George Marcus suggest that intolerance of groups in America is no threat to democracy as long as there is a level of 'pluralistic intolerance', a variety of different groups to be hated. 'The consequences of high levels of intolerance may be mitigated by the extent to which the antipathy of citizens . . . is dispersed among an ideologically heterogeneous set of groups' (Sullivan et al., 1982, p. 139). Conversely, when intolerant opinion coalesces around one particular group, as it did in the McCarthy era around communists, the change in politics and policy can be swift and repressive against the targeted group existing *within* the community. Thus, Putnam's results, in light of this analysis, suggest that there is, at the very least, the potential for a pluralistically intolerant America to shift towards a more homogeneous and focused antipathy, particularly in the event of another attack.[23]

The other finding in the 2001 study that gives further cause for concern is the change in attitude towards immigrants since 2000. While the vast majority of indicators show a positive increase in civic attitudes, one important exception is the support for immigrant rights. The change in the percentage of Americans supporting immigrant rights before 9/11 and after is −11 per cent.[24] New immigrants are clearly facing significant antipathy within the broader American society. Thus, to the extent that the focus of intolerance in America is a specific

---

[22] Amarjit Singh Buttar, chairman of the American Region of the World Sikh Council, comments: 'When you put my picture next to that of Osama bin Laden, for the man on the street, we both may look alike' (Brown, 2001).

[23] James Gibson has argued that protection against the repression of cultural minorities is less a factor of pluralistic intolerance than constitutional protections of individual freedoms (Gibson, 1989, p. 570). However, the shift from state to community (in the current administration's faith-based initiatives and USA Freedom Corps) brings such robust constitutional protection into question (as is discussed shortly).

[24] See www.ksg.harvard.edu/saguaro/press.html for 15 January 2002; accessed 5 June 2002.

ethnic group, or 'immigrants' more broadly defined, the underlying notion that pulls these attitudes together is the sense that these individuals are more likely to be 'terrorists' and therefore threats to American society. In building community, in light of 9/11, the state needs to be very careful that it does not exploit or fuel these attitudes but works to counter the cohesive antipathy towards any particular ethnic or religious group.

Thus, since *Bowling Alone* was published two general themes have emerged in Putnam's social capital theory, partly in response to subsequent research and partly in response to world events: the Church as the engine for social capital building in America, and the linking of a revival of American community to national security interests in the wake of 9/11. Each of these recent thrusts in social capital theory has its real world counterparts in President Bush's domestic policy framework, namely the faith-based initiatives and the USA Freedom Corps (particularly the new Citizen Corps) respectively. We turn to consider this domestic agenda in more detail, and the ways in which some of the fears with respect to the blurring of Church, state and community work out in the concrete debates surrounding these specific policy initiatives.

Social capital and the Bush administration's domestic agenda

On 29 January 2002 President George W. Bush gave his first State of the Union address since 11 September 2001. Not surprisingly, the events of that day were a central theme in his speech before Congress. Bush made the case that America needed to respond 'resolutely' to 9/11, suggesting that there was a role for both the military and civilians in the ongoing 'war' against terrorism. While the American military and intelligence agencies would be called upon to bring those responsible for 9/11 to justice, to defeat any states harbouring terrorists and to prevent future attacks from occurring on American soil, civilians, as Putnam had first suggested in the *New York Times*, also had an obligation to heed a civic call to duty in the wake of terrorist attacks. 'We want to be a nation that serves goals larger than self. We've been offered a unique opportunity and we must not let this moment pass. My call tonight is for every American to commit at least two years – 4000 hours over the rest of your lifetime – to the service of *your neighbors and your nation*' (emphasis added).[25]

---

[25] See www.whitehouse.gov/news/releases/2002/01/20020129-11.html; accessed 4 July 2002.

Bush echoes Putnam's theme, in the final sentence, that the connection between community service and national purpose is a close one.

In March 2002 Bush reiterated the need for public service as a civilian response to 9/11, so as to bring together the interests of country and community into one overarching goal defined as 'good'. Social capital became part of the explicit fight against terrorism worldwide:

> There are social entrepreneurs in our society who help define America . . . I believe out of this evil [9/11] will come incredible good. And one of the good things that will happen is Americans will ask the question about how I can help fight evil by doing something good . . . If you're interested in doing something for your country, help somebody in need; write a check, give your time, volunteer.[26]

In the State of the Union address, Bush was explicit about how the federal government planned to facilitate the building of community:

> Many are already serving, and I thank you. If you aren't sure how to help, I've got a good place to start. To sustain and extend the best that has emerged in America I invite you to join the new USA Freedom Corps.

In the two days following his speech to Congress Bush launched the USA Freedom Corps, and, as we shall see, explicitly anchored it in Robert Putnam's social capital thesis.

USA Freedom Corps

The USA Freedom Corps has four elements: an improved AmeriCorps (first introduced by the Clinton administration as community service at home); a Senior Corps (for seniors to engage in civic service); a strengthened and redefined Peace Corps (first introduced by the Kennedy administration for American citizens who wish to serve abroad); and a brand new element, the Citizen Corps (which seeks to marry civic activity with homeland security). The explicit theoretical anchors for this initiative are Putnam's decline of community thesis, articulated in *Bowling Alone*, and the catalytic power of 9/11 to reverse this trend, as expressed in his subsequent articles. Thus, the USA Freedom Corps' *Handbook*, published in January, makes specific reference to *Bowling Alone* and quotes directly from Putnam's *New York Times* op-ed piece. 'There is more that we can do to tap this spirit [Putnam's call for civic renewal] and one key strategy is for individuals in communities to seek greater involvement with fellow citizens' (USA Freedom Corps, 2002, 9). A second report, produced in April 2002 and entitled *Principles and Reforms for a Citizen Service Act:*

[26] See www.whitehouse.gov/news/releases/2002/03/20020312-3.html; accessed 4 July 2002.

Fostering a Culture of Service, Citizenship and Responsibility,[27] also begins with a reference to *Bowling Alone*.

Putnam, in turn, has publicly supported the USA Freedom Corps initiative in the wake of 9/11 as an example of the federal government facilitating social capital building. In an article published a month after the 2002 State of the Union address, authored jointly by Putnam and Thomas Sanders, the conclusion is drawn that this kind of initiative is an excellent foundation for social capital growth; it simply needs to be built further.

> What institutional changes ought we [to] make today? President Bush's plan to seek $1 billion for the USA Freedom Corps is a bold first step. He hopes to galvanize Americans willing to serve through an expanded AmeriCorps, Senior Corps, and Peace Corps as well as a newly established Citizen Corps to help local communities prepare for threats of terrorism. More could be done. (Sanders and Putnam, 2002)

Both Bush and Putnam seem to view the conflating of national security with community service as largely positive; but, through our analysis of two of the four elements of the USA Freedom Corps, namely the brand new Citizen Corps and the refocused Peace Corps, troubling questions arise about the dangers inherent in conflating such agendas with respect to justice and diversity in terms of both a liberal concern with the civil rights of individuals and a multicultural concern with the impact on particular cultural minorities.

The Citizen Corps includes a number of community-based emergency preparedness initiatives in the case of another terrorist attack. In addition, however, when it was first introduced it also included local mechanisms for gathering information on potential terrorists in the community. For example, the White House recommended doubling Neighborhood Watch with an added 'Terrorism Prevention Component' (USA Freedom Corps, 2002, p. 15) and the establishment of a Terrorist Information and Prevention System, 'a nationwide mechanism for reporting suspicious activity – enlisting millions of American transportation workers, truckers, letter carriers, train conductors, ship captains and utility employees in the effort to prevent terrorism' (p. 17). While the amount of money initially dedicated to each of these purposes was relatively small ($6 and

---

[27] Putnam is quoted in the executive summary of the USA Freedom Corps' *Principles and Reforms for a Citizen Service Act*, available at http://www.nationalservice.org/about/principles/index.html. There has been congressional activity around this issue as well. John McCain and Evan Bayh introduced the Call to Service Act into the Senate in November 2001 in the aftermath of 9/11. In June 2003 McCain, Bayh and Senator Ted Kennedy held a press conference to 'reauthorize the National and Community Service Act'. In addition, Peter Hoekstra and Tim Roemer introduced into the House in May 2002 the Citizen Service Act of 2002.

$8 million respectively), one gets the sense that what was envisaged here was the community (in the form of either neighbour or local technician) as terrorist watchdog. The idea that 'millions of Americans' were being encouraged by their own government to watch their neighbours or clients for signs of 'terrorist activity' and report to federal authorities raised concerns in the media and beyond.

In an editorial published in July 2002 the *Washington Post* challenges the TIPS programme: 'Americans should not be subjecting themselves to law enforcement scrutiny merely by having cable lines installed, mail delivered or meters read. Police cannot routinely enter people's houses without either permission or a warrant. They should not be using utility workers to conduct surveillance they could not lawfully conduct themselves' (*Washington Post*, 2002a). The American Civil Liberties Union also questioned the programme, suggesting that the government was turning 'local technicians' into 'government-sanctioned peeping toms' (ACLU, 2002). TIPS was ultimately shelved when Congress passed the Homeland Security Act in November 2002 (H.R. 5005) and included a section:

Any and all activities of the Federal Government to implement the proposed component program of the Citizen Corps known as Operation TIPS (Terrorism Information and Prevention System) are hereby prohibited. (United States Senate, 2002, sect. 880, p. 280)

Another programme within the Citizen Corps is the Volunteers in Police Services. 'Volunteers in Police Service is a locally-driven Citizen Corps program that allows community members to offer their time and talents to their local law enforcement agency. VIPS serves as a gateway to information for and about law enforcement volunteer programs and meets a volunteer's desire to serve as well as an agency's need for support.'[28] In the inaugural issue of *VIPS in Focus*, an electronic newsletter about this programme, VIPS is linked to the Neighborhood Watch programme, and both are connected to 'neighborhood cohesion' and civic engagement:

This inaugural edition addresses a central focus for many law enforcement volunteer activities – advancing community crime prevention efforts by building on Neighborhood Watch activities. The purpose of this edition is to examine how agencies are linking such programs to increase neighborhood cohesion and extend community policing activities by engaging the citizenry.[29]

While both Neighborhood Watch and volunteer police service programmes have been around for a long time and provide important

---

[28] See http://www.policevolunteers.org/law/faq.htm#008; accessed February 2004.
[29] See http://www.policevolunteers.org/; accessed February 2004.

supporting roles to local police units, it is the link, under the auspices of a 'Citizen Corps', to 'terrorism' that begins to blur the lines between 'national security' and 'community service'. Moreover, the original TIPS programme provides evidence of how far the White House may be willing, particularly in the event of another attack, to go down this path of using local people in the community as 'spies' on their neighbours. Thus, the degree to which either of these networks (Neighborhood Watch or VIPS) could be used as tools for the police or federal authorities to collect information on individuals in the future, without having the civil rights training or knowledge to which federal, state and city officers are subject, remains unclear.

Although the civil rights of individuals in their homes is of vital importance to a liberal democracy, an equally troubling but hidden dimension to such programmes is the ethnic/religious subtext, left unstated by both the government itself and many of the critics. It is not *Americans* as a whole who will come under surveillance in the community in these programmes, but ethnically and culturally demarcated groups that will be targeted. The White House would deny any risk of racial profiling in these community-based programmes but, in light of Putnam's findings on the increased levels of suspicion towards Arab-Americans and new immigrants more generally, it is not difficult to surmise where the focus of community surveillance would probably be with respect to 'terrorism prevention'. Moreover, while the *Washington Post* editorial rightly suggested, in relation to the TIPS programme, that the replacement of professionally trained police officers by utility workers for surveillance in people's homes would have circumvented the law with respect to *individuals*, there are, in addition, ethnic or racial dimensions to all the rules, professional training and appeal mechanisms used by police officers; these mechanisms are removed when the task is handed over to local volunteers within the community.[30] Thus, the 'community' may be a useful device to avoid the thorny issues raised regarding the privacy of individuals in relation to state power (the concern raised by liberal justice) *and* ethnic group targeting (the concern raised by multicultural justice). Put simply, by generally blurring the line between civic engagement and national service through the programmes established in Citizen Corps, the Bush administration has created the possiblity that the rules, laws and practices that prevent local police and state authorities from violating the privacy rights of individuals or from racially profiling

---

[30] Needless to say, many critics in America would suggest that police officers often fail in their professional responsibilities over race, but at least the issue, the rules governing their conduct, and the mechanisms for challenging police who overstep the line are all in place.

particular groups of American citizens may be circumvented by individual citizens in their local neighbourhoods as they respond to the call for civic participation.

The other element of the USA Freedom Corps that raises concerns is the new focus of the Peace Corps, the overseas service organization first introduced by President Kennedy. The Bush policy handbook suggests that this programme will be doubled over the next five years, boosting the existing Peace Corps 'to near historic highs of 15,000 volunteers, last achieved in June of 1966' (USA Freedom Corps, 2002, p. 8). This increase is completely consistent with Putnam's idea of a renewed civic engagement, but the specific goals of this latest Peace Corps include religious education as well as patriotic service. The handbook suggests, for example, the need to expand the number and *kind* of countries with volunteers. In particular, it is suggested that 'the administration will work with other countries that do not have Peace Corps volunteers, including *more Islamic countries*' (p. 27, emphasis added). President Bush clarifies the underlying purpose of this new Peace Corps as well as the emphasis on Islamic countries in answers he gave in Philadelphia in March 2002:

If there are any people interested in *spreading US values around the world*, the Peace Corps is a wonderful place to do so . . . Our goal is . . . to make sure we have the Peace Corps go to nations, particularly Muslim nations, that don't understand America. They don't understand our heart; they don't understand our compassion; they don't understand that we share the same values . . . [T]he Peace Corps is a good way to spread that message.[31]

Thus, under the Bush administration, the emphasis has shifted from the original idea of 'helping others to help themselves' to 'spreading' American values, particularly in Islamic nations. As a consequence the mixing of religious and political objectives, packaged again under the rubric of community service, is not limited to American communities but expands to include the globe, especially the Islamic world.

---

[31] Remarks by the president in 'Conversation on Service', Kimmel Center for the Performing Arts, Philadelphia, emphasis added; available at www.whitehouse.gov/news/releases/2002/03/20020312-3.html; accessed 4 July 2002. It is important to note that many of the volunteers in the Peace Corps do not necessarily endorse this new thrust and find that the reality is often very different on the ground. For example, one volunteer, Jay Davidson, who went to Mauritius, an Islamic country, found that both religion and government were less important than the concrete relationships he established with people. 'Davidson said that when people deal with each other on a one-to-one basis, labels like "American", "Muslim" or "Christian" fall by the wayside. "When we express our friendship to each other, we do it because of the way we treat each other and not because of anything our governments do."' See www.worldvolunteerweb.org/news-views/news/muslim-countries-ask-for-974/lang/en.html (accessed February 2006).

Faith-based initiatives

The other significant initiative undertaken by the Bush administration that mixes Church and state under the rubric of community service consists of the 'faith-based and community initiatives'. President Bush, when he was governor of Texas, introduced faith-based initiatives in that state, and as president he began to develop the necessary infrastructure to expand his original state programme into a national one. He found some philosophical support in both the meetings of the Saguaro Seminar and the recommendations arising out of the *Better Together* report on the rebuilding of American communities. The first recommendation in the chapter on religion and social capital in this report, based on the June 1998 meeting of the Saguaro Seminar on religion and communities, is to 'increase secular funds for faith-based organizations'.[32] It is worth noting that the Saguaro Seminar included amongst its participants John J. Dilulio, the first director of the White House Office of Faith-Based and Community Initiatives, serving as assistant to the president during 2000–2001, and Stephen Goldsmith, chief domestic policy adviser to George W. Bush during the 2000 campaign, and a special adviser after his election to the presidency on 'faith-based and not-for-profit initiatives'.[33]

Within a month of the publication of *Better Together* President Bush (on 29 January 2001) signed two executive orders, creating the high-level White House Office of Faith-Based and Community Initiatives and instructing five Cabinet departments – Health and Human Services, Housing and Urban Development, Education, Labor and Justice – to establish 'Centers for Faith-Based and Community Initiatives'. In the latter case, each of these departments was required to conduct a department-wide audit and identify any barriers to the participation of 'faith-based' and other community organizations in the delivery of social services. The White House was explicit in making the link between social capital and these new initiatives: 'Our goal is to energize civil society and rebuild social capital.'[34] While the language is broadly inclusive, it is clear that most of these 'faith-based initiatives' are really Churches. Don Eberly, former deputy director of the White House Office of Faith-Based and Community Initiatives, and deputy assistant to the president, admitted during a discussion (which also included Robert Putnam and Amitai Etzioni) on the National Public Radio programme *Talk of the Nation* that,

---

[32] 2001 *Better Together* report, available at www.bettertogether.org/pdfs/Religion.pdf (accessed 21 August 2002), chapter 5, 'Religion and social capital', p. 6.
[33] See www.ksg.harvard.edu/saguaro; accessed 23 July 2002.
[34] See www.whitehouse.gov/news/reports/faithbased.html; accessed 2 July 2002.

while the White House was not trying to 'pit' Churches against secular organizations, in most cases it was small-scale congregations that were fulfilling this function.[35] Put simply, under this programme the federal government uses Churches to deliver governmental social benefits and policies.

President Bush was clear in his original announcement that the delivery of social services had to 'value the bedrock principles of pluralism, nondiscrimination, evenhandedness and neutrality'.[36] But one wonders how Bush believed such goals could be achieved within the context of the 'charitable choice' elements of the original White-House-backed plan: provisions that 'would have opened new government programs to religious groups and would have allowed the groups to maintain their exemption from civil rights laws' (Franzen, 2002). In the summer of 2001 the House of Representatives passed a bill supporting the White House initiative, including the 'charitable choice' provisions, making clear that these 'faith-based institutions' would not be subject to civil rights laws even in the delivery of federally funded social services. Concerns were immediately raised regarding the potential for religious discrimination against those employed to provide such services. Even the Churches that stood to gain from the new funds questioned this aspect of the House bill. The Methodist Church, in representations before the Senate Judiciary Committee in June 2001, makes the following case:

The United Methodist Church cannot support legislation that clearly endorses religious discrimination in the hiring and firing practices in community social service ministries paid by the federal government . . . It is one thing for the Church to require that their pastors, organists, sextons and other employees of the Church to be from their faith and conviction; another thing, entirely, for religious groups receiving tax dollars, in order to provide secular services, to be allowed to use the same criteria for hiring their employees for government-related programs.[37]

Concerns were also raised with regard to the fate of gays and lesbians, either as potential employees or clients (Lightman, 2001).

In November 2001 President Bush sent a letter to the Senate leadership; it reads: 'Since September 11, Americans have come together to help meet our national needs in this time of great crisis . . . [I]t is now time for America to stand by her charities . . . I believe the Congress must address these issues now. We must pass and sign into law an "Armies of

---

[35] 'What is communitarianism?', *Talk of the Nation* (with guests Robert Putnam, Don Eberly and Amitai Etzioni), National Public Radio, 5 February 2001, minute 23.

[36] See www.whitehouse.gov/news/releases/2001/08/unlevelfield.html.

[37] Contained in a press release by the Americans United for Separation of Church and State organization on 14 June 2001; see www.au.org/press/pr614012.htm; accessed 4 July 2002.

Compassion" bill this year.'[38] The Senate was concerned enough with the discriminatory potential of the House bill to propose a new piece of legislation. In February 2002 the Senate, under the leadership of Rick Santorum and Joseph Lieberman, hammered out a compromise bill that removed the controversial 'charitable choice' provisions of the House bill but, consistent with White House rhetoric, retained the title 'Armies of Compassion Initiative' (Gerstenzang, 2002a). In December President Bush grew impatient with Congress for failing to pass any legislation in the two years since he had first introduced the idea and signed an executive order implementing core elements of his faith-based initiative proposals for federal contracts. The decision to use an executive order riled some, who argued that Bush was circumventing the will of Congress. James Gerstenzang in the *Los Angeles Times* writes: 'Sidestepping Congress . . . Bush moved last week on . . . his faith-based initiative' (Gerstenzang, 2002b). An editorial in the *Washington Post* entitled 'Faith-based by fiat' argued that the controversy over Bush's initiatives was 'a fundamental debate' that should be worked out 'through the political process' rather than through presidential 'fiat' (*Washington Post*, 2002b). In April 2003 the Senate finally passed a bill, but while it expanded the tax breaks for charitable donations it also eliminated most of the original provisions for social service delivery through religious organizations.

Since his re-election in November 2004 Bush has recommitted himself to faith-based social services, saying that he will take his own initiatives by federal orders if necessary. According to Jim Towey, the director of the White House Office of Faith-Based and Community Initiatives, 'The president will continue to look at what are his tools as chief executive, what other executive actions he can take' (Marus, 2005). One specific avenue that is being pursued by the White House is to convince governors and state legislators to fund more social services through faith-based initiatives (Meckler, 2005). Richard Nathan, director of the Rockefeller Institute at the State University of New York in Albany, has argued until recently that there has been very little interest expressed by the states in faith-based social services, but that it began to change in the autumn of 2004.[39] According to Erin Madigan, as of January 2005 '[t]wenty governors – Democrat and Republican alike – have established faith-based outreach offices' (Madigan, 2005).

---

[38] Text of a letter from the president to the Senate majority leader and the Senate Republican leader, 7 November 2001; see www.whitehouse.gov/news/releases/2001/11/20011108-2.html; accessed 4 July 2002.

[39] 'Scanning the policy environment for faith-based social services in the United States: results of a 50-state study', *The Roundtable on Religion and Social Welfare Policy Report*, Rockefeller Institute of Government and Pew Charitable Trusts, October 2003. In the foreword to this study Nathan comments that the reaction has been 'muted'. More recently, however, he says that more interest is being expressed (Meckler, 2005).

The debate over faith-based initiatives between the House, Senate and White House largely centred around the issue of discrimination in hiring, which religious organizations viewed as a question of their right to hire adherents of their own faith. As an editorial in the *Washington Post* points out, the deeper questions raised by these initiatives fell out of view in these skirmishes between Congress and the White House:

> The real question is how engaged the government should be in the first place with groups whose religious missions are hard to separate from the secular functions the government wishes them to serve. Can America have a partnership between federal agencies and religious groups that harnesses the promise of faith-based action without the government sponsoring religious doctrine, coercing its citizens or otherwise endorsing religion? The issue of religious discrimination is only one feature of this larger question – one it should not be permitted to dominate. (*Washington Post*, 2003)

Under existing executive orders and with the potential expansion of the programme either under the auspices of the White House or through state budgets, troubling questions remain about the overlap between Church and state and its impact on vulnerable cultural minorities. For example, the degree to which Churches (or other religious organizations) may use federal funds to proselytize their religious message is still unclear. Certainly, Bush's plan allows religious institutions to continue to display religious art, icons, scripture or symbols as they provide social services. What the impact of this might be on religious or other cultural minorities is an issue that continues to be raised by representatives of various concerned groups. The American Jewish Congress was the first major American Jewish group to oppose the first Senate bill, while Hadassah and the American Jewish Committee have both expressed concerns over the need to keep the state and religion separated, pointing to examples in drug addiction programmes, where some Christian organizations have allegedly used federal money to convert people going through recovery from addiction to drugs or alcohol (*Los Angeles Times*, 2002; American Jewish Committee, 2002; Hadassah, 2001). Americans United for Separation of Church and State concur: 'Such displays [of art, icons, scripture] will make many religious minorities feel like second-class citizens at institutions providing social services with tax dollars. "It is simply wrong for a publicly funded job training facility to post a banner that reads 'Only Jesus Saves'" [Revd Barry Lynn, executive director] said.'[40]

While much of the debate over federal faith-based initiatives may still be hypothetical and speculative, a report by the Texas Freedom Network Education Fund on George W. Bush's first efforts at faith-based

---

[40] See www.au.org/press/pr020702.htm; accessed 4 July 2002.

initiatives while he was governor of Texas may provide some concrete evidence of the outcomes of religious-based social service provision. There
are a number of interesting aspects to the Texas initiatives. First, the legislation sought not only to increase state money for religious organizations
to deliver social services but, as importantly, to loosen the regulations with
respect to hiring, accreditation and regulation. For example, the Texas
Legislature in 1997 set up an alternative accreditation system allowing
faith-based children's homes and childcare facilities to be accredited by a
faith-based entity rather than regulated by the state.[41] Drug and alcohol
programmes were also exempted from state regulation.[42] 'Deregulation
of faith-based service providers is essential to the Faith-Based Initiative,
which essentially strives to bring more faith-based providers into the social
safety net – whether by increasing funding streams or by removing regu-
latory barriers for these programs' (Texas Freedom Network, 2002).

According to the report, the alternative accreditation system for childcare facilities was in place for four years (1997–2001) and was taken up
by only eight facilities. Two thousand other faith-based facilities chose
to continue operating under a state licence, which raises the question of
whether such deregulation was in fact necessary. Amongst some of the
eight that were accredited by the Texas Association of Child-Care Agencies there were irregularities and problems, to the extent that the Texas
Legislature chose in the spring of 2001 not to renew the state's alternative accreditation programme. The deregulation of substance abuse
programmes continued; faith-based drug treatment centres needed only
to register with the alternative Texas Commission on Alcohol and Drug
Abuse to become exempt from virtually all regulations governing state-
sponsored agencies (Texas Freedom Network, 2002).

Thus, it is not simply the question of funding for faith-based organizations that is worrying but the deregulation in the name of religious
freedom that can put vulnerable populations such as children and drug
or alcohol addicts at risk.

Faith-based deregulation endangers vulnerable populations. It has proven dangerous to exempt social service providers – simply because they are faith-based –
from the health and safety regulations expressly created to protect vulnerable
populations like children and chemically dependent people. There is no question
that eliminating basic health and safety standards made operations easier for a
few faith-based programs in Texas, but it has also jeopardized the well-being of
clients served by these facilities. (Texas Freedom Network, 2002, 'Texas lessons',
lesson 2)

---

[41] House Bill 2482 (75R) 1997; see www.capitol.state.tx.us; accessed 6 June 2003.
[42] House Bill 2481 (75R) 1997; see www.capitol.state.tx.us; accessed 6 June 2003.

The central lesson from Texas is that the 'charitable choice' provisions (which exempt faith-based institutions from state regulation of one kind or another) are potentially very dangerous. As the *Washington Post* editorial suggested, the debate is not simply about who gets to employ whom, but about the broader questions concerning the role of the state with respect to the vulnerable, and the necessity of drawing a line between the state's role on the one hand and the religious institutions on the other.

The White House seems to think that there is too *little* religion in the public realm, particularly at the community level. Thus, when pressed on the issue of the separation of Church and state on *Talk of the Nation*, Eberly concludes that 'most people would acknowledge that the pendulum might have swung too far in the direction of . . . an official secularism in public spaces in America'.[43] This challenge to 'secularism' in the public sphere is often accompanied by a weaker interpretation of the Jeffersonian wall of separation between Church and state. Thus, Eberly argues in the same discussion that the separation of Church and state is nothing more than the obligation of the state to have no *established* religion – which is the case, for example, in the United Kingdom (see also Eberly, 2000). The report of the original proceedings of the fifth seminar of the Saguaro Seminar on faith and civic engagement in June 1998 also subscribes to this minimalist interpretation of the separation of Church and state.

Contrary to our collective memories, the doctrine of separation of Church and state enshrines *two* beliefs: a prohibition on the governmental establishment of religion *and* the protection of religious expression from government interference.[44]

The foundation for this narrow view of the separation doctrine is from a particular interpretation of the constitution as it was written rather than from evolving rulings made by the courts, particularly within the public education system, in response to an increasingly multicultural and multi-religious society. As such, this view of the separation of Church and state seems to shut down any political debate beyond the idea that individuals should be free to engage in religious belief and practices and the government should not have an official religious position; what it leaves untouched is the enormous area in between, namely the semi-public sphere of the community.

---

[43] 'What is communitarianism?', *Talk of the Nation* (with guests Robert Putnam, Don Eberly and Amitai Etzioni), National Public Radio, 5 February 2001, minute 41.

[44] *Report of the Proceedings*, on the Saguaro Seminar website www.ksg.harvard.edu/saguaro; accessed 23 July 2002. In an updated version (accessed in December 2003) there is a change in wording: 'The Constitution does not specify the "separation of Church and state" but only the obligation not to establish, prefer or interfere with the practice of religion.'

Perhaps the most troubling aspect of the faith-based initiatives is the way in which the Bush administration has used social capital, and specifically the idea of 'community', as useful vehicles for sidestepping the whole debate about Church/state separation. As Eberly comments: 'Let us sort out the issues of Church and state in the context of public policy, *but separate out those questions* from the issue of the relationship of *religion to community.*'[45] This suggestion is deeply worrying, for the implication is that, if the federal government delivers social services through the community, the issue of Church/state boundaries should not apply in the same way. Thus, when the five federal social policy departments deliver social services as state institutions they are required to respect the rigid separation of Church and state, but when service delivery is transferred to the Churches (through faith-based centres) it seems that this strict separation is no longer as necessary since this occurs in the *community*. Moreover, given the result of the presidential election in November 2004, there may now be an electoral imperative for the Democrats to be seen as friendly to closing the link between Church and community. Indeed, on the eve of the inauguration of George W. Bush for his second term in office, Senator Hillary Clinton, touted by some as a future presidential candidate, said in a speech in Boston that she supported faith-based initiatives and called the debate concerning the respect for the separation of Church and state and faith-based social services a 'false division . . . There is no contradiction between support for faith-based initiatives and upholding our constitutional principles' (Jonas, 2005).

Conclusions

As Kenneth Wald has argued, the role of the Church and its push for social reform of the American state, through lobbying, committees and electoral campaigns, is part of a long and important democratic tradition; and the importance of religion to Americans in their private lives (particularly for women and African-Americans) is exceptional in comparison to other industrialized countries. This chapter is not challenging either of these traditional roles of religion in the United States; what it does challenge are the dangers (internationally) of exporting particular 'national' values to countries that adhere to other religious traditions under the rubric of 'service to others', and (domestically) of delivering social programmes to vulnerable individuals and religious minorities through Churches that are exempt from civil rights legislation. When these international or domestic

---

[45] 'What is communitarianism?', *Talk of the Nation*, National Public Radio, 5 February 2001, minute 42, emphasis added.

initiatives are financed by US taxpayers' dollars, the whole relationship between state as sovereign power and Church as moral gadfly is wholly changed, and the state has become (in part) the financial officer for the Church's expanding role, through the twenty-first-century equivalent of the Social Gospel, in defining community values both at home and abroad.

In his State of the Union address in January 2003 President Bush laid out four goals for domestic policy. The final one, hearkening back to the 'compassionate conservatism' of his presidential campaign, called on Americans to apply 'the compassion of America to the deepest problems in America'. Bush summarized the dual policy thrust of this compassion, consisting of the two initiatives analysed in the preceding section: 'I urge you to pass *both* my *faith-based initiative* and *the Citizen Service Act*, to encourage acts of compassion that can transform America, one heart and one soul at a time.'[46]

It is a curious and troubling question as to whether or not governments should be in the business of transforming 'hearts and souls' at all, either at home or abroad. And, if they are, whether that transformation should be married to either a patriotic or a religious agenda. As an editorial in the *Atlanta Journal and Constitution* concluded with respect to Bush's evangelical tone regarding both the USA Freedom Corps and his faith-based initiatives:

Such [evangelical] rhetoric does not suggest a president committed to guarding the wall that separates Church from state in this country, a wall that has long served the best interests of both parties. To the contrary, it suggests a willingness to subvert that constitutional directive on behalf of a goal that the president believes is more important: the changing of souls and hearts. But that goal, while important, is simply not government's business. (*Atlanta Journal and Constitution*, 2002)

Complicating the issue in this long-standing debate about the separation of Church and state, or national interests and individual voluntary service, is this new factor that has been introduced through the social capital literature into Bush's domestic policies: community or civil society. What I have tried to show in this chapter is the extent to which the invocation of 'community' can be used by state actors to get around the Church/state problem or the national security/civil liberties problem. By invoking the idea of 'community' initiatives, the government's attempts to change the 'hearts and souls' of its citizens through religion is made much

[46] 'State of the Union address', January 2003, available at www.whitehouse.gov; accessed 5 June 2003.

easier constitutionally; similarly, civil liberties, particularly for Muslim-Americans, are more easily circumvented if neighbours in 'Neighborhood Watch programs' or community members in TIPS or VIPS programmes are asked to do some of the work of the federal authorities. These are the potential dangers if 'community' revival is allowed to blur too easily into the idea of a reawakening Church and/or the needs of homeland security.

7   Justice in diverse communities: lessons for the future

We began this book by considering two different definitions of 'social capital'; the instrumental, aggregative and functionalist definition of 'capital' (participation and trust) provided by the 'American' school (Coleman and Putnam), versus the more critical, historical perspective (networks and resources) of the 'European' school (Gramsci and Bourdieu). According to the former school of thought, investment in social capital is apolitical (since it exists outside the realm of the state), functional (since it serves larger ends), aggregative (since it is simply the sum of the number of individual decisions to connect) and positive (for democracy and individual well-being). As individuals choose to increase the number of connections in their community, higher levels of trust, solidarity and generalized reciprocity will result, and these can be quantitatively measured; in turn, such increased connectedness will result in better neighbourhoods, greater economic prosperity, more health and happiness for individuals and stronger democracies. It is for these instrumental and aggregative reasons that social capital and social connectedness are seen as largely positive by Coleman and Putnam.

For all the emphasis on civic society and community in Putnam's thesis, at the end of the day the central units of analysis of this 'capital' are, in essence, the individual (whose interests, 'rightly understood', are being served by increasing cooperation) and the American nation (the democratic health of which depends upon the 'civic culture' in which it is rooted and the degree to which it is unified). Embedded in this analytical framework is a particular vision of the 'social' that is shaped by a normative commitment to neo-republicanism, as evidenced by the repeated emphasis on social cohesion, civic unity and 'coming together', and a nostalgia for the past that sees previous periods of American history (the Progressive Era and the long civic generation of the Second World War) as the gloriously socially capitalized apex from which contemporary civic society has 'fallen' or collapsed. Thus, there is considerable theoretical tension in the term 'social capital' as Putnam deploys it: between the analytical, aggregative and instrumental nature of 'capital' on the one hand,

and the normative, cohesive and republican impulse of the 'social' on the other. This underlying tension, particularly as it impacts women and cultural minorities, is explored in the concluding section of this chapter.

The other definition of social capital, as articulated by Bourdieu, based in part on Marx's critical theory of capital accumulation and Gramsci's (and more recently Cohen's and Arato's) analysis of civil society, or the social, as the contested site within which the battle for cultural hegemony occurs, provides us with a more critical theoretical starting point from which to analyse social capital accumulation. Social capital, for Bourdieu, is not just a story of individuals making decisions whether to be more connected in an apolitical social sphere but, rather, it represents the economic and cultural forces at play, at any particular time or place, that limit the range of possibilities that certain individuals or groups (based on their marginalized economic or cultural status) have for creating networks or drawing on the resources inherent in them, thus making the accumulation of social capital highly political (in the broad sense of the word) to the extent that it is shaped by these power relations and is often negative (to the extent that networks can be used to exclude as well as include). Consequently, for Bourdieu, social capital analysis cannot be limited to simply counting the aggregate number of individual connections in a functionalist account of social capital but must also address the *nature of the connections* themselves, including the extent to which they are shaped by historical conditions and how these relations may reinforce the inclusion and exclusion of certain groups of citizens within civil society. Thus, unlike the functionalist approach to social capital, Bourdieu's theory of social capital is rooted in networks and their resources;[1] as such, he has no room in his analysis for either shared norms or trust as the linchpins by which participation is transformed into cooperation.[2] Bourdieu's vision of civic society, in direct contrast with Putnam's, as a sphere for 'coming together' and unity, is marked by division and contestation, not only *against the state* (as the 'civic culture' version of civic society would argue) but also within civic society itself, particularly over the norms and boundaries created by those with cultural and social power.

Thus, in our examination of Putnam's thesis, we have reread his story of lost paradise and promised redemption in the social capital narrative with

[1] Mike Savage has argued recently (2005) that Bourdieu is somewhat limited in his analysis of 'social capital' relative to the enormous body of work in the sociological literature on networks, and suggests that we replace social capital altogether with the idea of social networks in order to tap into this other set of scholarly resources.

[2] '[Bourdieu's] definition is, in many respects, more parsimonious than that offered by either the World Bank or the OECD, excluding, for example, both norms and attitudes' (Privy Council Office, 2004).

a wary eye: one that uses the critical and historical approach suggested by Bourdieu but with the added gender and cultural lenses that allowed us to view these additional dimensions of social capital, in the past and present, from the contestation of norms to the broader context of power relations and to the particular meaning that 'community' had for women and cultural minorities through the course of twentieth-century American history. In this final chapter we use this same theoretical framework to turn to the future and ask, as Putnam did, how these histories of American community might inform our recommendations for the future. We begin with the lessons learned from the past.

A summary of the past and present: lessons learned

My analysis of the golden Progressive Era (chapter 2), used by Putnam in the penultimate chapter of *Bowling Alone* as *the* model for the way out of our current malaise, has provided the concrete historical evidence for a more *negative* and *political* side of the social capital story. Fraternal organizations, it turns out, were not simply positive builders of brotherly love but powerful venues for the exclusion of women. Similarly, women's organizations growing out of these forces of exclusion were not just the non-political builders of solidarity, shared norms and trust suggested by Putnam but politically minded sources of division, challenging the basic premises of community membership and heretofore shared norms. Moreover, the 'maternalist' language used by many of these organizations to make palatable their political aims reflected women's need to express their motivation, for engaging in public life, as a maternal interest in *others* rather than a direct interest in themselves. Thus, the principle that Putnam and Coleman argue is unique to social capital (a type of investment with benefits that are often enjoyed by others) is present in this early model of social capital accumulation; but the gendered nature of such 'other-oriented' civic activity is revealed through the distinction between the 'maternalistic' nature of women's organizations (capital building wholly for others, as 'mothers' are understood explicitly to be working in the interest of their 'children') and the 'fraternalistic' nature of men's organizations (capital building for themselves, as 'brothers', as well as others). Thus, women more than men, from the beginning of the twentieth century through to contemporary social capital theory, are repeatedly called on to lead civic renewal and to justify their civic activity in terms of the benefit it will bring to others rather than to themselves.

Exclusion was also found in the religious, cultural and ethnic parameters of the mainstream associations. African-Americans, in particular, were subject to the forces of exclusion, not just from the groups themselves but also from the projects with which these associations were engaged. But, beyond Bourdieu's analysis of exclusion, we also found in the educational and social welfare thrust of social capital accumulation in the Progressive Era a more insidious force of 'assimilation', to an overarching 'American' and – by extension – Protestant Christian norm and community. It follows that the 'shared norms' and 'dense social networks' of social capitalism in the Progressive Era were deeply problematic if subsumed within them was a particular set of cultural norms to which certain cultural and religious minorities were to be assimilated, particularly through the power of educational and social welfare projects. Thus, settlement houses and schooling, in the form of kindergartens for immigrants and residential schools for 'Indians', may have had some positive economic effects, but they also had profoundly negative cultural effects, given that they were designed to Americanize these 'cultural others' to a particular set of 'American' norms. The most extreme version of cultural assimilation was a policy of either separation or eradication for those who simply could *not* conform to particular cultural norms – an historical perspective taken towards both homosexuality and disability during the first half of the twentieth century. Not only is this history important in and of itself to illustrate the potentially negative effects of shared community norms on particular cultural minorities but, as has been shown, it is also critical to understanding why certain kinds of civic associations (rights-oriented self-advocacy and identity groups) grew up (in response to this history) around the gay/lesbian and disabled communities in the second half of the twentieth century.

Finally, it was necessary to recognize that subordinated groups were *agents* as well as victims in the creation of civic associations and their projects during the Progressive Era. We have found that associations run by cultural minorities themselves (African-Americans and some disabled groups) focused less on charity as their goal than on empowerment. Once again, the recognition of these associations is critical not only to understand the more complicated, but full, story of both agency and victimization of cultural minorities during this period of history, but also because these associations are the historical seeds for the advocacy and identity politics centred around empowerment that came to full bloom in the second half of the twentieth century through the civil rights and, more broadly, new social movements. The focus on empowerment also underlines the idea that civic society throughout history, as Gramsci has argued, is and always has been a site for contestation between differentially placed groups.

Thus, using a gendered and cultural lens to view America's shift from the Gilded Age to the Progressive Era has, ultimately, allowed us to consider not only the economic amelioration aspects of social capital building (largely positive, as Putnam's analysis suggests) but the more negative impact on women and cultural minorities. The analysis suggested that civic society is far more political, in the broad sense of the word (i.e. contested), than Putnam suggests, and had, due to the nature of accumulated power, profoundly negative as well as positive effects. 'Bad' social capital from this historical perspective is not simply a matter of a few associations (such as the KKK) gone wrong, as is often understood in the social capital literature, but a broader problem of dominant norms and values, along with the deployment of an appeal to solidarity either to assimilate or to exclude particular groups in American society.

This critical examination of the 'golden age' of social capital allowed us to look anew at the 'decline' of social capital and its wholly 'negative' character, as postulated by Putnam, in the latter half of the twentieth century (chapter 3). Using the same gendered and cultural lenses adopted for our examination of the past, I analysed the decline of the eleven women's civic associations chosen by Putnam as his barometer of female civic participation in America over the course of the twentieth century, and found that the majority of these organizations were products of the past: groups born of exclusion when women had no other avenue to political power. Their decline could be seen, therefore, as a positive development as much as a negative one, as women demanded, and won, a direct (rather than indirect) path to political and economic power. Moreover, these demands (and the feminist associations that developed out of them) were based on the idea, growing out of second wave feminism, of 'sisterhood' (capital building for themselves) rather than the maternalism (capital building for others) of the Progressive Era. The decline of such traditional women's organizations can also be seen as positive to the extent that they engaged in either exclusionary or assimilationist projects in relation to cultural minorities.

In addition to the fact that the 'decline' of what Putnam measured may not have been as negative as he thinks, the analysis also questioned whether he has been measuring the right kind of civic activity. The specific areas of increased engagement by women in American society overlooked by Putnam include the direct involvement of *women* in politics as candidates, elected representatives and senior party organizers, the exploding numbers of female athletes (girls and women) in various sporting activities (beyond bowling), the numbers of women joining professional organizations, the legions of working mothers engaged in various kinds of childcare activities, small group activity and, finally, those women involved in rights advocacy, from disability to same-sex rights to feminist organizations. In all these cases the levels of networks, social contacts and community development enjoined by such individual engagement could potentially represent an enormous increase in social capital amongst women over the latter half of the twentieth century (as Peter Hall argues is the case in the United Kingdom).

Chapter 4 contains an analysis of the reasons given by Putnam for his postulated decline in participation. With respect to generational change, I raised two questions. The first is whether or not it is appropriate to hold education constant in Putnam's account. As Hall argues, it is unclear why we should be concerned only with civic participation that is *not* caused by increasing levels of education. Indeed, the fact that there is an increase in educational attainment by one generation over another, countering other forces that lead to a decline in participation, should be highlighted rather than hidden. This generational issue of educational attainment has been of particular importance to women and cultural minorities alike over the last forty years (although, as discussed, there is still a considerable gap between white Americans and Hispanic/black Americans with respect to educational attainment – an issue that needs to be addressed).

The second question raised was whether Putnam's survey questions that remain constant over time adequately measure newer forms of civic activity, in the way that the changing surveys used by Hall in the United Kingdom could (notwithstanding the loss in methodological comparability). Hall, unlike Putnam, found no generational effects, in part due to his use of different and updated surveys, where the language and questions incorporated newer kinds of civic activity: ones in which a younger generation would be more likely to be involved. Finally, the generational change argument needs to be separated out in relation to gender, for, according to Hall, there is a very different story to be told about women's civic activity, which he concludes has doubled in the United Kingdom over the last thirty years; again, an important aspect is rising levels of educational attainment during this period.

At the same time, Putnam is correct to note that the mass entry of women into the workforce had an impact on social capital and civic engagement generally. The 10 per cent 'decline' in social capital that Putnam estimates is the result of full-time maternal employment was challenged not so much because it is not a factor in the decline of civic engagement (indeed, it is probably more important than Putnam suggests) but because the proposed solution to such time crunches (women should be 'allowed' to work part-time) was premised upon faulty analysis, which concluded women really *wanted* to work part-time rather than full-time. Paid family leave is another suggestion made more recently by Putnam, but once again one needs to be cognizant of the gendered implications of such a policy. In both cases, the disproportionate onus on women to give up full-time work for either part-time work or full-time leave, in order to facilitate social connectedness, is part of a longer tradition in the American social capital literature, beginning with Coleman, that has tended to embrace gender inequities as legitimate means in the drive towards a socially capitalized end.

The role of television as a central causal factor in the decline of civic activity was also examined. Television, in earlier versions of Putnam's social capital theory, was an almost uni-causal explanation for the collapse in social capital. Even in *Bowling Alone* it represents an enormously important factor, albeit hidden within the 'generational' explanation; for, as Putnam himself suggests, generational change is not a cause but a reconfiguration of the puzzle that still requires an explanation as to what the anti-civic 'X-ray' might be that made the generation after the Second World War less civically engaged. This leads him back to television. Thus, television (in its own right and through the secondary category of generational change) continues to be the major causal variable in *Bowling Alone* for civic decline. However, the foundation for a *causal* relationship between television and social capital is very shaky indeed. The Canadian study of Notel, Unitel and Multitel that Putnam uses as his definitive evidence for a *causal* relationship is, quite simply, unable to bear the heavy burden of proof placed on it by his analysis. What Tannis MacBeth, the author of this study, actually concludes is that the introduction of television had a negative impact on some activities in the community, most particularly sports, but had little or no effect on 'civic activity'. Moreover, she cautions readers against extrapolating her findings to a universal theory of the impact of television, and against making a simple time-displacement analysis, when there are a whole range of factors involved. We were left at the conclusion of this chapter with the sense that the 'causes' offered by Putnam for the changes that occurred in American community over the course of the twentieth century, most particularly the changes in the nature of participation and the growing decline/gap with respect to generalized trust, were not up to the task, setting the stage for an alternative causal explanation.

In chapter 5, before developing this alternative explanation, it was first necessary to consider two other key concepts in social capital theory (along with participation), namely 'trust' and shared norms. While Putnam tends to conflate 'trust' and 'participation' together in his theory under the general rubric of 'capital', and makes the former a functional vehicle through which the latter creates cooperation in communities, it was argued that these two very different phenomena need to be analysed independently from each other, and that the specific *reasons* for the decline in trust should be considered independently of the reasons for any changes in the nature of civic participation. The first task at hand was to look at the empirical dimensions of 'trust' amongst Americans. Like Putnam, and many other theorists on the subject, I concluded that trust (unlike participation) clearly has declined over the last thirty or so years in the United States (as it has elsewhere). However, there was another dimension to the data on trust, largely overlooked in Putnam's theory, that needs to be given equal weight in any social capital analysis: the enormous *gap* in trust between the privileged and the marginalized.

Having outlined the empirical dimensions of trust, we turned to consider the role it serves in social capital theory. Trust, it turns out, is the linchpin: it serves both the individual and the state, by facilitating social cooperation between individuals and creating civic unity in American society, respectively. In the first instance, civic trust turns civic participation into generalized reciprocity and is, therefore, pivotal in the transformation of participation into actual positive outcomes for the individual, by reducing the costs of social cooperation. In short, it is the 'lubricant' in communities. Trust, in other words, is good for the individual; distrust is bad. There are exceptions, of course, where one should *not trust* particular organizations that are not worthy of trust, but social capital theorists do not seem to allow that distrust at the societal or community level might be either an appropriate response, or even a good thing, in terms of providing a motivating force for seeking justice on the part of particular groups that have been 'betrayed' by the larger society.

The second function of trust in social capital theory is that, as well as serving as a lubricant between individuals, it provides the 'glue' that unites communities, and even nations. This neo-republican aspect of social capital was analysed in some depth, including the dangers of a transcendent unity to those individuals or groups who might be on the margins. Under the rubric of civic unity, I also examined the idea of 'shared norms', which at first appear as nothing more than the reciprocity and trustworthiness that simply 'arise' naturally from increased connectedness. But, it became clear that Putnam's theory is undergirded by implicit shared cultural values that go beyond naturally arising procedural norms. The broad cultural norms, as seen in his theory, are the general commitment to the Church as the engine of civic renewal and the renewal and revival of the 'silent' middle class at the expense of the 'cultural margins'.

Finally, I proposed an alternative explanation for the two dimensions of trust (the *decline* and the *gap*), based on the intersecting influences of cultural, economic and social forces in the last thirty years. I argued, in essence, that both the decline and the gap in trust result from the impact of economic inequality and turbulence, the political duplicity of key events in recent American history, the changing nature of the media with respect to politicians as well as society and the impact of the so-called 'cultural wars' on American society, as the inclusion of both women and cultural minorities comes home to roost in the daily life of American politics (specifically, the kind of deeply personal identity politics unleashed, for example, by the debate over abortion or same-sex marriage). I concluded that, while there are some real costs in a society that lacks trust, there are also times in American history when distrust not only constitutes an appropriate response to a collective sense of betrayal within a group of people but may even be productive to the extent that it galvanizes people to take steps to bring about changes in the dominant norms in the name of justice and diversity.

Finally, in chapter 6, I examined recent developments in the practice and theory of social capital (including Putnam's research on forty communities in America, and 9/11 and its aftermath) in order to analyse what new light they might cast on the preceding analysis of *Bowling Alone*. The Social Capital Community Benchmark survey, published in March 2001 (and updated in the autumn of that year), yielded two significant findings: the centrality of religion to civic engagement in America and the inverse correlation between social capital and ethnic diversity. The call by Putnam, in the closing chapter of *Bowling Alone*, for a 'Great Awakening' of Christianity to spearhead civic engagement was analysed in some depth, and in relation to the secondary findings of Putnam that religious affiliation was correlated with intolerance towards cultural minorities. This analysis highlighted the profound difficulty in reconciling the goal of a unified community, particularly if it is premised upon a specific set of shared norms, with the rich multicultural diversity of American life. These concerns over multicultural diversity and social capital were reinforced by the second main finding of the Community Benchmark survey, namely the inverse correlation between ethnic diversity and social capital building in specific communities. Putnam addresses this question of diversity, both in *Bowling Alone* and within the summary of the survey: his solution is 'bridging' social capital. I raised three specific issues in relation to this solution. Is it strong enough? Is it appropriate to all cultural minorities? Can it be measured? Finally, this section concluded with a consideration of the broader question (first broached in chapter 5) as to whether diversity and social capital building are fundamentally contradictory. John Helliwell has provided one answer to this question, suggesting that the tension between diversity and social capital is not a 'natural law' but, rather, can be affected by governmental policy, particularly in the case of newly arrived immigrants. Thus, he argues that Canada provides a model for reconciling social capital and diversity through the implementation of an integrationist and multicultural immigration policy rather than an assimilationist one.

Chapter 6 concluded by examining the specific impact of 9/11 on social capital. Putnam has argued that the strong patriotic feelings in the immediate aftermath of 9/11 should be used to rebuild civic America. This recommendation raised concerns with respect to the impact on both individual rights and cultural minorities of merging national security concerns with community service. Indeed, as was shown, one of the two major domestic policy initiatives undertaken by President Bush (the USA Freedom Corps) was explicitly linked to Putnam's social capital thesis, raising just such concerns with respect to both the Citizen Corps and the new mandate announced for the Peace Corps. In both cases civic voluntary service was deployed by the state to serve national interests in the 'war on terrorism', through, respectively, spying on one's neighbours to ensure domestic security and spreading US values internationally, particularly to Islamic countries. The other major domestic programme rooted in social capital was Bush's faith-based initiatives, directed at shifting the delivery of social services from the state to the Church. The question in both cases is whether the sharp demarcation between society and government, and state and Church, that has been extolled by liberalism since its inception has become blurred in these initiatives, behind a seemingly harmless mask of either community or civic engagement. Thus, it was necessary to consider, through the lenses of both liberal and multicultural theories of justice, the extent to which the rights of either individuals or particular cultural groups are put at risk by such initiatives.

The key lesson learned

There are a number of lessons to be found throughout this summary, but perhaps the main message to be taken from the analysis of the past and present of social capital in America is this: when talking about the changes in American community during the twentieth century, it is imperative that the experiences of different groups of Americans, most particularly those who were historically subordinated but gained important ground during this time (women and cultural minorities), be taken out and analysed separately from a generalized theory of the community as a whole. Otherwise, the very different experiences of women, gay and lesbian Americans, African-Americans, Asian-Americans, Hispanic-Americans and disabled Americans in relation to the wider American community and its norms – and, especially, what the last three decades represent to them – will be entirely lost in a meta-narrative of 'decline' and collapse.

When these groups are fully recognized, the social capital vision of both the past and the present is profoundly altered. The past is suddenly not as idyllic as painted, either in the Progressive Era or in the 'long civic generation' after the Second World War. The so-called collapse in civic *participation* in the current era, when the perspectives of women and cultural minorities are fully recognized, raises the empirical question of whether one is counting *older*, more traditional (and outdated from the point of view of equity and diversity) forms of association and/or failing to recognize the number of *new* kinds of civic activity, from female athletics to professional associations to advocacy groups to childcare activities, as well as the normative question of the meaning one attaches to the changes in civic activity. At the same time, social capital's focus on the *decline* in civic *trust* may be, from the perspective of cultural minorities, less important than the profound *gap* in trust between the marginalized and the privileged.

Finally, the causes proposed by Putnam for the decline in civic trust – for example, the introduction of television – seem a far less plausible explanation if specific cases (such as the greater absence of trust amongst African-Americans) are separated out for consideration. This is why the 'revival' of community, based on the models of the past, as countenanced by Putnam in theory and Bush in practice, is of such potentially grave concern. The language of 'revival', 'renewal' and 're-engagement' strongly suggests, within the overall context of this theoretical paradigm, a return to the past; a 'coming together' of American community around the models provided either by the Progressive Era or by the 'long civic generation' of the 1940s and 1950s and in reaction to the more recent 'divisive forces', the cultural rip tides of the last thirty or forty years. If successfully brought about, such a future community would pose real threats to the hard-fought-for victories that each of these subordinate groups has struggled to achieve over the last three decades, all under the seemingly progressive and friendly rhetoric of civic service and community revival.

Looking to the future: the principles of a just community

In light of our analysis of social capital, in the past and at present, what can we say about the future of diverse communities in America? First, it should be made clear that the call by Putnam, and by communitarians and third way theorists, for a focus on the community and civic society is an important normative claim: one that clearly resonates in both the theoretical and practical worlds of liberal democratic politics. As was stated at the outset, there are a number of good reasons why it should be taken seriously. If one accepts the communitarians' challenge to an overly exuberant liberal individualism and the third way's critique of the many deleterious effects of social welfare states, the future aspirations for a better society may well lie beyond both the individual and the state, in this intangible sphere known as civic society or community. But, rather than assuming that the normative appeal of community is a given, or that the norms inherited from the past implicitly serve the needs of diverse communities in the future, it is necessary – as the Canadian Royal Commission on Economic Prospects first argued in 1957 – that the community be analysed as an end itself, and the normative principles that govern civil society into the future be made explicit and debated by all.

In developing the set of principles listed below, we must bear in mind the lessons of history, paying particular attention to the specific counter-narratives of historically subordinated groups. A just community in diverse societies would be mutually respectful, equitable and inclusive, as well as the site of division and contestation, for the foreseeable future. The principles outlined below provide a starting point for thinking about an alternative kind of civic society.[3]

The first principle of a just community is to acknowledge the historical reality of exclusion, assimilation and eradication in the civic life of America. Rogers Smith's vision of American political history as one of 'multiple traditions' provides one theoretical starting point. Smith argues that the Tocquevillean America that dominates much of American political theory must be 'severely revised to recognize the inegalitarian ideologies and institutions of ascriptive hierarchy that defined the political status of racial and ethnic minorities and women through most of US history' (Smith, 1993, p. 549). Smith's focus in this article is on the Progressive Era as the case study for these conflicting normative claims between liberty on the one hand and discrimination on the other, and how this shapes the definition and meaning of *political citizenship* in America. I would argue that his analysis could be applied equally to explain the nature of *community membership*, but would add two additional important points to Smith's theory of multiple traditions.

First, it is necessary to recognize that this hierarchical tradition exists in relation not only to racial and ethnic minorities but also to more broadly

---

[3] These principles are the mirror image of the critique I have been developing of the social capital theory of community in the previous chapters. My purpose here is to move beyond simply critiquing the social capital model to providing some constructive and concrete ideas about how an alternative vision of community might be theorized. These principles are, necessarily, no more than a preliminary step in what should be a much broader debate in liberal democracies about civil society. Finally, it should be noted that these principles are focused, as Putnam himself is, on the future of community in the United States. As such, they assume the existing broad political framework, including a stable democratic state and the protection of rights through the current body of law.

construed 'cultural minorities', including people with disabilities and gay and lesbian Americans; for the latter two groups, as discussed, faced the most profound form of discrimination during this period of time, namely attempted eradication, through either sterilization or psychotherapy, respectively. Secondly, the historical injustices visited upon groups of American citizens during the Progressive Era may go beyond being simply a 'different tradition' living 'alongside' a pure Tocquevillean liberal democracy, as Smith argues. Is it possible that such demarcations between groups of people are inherent, at least in part, in the liberal tradition itself? This question goes beyond the scope of this analysis to the heart of current debates within political theory as to whether *liberalism* is an ideology flexible enough to respond to the various historical injustices waged upon particular groups of Americans, or whether a more radical theoretical project is required – one that seeks new principles upon which to build a just society. As Desmond King (1999, 2005) and Uday Mehta (1990, 1999)[4] argue, the persistence of illiberal practices in liberal states (assimilation, segregation) needs to be acknowledged and explained. How is it that America at the turn of the twentieth century, in the so-called 'Progressive Era', could engage in such practices as the institutional segregation of African-Americans and the sterilization of the mentally disabled? Are such practices completely anathema to, or intertwined with, liberal norms of 'reason', 'industry' and 'progress'? The critical point here is that exclusion and assimilation may exist in some kind of parallel formation to the liberal tradition, as Smith suggests; or they may be implicated and enmeshed in each other, as Honig, Brown, Mehta and King have argued.

The second principle of a just community is to recognize the collective, as distinct from aggregative individual, experience of American citizens. Americans exist not only as individuals but as members of collectivities. These collectivities, moreover, have differential measures of power. Belonging to a cultural minority, for example, has enormous implications both for participation in civic activities (and the nature of those activities) as well as for levels of trust, as we have seen. This means that the gap between groups, within a given period of time, with respect to trust or participation must be given as much weight in the analysis

---

[4] As Uday Mehta comments: 'When it is viewed as a historical phenomenon . . . extending from the seventeenth century, the period of liberal history is unmistakably marked by the systematic and sustained political exclusion of various groups and "types" of people. The universality of freedom and derivative political institutions identified with the provenance of liberals is denied in the protracted history with which liberalism is similarly linked. [. . .] Something about the inclusionary pretensions of liberal theory and the exclusionary effects of liberal practices needs to be explained' (Mehta, 1990, p. 427). See also Wendy Brown (2004) and Bonnie Honig (2001).

of community as the change across time amongst individuals. Needless to say, analysis aggregating individual experience provides important insights into what is happening in communities, but this must never be thought of as synonymous with the collective experiences of groups. Groups are notoriously difficult to define, and thus recognizing collectivities will require a subjective and historical analysis. While this kind of analysis will challenge some of the 'scientific' precepts that accompany the methodological individualism underpinning American social capital theory from Coleman to Putnam, it is likely that the recognition of collective experience will help to address the empirical realities found in the data (such as why African-Americans experience a generalized gap in trust).

At the same time, the recognition of groups as collectivities is consistent with the normative prescriptions of multicultural theories of citizenship (Kymlicka, Taylor), in which it is argued that ethno-national groups need to be recognized and in some cases protected through group rights. As such, the recognition of groups opens up not only an empirical but a normative dimension of analysis at the level of theory and practice. Theoretically, such recognition challenges the normative commitment in Putnam's theory to a transcendent unity and shared norms, and instead suggests, as John Helliwell argues, a more multicultural approach to diverse communities. At the more practical level of associational life, it means recognizing groups and not just individuals in society. One specific example provided in chapter 3 was the Girl Scouts of America's approach to the Hispanic-American community, in which the focus was not so much on the incorporation of individual girls to the Girl Scouts as an existing association but, rather, working to change the organization in some very basic ways in order to accommodate the collective cultural norms at work within that specific community.

The third principle of a just community (which emerges from the first two) is to recognize and address the particular and different justice claims made by specific cultural minorities in civic society. Thus, it is necessary to think carefully about the historical experience of different groups in American society in terms of what may be needed to create a more just multicultural community for all. In some cases this will entail emphasizing the liberal principles of rights, inclusion and the same treatment, and in other cases emphasizing the multicultural principles of difference, cultural protection and diversity. Moreover, the recognition of difference and diversity will have implications with respect to the differing emphasis placed on bonding and/or bridging capital.

In the case of groups that have experienced a history of segregation and exclusion as well as cultural discrimination, the focus will be on inclusion, equality and rights. Two specific examples are African-Americans and people with disabilities, where the search for justice is largely framed through a liberal commitment to positive and negative rights, along with a need to bond around positive notions of 'black pride' or 'independence' in order to counter the negative language and stereotypes that have been accorded to both these groups of American citizens.

Thus, African-Americans may want to build a civic society that emphasizes integration through 'bridging capital' (to overcome economic and civic exclusion in the past) without giving up entirely on 'bonding capital' (to provide forums for the building of cultural pride against a history of degradation). The profound nature of exclusion, in the case of the African-American community, however, requires a much more radical agenda than the one suggested by Putnam in his 'Agenda for change', where the singular focus with respect to bridging capital was on 'arts and culture', as discussed. Thus, addressing the continuing experience of exclusion and the disproportionate levels of poverty amongst African-Americans will require not just civic groups but the power of the state and courts in order to maintain affirmative action while implementing economic measures aimed at shrinking the disparity in wealth. Americans with disabilities also seek to be fully included in the mainstream of civic life, through the principle of accessibility and liberal rights enshrined in the Americans with Disabilities Act. At the same time, the 'independent living' movement, along with disability scholars, seek bonding capital in order to advocate a change in the medicalized meanings of 'disability', 'rehabilitation' and 'abnormality'.

New immigrants will also appeal to both multicultural and liberal theories of justice and will need the two kinds of social capital building (building and bonding), necessary equally for their cultural survival and integration into the larger community. For example, the growth of Asian-American Churches suggests the desire as well as the capacity for bonding and bridging capital in order both to preserve cultural difference and integrate into American mainstream culture, respectively. But, once again, as Helliwell has argued in relation to Canada and the United States, the state can play a pivotal role as to whether or not new immigrants are able to balance integration with cultural preservation, concluding that Canada's multicultural policy is pivotal to the higher levels of trust felt by new Canadians in comparison to their American counterparts.

There are some groups who will put more of an emphasis on multicultural theory and bonding capital in order to preserve themselves from assimilation into a dominant community. Thus, the 'Deaf' community, which sees itself as a linguistic cultural minority, requires not so much inclusion into mainstream 'oralist' society through a liberal theory of individual rights as respect for difference and protection from assimilation to a dominant majority culture. For Native Americans (or First Nations in Canada) the call for a disengagement from the larger (non-aboriginal) community in order to further their own forms of self-government is consistent with multicultural theories of justice that seek to preserve cultural integrity and diversity, but inconsistent with the goals of 'bridging capital' (to the extent that it means transcending identities). Again, this goal to recognize difference is a direct response to the historical experiences of Native Americans of both colonization and assimilation. Similarly, while some gay, lesbian and queer American citizens seek equity and inclusion through the liberal model of civil rights, others seek to protect themselves, as a group, from the forces of assimilation.

Put simply, while the liberal goal of inclusion through 'bridging capital' may fit some groups who have been excluded or segregated from civic society, it may also be exactly the opposite of what is needed with respect to other cultural minorities who see their normative priority as the preservation of their unique identity against the threat posed by a dominant cultural force.

The fourth principle of a just community is that communities are better conceptualized as agonistic processes where the norms are still under negotiation than *solidified entities* of shared values. Thus, it may be that the community still needs to 'come apart' further in order for the principles of justice to be articulated fully and the needs of different groups to be voiced fully. This should not necessarily be seen in a negative light. As Jean Cohen comments:

Contestation over past institutionalizations and struggles over cultural hegemony . . . are not necessarily signs of social disintegration or moral decay. Instead, open, public, even conflictual pluralization and individualization of forms of life can be a response to change that has potential to realize these principles in less exclusionary, less hierarchical ways . . . Social contestation . . . *is* evidence that a once-hegemonic conception of the American way of life is being challenged and decentered. (Cohen, 1999, p. 231)

Put simply, the norms, parameters and boundaries of the community have been and continue to be under negotiation by those who still perceive barriers either to their full participation or to the recognition of an authentic difference. Contestation over norms and boundaries exists not only at the level of state legislation but also at the level of civic society. It is for this reason that supporters of civic engagement should not automatically dismiss groups engaged in advocacy over those traditionally dedicated to service. History has shown that advocates, in attempting to renegotiate the underlying norms of a given community, are often divisive in the short to medium term in their search for justice in the long term. To the extent that society continues to experience injustice with respect to culture or gender, this kind of contested politics will continue for the foreseeable future. As part of this agonistic conception of civil society, a lack of trust is not *necessarily* or always an inappropriate or bad thing, particularly if it serves as an impetus for change.

The fifth principle of a just community is that civic associations must be evaluated not only on the basis of their membership size but include other (normative) variables in a broader assessment exercise. Thus, as social capitalists analyse the actual associations and organizations that constitute civil society, it is important to pay special attention to the *kind* of connections manifest in any given organization. One of the great downsides of social capital and the aggregative model of individual choice is the tendency simply to count membership numbers rather than evaluate the collective impact that civic associations have on the community as a whole. To use a specific example, if we simply counted the membership of the Boy Scouts of America, we would seem to have a positive story in terms of their impact on the many American communities in which they are located, but the numbers would overlook one specific negative aspect of this group in American society as a whole. For gay men in America, the Boy Scouts of America represent a profoundly painful contemporary manifestation of their exclusion from the membership and norms of American civic life. Put simply, it is necessary to address explicitly the normative as well as the empirical dimensions of associational life in America if one is to get a full picture of its impact on a diverse American community.

The sixth principle of a just community is the need for a careful examination of the role that religion, and, more specifically, the fundamentalist Christian Church, should play in relation to community building in America in the future. As discussed, the Church has had a profoundly important role in the development of civic society in America, and it has particularly significant (and positive) meaning for women, African-Americans and Hispanic-Americans, both in their individual lives and in their collective search for justice. But, while the Church and other religious institutions will, and should, play an important role in social justice and civic society in the future, as they have done in the past, those who support an inclusive and respectful community must be extremely careful about calling for a 'Great Awakening' of the Christian Church as the centrepiece of a 'revival' of a collapsed American community, particularly given the growth of the fundamentalist Church (with potentially negative implications for specific cultural groups, such as gay and lesbian Americans) and the conjoining of the revival of the Church with a 'coming together' around a shared set of values.

There are a number of worrying signs in Putnam's theory with respect to religion and the 'revival' of community. The references in *Bowling Alone* to 'Churches' to describe all kinds of religious institutions overlook the very different nature of religious traditions in America. It is precisely because the Christian Church is so dominant in American life (Wuthnow's exceptionalism) that particular care must be taken to acknowledge past mistakes and prevent (in a rigorous way) the potential for such injury in the future. Although the Church has played a positive role in relation both to individual Americans' sense of spiritual well-being and to the collective aspirations of African-Americans during the civil rights movement, as well as to socially outcast and impoverished individuals throughout American history, the negative side of the Church's history must also be acknowledged and addressed. Thus, the historical (and, in some cases, current) injustices visited upon gays and lesbians, Asian-Americans and Native Americans by the Church, through discrimination, assimilation and exclusion, must be borne in mind. These concerns take on more significance when it is the state acting as the social engineer. Thus, a just community requires that any erosion in the wall between Church and state (such as by funding social services through a deregulated sphere of faith-based institutions) needs to be repaired and strengthened if the rights of religious and cultural minorities are to be fully protected in the American community of the future.

The seventh principle of a just diverse community is to address the issues of trust and participation as separate questions, seeking the specific causes and remedies for each independently of the other. By addressing these complex phenomena as if they are all part of one conflated syndrome within a functional model of capitalization, Putnam is unable to discern that what might have caused the decline in trust could be something quite different from the decline in political participation or the changes in civic activity. Indeed, given that trust, in a functional model, serves simply as the vehicle through which participation is transformed into cooperation, trust itself is not given the same focus as participation in Putnam's thesis; and there is no consideration that there may be a completely different set of causes at the heart of the patterns seen with respect to trust.

Because, as I argued in chapter 5, the causes of the decline and the gap in trust are different from those that explain the changes in participation (of either a political or a civic nature), this suggests that the possible solutions for the problems identified by Putnam are likely to be different as well. For example, with respect to the decline in political participation, Arendt Lipjhart, in his American Political Science Association presidential address of 1997, suggests the introduction of compulsory voting (as practised in Australia) in order to address the problem of declining political participation and low voter turnout (Lipjhart, 1997).[5] This is a worthy suggestion for debate, linking the rights of citizenship in a liberal democracy with its attendant responsibilities. Such a solution in the civic sphere (forcing people to join any particular association) would be anathema, however, to the precepts of a democratic society. Thus, the solution for one problem, if attacked directly, might be quite different from that for another.

Similarly, if social capital theorists are serious about addressing the lack of 'civic trust' in American society then it will be necessary to consider both the decline and the gap independently of either political or civic participation. The solution to the problem of civic trust will be complex and multifaceted but must address the root causes and the sense of injustice or betrayal arising from them, including economic inequality, cultural warfare and political duplicity. At the same time, the content of a ubiquitous media that seeks to sell its products twenty-four hours a day, often in a confrontational and sensational manner, also needs to be challenged as another culprit in the undermining of civility and trust, particularly amongst a younger generation. Any challenge to media content must be done so that it does not compromise the democratic right of citizens to know what those in authority are doing in their name.

The eighth principle of a just community is to use the power of the state (and courts) to help address any remaining obstacles to civic participation and, most importantly, the root causes of the decline and the gap in trust. There are a number of different dimensions that can be addressed with respect to state intervention in civic society. Some theorists concerned with civic society argue that the government, particularly the welfare state, is too strong and has crowded out community. The concern, as articulated by neo-liberals (and third wave 'New Labour' thinkers), is that an overly large and bureaucratic welfare state can overtake or displace civil society and the organizations that constitute it. One particular area of focus is the social services, where, it is argued, community associations would be better and more efficient delivery mechanisms than state bureaucracies. In essence, this school of thought argues that by pushing back the boundaries and functions of

---

[5] I have not addressed the question of political participation in earlier chapters in any depth, so it is perhaps foolhardy for me to suggest a solution, but it is meant simply to illustrate the principle that different kinds of questions with respect to participation require different kinds of answers.

the state one will expand the available space for the growth of voluntary activity and civic society. For the neo-liberals it is a matter of removing the state as both delivery mechanism and financier of social programmes; for third way thinkers, such as Anthony Giddens (2000) and Tony Blair, the state should continue as financier (albeit with less money) but transfer the delivery of social programmes to civic organizations.[6] George W. Bush has embraced the neo-liberal vision of a smaller state through tax cuts and welfare reform, as well as through the 'third way/social capital' idea of changing delivery mechanisms by means of his faith-based initiatives (which were discussed at length, including the problems that potentially arise concerning the separation of Church and state, in the last chapter).

There are certain aspects of this argument that are attractive, particularly when one looks at the problems that can arise in a highly bureaucratized system of social welfare – from the perspective of single mothers, for example (who often face an invasive and punitive welfare apparatus in order to qualify for funds), or people with disabilities (who face a paternalistic 'one size fits all' bureaucracy).[7] There is a danger, however, in this vision of a reduced or reformed welfare state, that 'social capital' is used to justify simply offloading the state's responsibility to provide a safety net for the vulnerable and needy onto the 'community' (which may or may not be able to absorb such responsibilities). Thus, there is a risk if the focus is *only* on shrinking the state without addressing in a multifaceted way what exactly the civic side of the equation is going to be. People may simply fall through the cracks and certain populations may be made more vulnerable by such changes.

In addition to the implications for those who might be accessing social services, the shift in responsibility from state to community also has implications for those who will potentially provide the community care. Transferring the labour for caring (for the young, elderly or disabled) from the state to the community entails a shift from public to private caregivers, and often a change from *paid* unionized women to *unpaid* non-unionized women, as feminist critics of neo-liberal cuts to social spending have

---

[6] In the lead essay of a special volume on the subject of social capital in the Labour journal *Renewal*, Tony Blair observes that '*the state can sometimes become part of the problem*, by smothering the enthusiasm of its citizens' (Blair, 2002, p. 12, emphasis added). Blair concludes: *We . . . need to do more to give power directly to citizens.* [. . .] [T]he key now is to [free] up the public sector' (p. 11, emphasis added).

[7] For many disability advocates, the welfare state is seen as a largely paternalistic and inflexible provider of a 'one size fits all' standard of services and equipment. In particular, the 'independent living' movement has emphasized the need for individuals to have control over choosing whatever goods and services are required to lead a full and independent life. Welfare states, in essence, by making decisions *for* 'clients', remove this capacity for free choice and autonomy.

argued (Bashevkin, 2002). In other words, there is a gendered and collective bargaining dimension to this shift from state to community that needs to be recognized and addressed. On the other hand, to take just one example, there are 'independent living' centres and 'community living' organizations that make a very strong argument that community organizations are often far better placed than bureaucrats in the welfare state to facilitate independent living for people with disabilities. Such a shift has the potential to transform 'clients' of the welfare system into 'citizens' of a nation state.

The second (and opposing) argument, made by neo-conservatives, such as within the Bush administration, is that the state should *not* shrink in relation to civic society but should be expanded specifically in the area of national security, as part of the national arsenal for the 'war on terror'. Thus, the White House engages in a national call to service, and facilitates and directs it through such programmes as the USA Freedom Corps. A just community, as argued in the previous chapter, must reject this conflation of civic service and homeland security (in the name of both liberal and multicultural justice) and, instead, preserve and protect the independence of civic society and cultural minorities from a militarized state on a war footing.

Ultimately, the state does have a critical role to play with respect to diverse communities. The crucial question is *what* it should be, if neither the neo-liberal/New Labour (shrinking state) nor the neo-conservative (blurring of civic service with national interests) visions will suffice. Theda Skocpol makes the case for a renewed focus on the state as necessary to the facilitation of civil society by challenging the neo-liberal and New Labour's call to shrink the state in the name of civic revival:

Liberals and thoughtful centrists are rightfully reluctant to conflate business and the market with civil society, while pitting voluntarism and charity in zero-sum opposition to government . . . Organized civil society in the United States has never flourished apart from active government and inclusive democratic politics . . . If we want to repair civil society, we must first and foremost revitalize political democracy. (Skocpol, 1996)

I would argue, like Skocpol, that the state can and should play a role in building civic trust and participation. The state can play a role in fostering civic participation by breaking down long-standing obstacles that might bar individuals or groups from participating fully in civic society. Indeed, it is *only* the state (and the courts interpreting the legislation passed by the state) that has the necessary power to overcome the long-standing obstacles to the full participation of certain groups of American citizens. Over the last two to three decades legislation passed by the American Congress and decisions made by the Supreme Court have provided evidence that this is the case: specific examples are civil rights legislation for African-Americans and the ADA for people with disabilities. It may also be achieved through affirmative action legislation, such as Title IX, which, as discussed, has unleashed enormous amounts of female civic participation by simply levelling the playing field for female and male athletes. Are there similar kinds of legislative initiatives that may be taken to remove any remaining barriers?

The state could also develop specific policies that have been found to be effective in other countries (most notably the United Kingdom) with respect to civic participation. Hall's analysis of the increase in social capital in the United Kingdom provides some insights into the role of the state that may have application to the United States and beyond. Hall argues that two of the main reasons why British social capital has continued to increase are a 'massive expansion of both secondary and postsecondary education' and 'forms of government action that have done much to encourage and sustain voluntary community involvement' (Hall, 1999, p. 434). While there are important cultural differences between America and Britain, specifically on the appropriate role of government, Hall's recommendations, given that they have proven to be successful in building community in Britain, should nevertheless be looked at in the American context. In particular, the gaps in educational attainment between different cultural groups in America need to be addressed by the state. Beyond Hall's analysis, there are important ways that the state can address the specific burden that women face with respect to care-giving by providing more childcare services and facilities, as Vivien Lowndes has argued (and, more generally, addressing the broad issue of care-giving for the elderly and disabled as well), and thereby ease the time/energy pressures on working women especially. The study by Nancy Burns, Kay Scholzman and Sidney Verba suggested that childcare for pre-school children is perhaps *the* critical factor for women with respect to civic activity (losing twice as much free time as men as a result of a pre-schooler in the home) (Burns et al., 2001, p. 185).

The third role that the state could play is addressing both the gap and the decline in 'trust'. The analysis in chapter 5 suggests that if the state is to help rebuild trust, particularly amongst the marginalized, it must address three root causes: economic inequality and turbulence, political duplicity with respect to the people it serves (particularly in the case of military campaigns) and the origins of the cultural 'wars', most particularly the continuing inequality and misrecognition of women and cultural minorities. The state, once again, is unique in its power to tackle economic marginalization and inequality. How to effect change is, of course, the stuff of current political debate, but some possibilities include tax cuts to encourage the private sector; redistributive and/or employment policies to speak directly to the unemployed or marginalized; and affirmative action policies to encourage the employment of the economically and culturally marginalized. Which of these policies or which combination would work best is beyond the scope of the current analysis, but suffice it to say that this area is a critical element in building trust and shrinking the gap. If economic equality is one of the key factors in sowing the seeds of trust, in any society, then it stands to reason that this should be a central goal of seeking to rebuild the trust of economically marginalized people. Why African-American or Hispanic-American citizens are disproportionately poor, and how to rectify the situation, are profound and complex questions, but it is clear that both civic society and the market left to its own devices will do little to solve these deep and intractable problems; the state, through the variety of policy tools at its disposal, is an important part of the solution.

With respect to political duplicity, the revelation that there were no weapons of mass destruction in Iraq, despite both the American and British governments using the claim to that effect as the basis for waging war, suggests that states still have some distance to go in recognizing the deleterious long-term costs to civic trust of deploying such convenient political arguments in order to meet short-term military objectives. Finally, the culture wars will continue, and there is no easy solution to be found with respect to the divisive and often irreconcilable positions in the area of identity politics. But the state should be under no illusion that moving backwards (towards the criminalization of abortion, for example, or the constitutional exclusion of same-sex marriage) will do anything but fuel the flames of cultural anger. What the state and courts can do at a minimum is to protect the gains made by women and cultural minorities over the last thirty years.

The ninth, and final, principle of a just community must be gender equity; communities cannot ask women to pay a higher price than men in the creation of social capital. Putnam suggests in his chapter on the pressures of time and economy that one of the solutions to finding more resources for civic participation is to 'allow' women to work part-time. As discussed, Putnam's argument that such a solution is consistent with women's equality because women actually *want* to work part-time is deeply flawed. This tendency in the functional social capital literature to place the onus on women, beginning with Coleman's suggestion that children's educational outcomes will be improved if a 'parent', assumed to be the mother, stays home, is transformed by Putnam into the suggestion that women should 'be allowed' to work part-time. This focus on expanding women's role in the private sphere (at the expense of hard-won gains to enter the public sphere) as the answer should be replaced by an emphasis on the *structural* obstacles to fulfilling the triad of important responsibilities faced by *all* adults (particularly parents or those looking after dependent family members) in contemporary society: family, work and community. This would require radical new thinking about the relationship between care-giving and work, rather than simply reducing women's paid employment. Putnam does speak of a new 'workplace agenda' but, if it is to be just, gender equity must be a central element in the equation.[8] Moreover, as Jean Cohen has pointed out, there is implicit in Putnam's social capital theory a vision of the nuclear family as 'the most fundamental form of social capital', where the loosening of bonds and the disintegration of the family is a contributing factor to 'social decapitalization' (Cohen, 1999, p. 240; see also Levi, 1996). A critical examination of the 'family' (and not simply an assumed reliance on one particular nuclear model) must be part of any analysis that addresses the principle of gender equity either outside the sphere of the market or that of the state.

While the idea of paid family leave, championed by Putnam more recently, is a useful suggestion in response to the problem of the time crunch between family, work and civic activity, careful consideration must be given, as countries such as Sweden and Norway have demonstrated, to the systemic gender inequities that arise with generically worded family leave policies. The burden is often borne by women. Finally, there is room not only on the work front but also on the associational side to address this problem. As Moose (Women) have demonstrated, there may be ways that civic associations can allow parents to overlap the time devoted to family with that required for civic engagement. For the individual, it will be necessary to find ways to overlap civic activity with either work or family responsibilities – indeed, this is one of the key challenges for the future. As Putnam himself concludes: 'Figuring out how to reconcile the competing obligations of work and family and community is the ultimate "kitchen table" issue.'[9]

Justice in diverse communities: is social capital the means to this end?

Having laid out an explicitly normative vision of what a diverse and just community of the future might look like based on the lessons learned from the past, I now consider whether social capital, as articulated by

[8] Nancy Fraser has argued this case eloquently in her article on justice, gender and the welfare state (Fraser, 1994).
[9] 'Lonely in America': interview with Robert Putnam, www.theatlantic.com/unbound/interviews, 21 September 2000.

Putnam, can, at the end of the day, provide the means for reaching this goal. Thus, this last section will take us beyond consideration of how social capital theory might be amended to whether it should be deployed at all, as a theoretical framework, if the objective is to build a just civic society or community, particularly with respect to women and cultural minorities. I address this question through a close examination of both the explicit and implicit meanings of each of the two basic terms used by Putnam ('social' and 'capital') in order to ascertain the extent to which they help or hinder the realization of justice in diverse communities.

The 'capital' of social capital: the 'science' of community building

One might well wonder why Putnam uses the terminology of 'capital' at all in relation to civic society. As we shall see, while the 'social' aspect of this term is long connected with the space between the individual and government, the use of the word 'capital', so closely linked (in the case of human or financial capital) with the individual, is at odds with the emphasis on community and solidarity. For Putnam, using the word 'capital' is an attempt to bridge disciplines and achieve a two-way link between economics and the other social sciences; by making economic analysis more sensitive to the significance of trust and cooperation in its analysis of collective action, while simultaneously making the soft, normative theories of a declining civic society (represented by third way theory, communitarianism and neo-republicanism) more scientific and empirical. Capital, according to this empirical kind of analysis, acts in accordance with certain universal laws. Like economic capital, social capital is defined as an investment made by individuals today that will create a quantifiable benefit tomorrow. If understood as such, social capital can be measured, much as its economic counterpart can be, in terms of both the aggregate investment (the amount of time invested by individuals in civic or political organizations, the aggregate degree to which they trust) and the utility of that investment over time (individual outcomes or democratic well-being). Capital is thus a very powerful tool for practitioners and scholars alike, in that it makes the study of community a quantifiable aggregate science. Ultimately, however, the use of the term 'capital' in Putnam's theory has three effects, all of which in the end, I argue, stand in the way of it being an appropriate conceptual tool for working towards a *just* community in diverse multicultural societies.[10]

---

[10] I leave to one side the question of whether social capital if conceptualized in a more critical fashion (e.g. Bourdieu's formulation) might be consistent with the claims of justice described above, as my focus is on Putnam's formulation. Others have made the case that a different version of the concept (rooted either in network analysis or Bourdieu) might still be very useful (Baron et al., 2000; Privy Council Office, 2003, 2004).

The first is that civic society in Putnam's theory of capital is not a good in and of itself, but exists largely for instrumental reasons in relation to a particular set of outcomes (namely, democracy in the state and the well-being of the individual). The focus, therefore, in social *capital* theory is necessarily on specific outcomes of robust and connected communities (are they united or cooperative?) rather than the nature of the connections that produce them. The second problem is that social capital combines several different indicators (notably trust and civic participation) under one general rubric. As such, it combines both these separate phenomena within one 'coherent syndrome', and moves the analysis of community away from examining them independently of each other. The third, and most intractable, problem in the use of the term 'capital' is the particular nature of the aggregative economic science underpinning it. The 'science' of social capital precludes analysing collective social configurations in the 'civic sphere' as anything more than the sum of their parts. The 'science' of social capital also tends to obfuscate both the moral and nostalgic feelings underpinning the analysis (which explain its popular appeal) behind the guise of objective 'number counting'. Moreover, by appealing to the overwhelming 'evidence' of his data, Putnam uses the science of capital in order to narrow the terms of what should be a broad democratic debate about what the nature of the problems are in contemporary American society to a more technical question of how to 'fix' the scientifically proven collapse or decline. Let us consider each of these problems in turn.

The first obstacle to the realization of a just community through social capital theory is the instrumental nature of 'capital', which is why Putnam's theory (and James Coleman's) are often referred to as 'functional theories'. Capital, according to Kenneth Arrow, means 'deliberate sacrifice in the present for future benefit' (Arrow, 2000, p. 4). The first implication, therefore, of a capitalized theory of community is that social relations, and even community itself, are valued largely for their functional usefulness to other (either private or public) ends in the future. Indeed, the whole structure of Putnam's book bears this out, as he moves from the empirical question of defining the scope of the decline to why it has occurred and, *ultimately*, explaining the resultant negative outcomes. Thus, section four of *Bowling Alone* emphasizes that community is important because it has a functional role in keeping America 'healthy, wealthy, and wise' (in the form of individual well-being as well as the democratic state). It necessarily follows that the measurement or evaluation of community, and the civic connections that constitute it, is carried out largely in relation to these larger purposes rather than in and of themselves. If connectedness is simply a means *in order to* create other ends, the normative nature of these connections becomes largely irrelevant (unless they are interfering with other kinds of connectedness or trust amongst individuals). With a largely functional analysis of civil society, the focus becomes the *number* of connections in civic society rather than their *nature*. As we have seen, however, it is the latter aspect that is critical to whether or not a diverse community is just.

Moreover, unlike other kinds of capital, social capital is a unique kind of investment, for it alone can benefit others rather than the investor him- or herself. Evidence of how the 'other'-oriented nature of social capital can result in inequitable results was provided in the recommendations made by Putnam and Coleman regarding the conflict between building social capital and women working full-time. For the good of community and/or their children, women provide optimal social capital building if they stop working full-time and engage instead in their community, specifically (from Coleman's perspective) in their children's schools, (in Putnam's theory) leading in civic and social activities. While such a community would be inequitable with respect to gender, this is *theoretically irrelevant* (although Putnam tries to address this problem by arguing that women actually *want* to work part-time) from the strict perspective of capital investment theory, because it is not the investment itself that matters as much as its future utility (in this case either to children in school or to the broader society as a whole). We shall return to this theme of the functional nature of social capital in the next section, when we consider the meaning of 'social' as well.

The second effect of the use of the term 'capital' in the analysis of American community is the tendency, referred to in principle 7 above, to conflate different kinds of phenomena into one generalized category of social capital, with the general causal flow moving from participation to trust. As a result trust, civic participation and political participation are all seen as aspects of one phenomenon, namely individuals choosing no longer to 'invest' in their communities. It is not surprising, therefore, that both the causes and the solutions for each of these particular 'problems' are the same in social capital theory. This conflation of trust with participation (and the sense that the latter causes the former), as argued in detail in chapter 5, is ultimately an obstacle both to analysing what may be causing a decline in trust as something separate from a change in participation and to delineating solutions specific to each kind of change. This is why, when Putnam comes to the conclusion of his book, he is focused mainly on how to encourage participation and voluntary service, assuming that trust will just naturally arise from a more connected society, rather than asking how one might increase trust.

The third effect of deploying the language of 'capital' is to mask an emotive appeal to the past (the 'long civic generation' or the Progressive

Era) in seemingly hard, empirical, scientific data. Thus, Putnam believes, unlike the softer, more normative utopian visions of community that animate communitarian, civic republican or third way theories, his theory escapes emotional biases. This *science* of community is manifest in his claim that the collapse of community is not simply a nostalgic yearning for the past but a hard, cold, present reality that can be documented through the 'objective' counting of 'capital' investment. Indeed, in the introduction to *Bowling Alone*, Putnam explains his use of data explicitly as a way of countering such appeals to the past: 'One way of curbing nostalgia is to count things' (2000, p. 26). However, as the analysis in this book has shown, how you measure social capital and what you decide to count may actually *feed* nostalgia rather than curb it. Thus, by choosing to count the membership of largely traditional organizations, by using questions first devised in surveys of the 1950s, by using the Progressive Era as his point of reference, Putnam's longitudinal empirical 'science', as I have argued, is actually embedded in a nostalgia for the past.

The larger point, however, is not that Putnam should improve the method by which he counts social capital investment and make it devoid of any feelings towards the past or future but, rather, the need to raise the question as to whether there can be a science, particularly of community, completely divorced from culture or normative commitments. My own view is that this belief is itself a (powerful) kind of fiction. I would argue that Putnam's notion of 'capital' and the 'scientific approach' underpinning it is rooted in a particular kind of Anglo-American epistemology: an aggregative methodological individualism[11] that owes much to the economic theories of James Coleman and Gary Becker but can also be found in earlier political forms in the analytical methodology of Thomas Hobbes and J. S. Mill. The assumption behind such 'science' is that collective enterprises (be they the market, the community or society as a whole) can be analytically broken down into their constituent parts.[12] These parts are individual human beings, who, with the introduction of the idea *homo economicus*, can be viewed as largely interchangeable, in that it is assumed that all are fundamentally motivated by rational self-interest and utility maximization. Thus according to classical economic theory, economic capital accumulation is the result of aggregate individual investments based on rational decisions about presumed future utility. In the

---

[11] For an insightful review of this idea from the point of view of economics, see Fine and Green (2000).

[12] As C. B. Macpherson comments: 'In short, the resolutive stage of the Galilean method, as applied to political science, consisted in resolving political society into the motions of its parts – individual human beings . . . which, compounded, could be shown to explain [political society]' (Macpherson, 1968, p. 27). See also Easton (2002).

case of social capital theory, civil society becomes a compound of individual behaviours to participate, trust or network, which is then aggregated to explain the whole. Skocpol describes the shortcomings of Putnam's approach in the following way:

> Ironically for a scholar who calls for attention to social interconnectedness, Putnam works with atomistic concepts and data. He writes as if civic associations spring from the purely local decisions of collections of individuals . . . He tries to derive group outcomes by testing one variable at a time against such highly aggregated individual-level data . . . Putnam largely ignores the cross-class and organizational dynamics by which civic associations actually form and persist – or decay and come unraveled. (Skocpol, 1996)

The larger point I am making is that the methodology chosen necessarily constructs what is discovered. As Chandra Mohanty reminds scholars, there is always a 'need to examine the *political* implications of our *analytic* strategies and principles' (Mohanty, 1988, p. 65, emphasis added). The political implications of Putnam's methodological individualism are that a multicultural normative analysis is precluded, because it works against locating individuals either in time (history) or space (cultural or geographical identity). As Michael Shapiro describes Putnam's project:

> Those invoking Tocqueville of late . . . [efface] spaces of difference and [aggregate] the social domain within a unifying grammar, they promote inquiry into the relationship of social solidarity and civic-mindedness to a nation's . . . democratic performance. This undifferentiated view of political actors, functioning within a homogenized national space (the undifferentiated space of citizenship), conceals specifically situated historical bodies as sites of the investment of power . . . that enables some and disenables others. (Shapiro, 2001, p. 105)

Thus, methodological individualism makes the possibility of recognizing the collective dimensions of social capital associated with the specific experiences of particular cultural minorities within the civic space of America, and the differential narratives that underpin them, difficult if not impossible.

Perhaps what is most ironic about the scientific assertions of social capital theory, however, is the impression one gets in reading *Bowling Alone* that Putnam's analysis and prescriptions for the future are fundamentally driven not so much by a dispassionate scientific mind at all but, rather, by a *passionate* commitment to the normative importance of Americans participating in their communities and 'coming together' again, fuelled by a deep sense of moral disquiet with respect to the current state of affairs in contemporary America. It is a curious, and unfortunate, fact, no doubt the result of the hegemonic power of the scientific paradigm in contemporary Western discourse and political science more specifically, that so many modern scholars who are actually motivated by strong moral sentiments feel compelled to make their argument in the language of 'scientific' analysis and 'objective' empirical realities because only this will give legitimacy to their normative claims.

Another famous example, from a different part of the political spectrum, of a modern scholar who claimed to be engaged in science but where one has the strong sense that it is moral outrage driving his theories and conclusions is the *scientific* socialism of Karl Marx. Like Putnam, Marx argues that his theories are not rooted in normative prescriptions (he leaves that to the utopian socialists) but are dictated by the scientific laws of *capital* (in his case, economic rather than social). While both Marx and Putnam are no doubt sincere in the belief that their particular theories of economic and social capital, respectively, are 'scientific', and thereby provide an objective edge to their visions of society, the appeal to a transcendent science of society often obscures the normative and emotive underpinnings of each man's scholarly commitments and dampens democratic debate about what is to be done. In raising questions about the 'science' of capital, I am not suggesting that either the empirical or scientific dimensions of such analyses are without merit; indeed, both Putnam and Marx provide enormous and much-needed insights (in their very different ways) into the mechanisms by which social and economic 'capital' develop, and empirical analysis provides, in its best form, a certain kind of discipline to 'mere feeling'. But their arguments cannot be allowed, solely by virtue of their claim to *be* scientific, to trump other kinds of claims. More importantly, it is folly to suggest that there can ever be a pure social science, independent of the convictions or political context of its scholarly authors and free from the socially constructed language and categories deployed within which it is expressed. Working out the role of science in the study of politics, particularly when it is used to underpin a prescriptive vision for the future, is a complex task and beyond the scope of this book. But, in line with Ian Hacking (2000), it is clear to me that one cannot subscribe to either the 'science studies' vision of the empirical method as a wholly socially constructed entity, nor the argument made by some social scientists that the study of politics and society can be made fully 'objective'.

Ultimately, I believe that debate, both academic and democratic, is best served, particularly when the subject is the *future* of community, when scholars of all stripes use the tools at their disposal (empirical and normative) to provide insights into the nature of civic society, without making transcendental claims of scientific objectivity that serve to trump other competing theories and stifle a broader discussion amongst citizens about the nature of the problem based on having 'proven' what it is.

Thus, such a debate needs to be within the reach of ordinary citizens, and the terms need to be broadened to include not simply the fixing of a problem but a discussion of what the problem is that needs to be fixed. This seems to me to be both an honest and a democratic footing from which to launch the debate over the future of American community, opening up the possibilities of discussing the historical, collective and cultural dimensions of civic 'justice' alluded to in the principles above, as well as keeping the door open for new insights provided by the continued application of empirical analysis.

The 'social' of social capital: the dangers of neo-republicanism and nostalgia

The idea of 'social' in social capital has a number of constitutive threads. The first links Putnam to a very deep theoretical vein of American political thought, stretching from Tocqueville to Almond and Verba's classic text *Civic Culture*, namely a healthy and robust civic life amongst the American public. Will Kymlicka has called this distinction in liberal theory between the state and society one formulation of the public/private divide. He concludes: 'Liberalism involves a "glorification of society", since it supposes that the private (non-state) associations which individuals freely form and maintain in civil society are more meaningful and satisfying than the coerced unity of political association' (Kymlicka, 2002, 388–9).[13] While this conception of civic society is entirely consistent with the liberal democracy envisioned by Tocqueville and Almond and Verba, Putnam's conceptualization of the 'social' (and the source of its popular appeal) goes beyond this classical notion of voluntary association of civic-minded individuals to a more republican idea of civic unity, manifest in his explicit call for a 'coming together' of American communities and families and, more importantly, embedded in the theory itself through the mechanisms of shared norms and trust. Thus, where the 'capital' of social capital pushes the debate towards the individual and the need for lubrication to facilitate collective action, the 'social' in social capital moves in the opposite direction, towards a trusting society that needs to find the glue that not only binds individuals together (cohesion) but, in transcending difference (unity), protects all Americans from the threats of factionalism and division.

---

[13] This implies that civic society (as opposed to political association) is a sphere free of 'coerced unity'. One of the key arguments throughout this book is the need to recognize, as J. S. Mill did, the power of 'community' or 'society' to coerce individuals in a multitude of ways.

Putnam first articulates the goal of 'civic unity', or the coming together of America, in the introduction of *Bowling Alone* as the need to reverse the forces of division and diversity that have pulled apart America over the last three decades in favour of something that will give Americans a shared sense of identity and civic purpose. Indeed, he describes this as the 'dominant theme' of his book.

> The dominant theme [of *Bowling Alone*] is simple: for the first two-thirds of the twentieth century a powerful tide bore Americans into ever deeper engagement in the life of their communities, but a few decades ago – silently, without warning – that tide reversed and we were overtaken by a treacherous rip current. Without at first noticing, we have been *pulled apart* from one another and from our communities over the last third of the century. The impact of these tides on all aspects of American society, their causes and consequences and *what we might do to reverse them, is the subject of the rest of this book.* (p. 27, emphasis added)

Put simply, Putnam is concerned not only with a *lack of participation* but with the failure of Americans to transcend difference. It is not surprising, therefore, that the report published by the Saguaro Seminar and Putnam's recently published book (with Lewis Feldstein) both share the same title: *Better Together*. The 'coming together' of American community ultimately shifts the vision of civic society from a site of contestation and resistance to a more republican or communitarian vision, of commonly shared civic identity, values and purpose that transcend difference.

These two visions of civic society are described in Michael Mosher's concluding essay of the volume entitled *Alternative Conceptions of Civil Society*, edited by Simone Chambers and Will Kymlicka.

> In thinking about these essays, I asked how many authors recognize the significance of the following choice in models of civil society. Either you want civil society because it is a transmission belt for the dominant republican values . . . or you want civil society because it entrenches diverse values. (Mosher, 2002, p. 208)

The former definition ('a transmission belt for dominant republican values') underpins Putnam's social capital theory, in which the dominant values to be transmitted are from the past (the Social Gospel in the Progressive Era, the shared civic commitment to America of the 'long civic generation') via a contemporary reassertion, tinged by nostalgia, of the 'shared norms' of the traditional middle class against the divisive forces of the new, postmodern 'cultural margins' in American society.[14] This

---

[14] It is worth noting that Mosher concludes, in a volume explicitly devoted to the principle of diversity, that the deployment of the term 'civil society' in and of itself seems to lead ineluctably to moral convergence around a dominant set of values from the past. 'I offer a preliminary observation [on these essays] . . . many of the contributors seemed

normative commitment to unity is embedded theoretically in the fundamental link that Putnam makes between participation and trust, as
detailed in chapter 5. At the point at which trust becomes the theoretical linchpin by which individual decisions to participate, to join or to
network become the basis for social cooperation (and so much more),
Putnam's theory turns from neo-Tocquevillean to neo-republican, and
civic participation is transformed, through the need to build trust, into
the imperative to unite.

As a consequence, it should come as no surprise that government ministers in the United Kingdom adopt the language of social capital to
underpin not only the principle of 'active citizenship' but the search for
both 'community cohesion' and – more strangely in a country not republican by disposition – national unity, as evidenced by a series of min-
isterial speeches that link social capital or civic renewal with finding a
transcendent 'Britishness' through common shared norms. Such appeals
to civic and national unity are used as a balm in insecure times, and as a
means by which to counter such potentially threatening forces as terrorism, immigration and multiculturalism. Thus, like Putnam, Tony Blair
(2002), former Home Secretary David Blunkett (2004) and Chancellor
Gordon Brown (2004) speak of social capital in the context of forces that
are 'pulling apart' Britain and provide a new, united way forward that is
ultimately rooted, again like Putnam's analysis, in a nostalgic view of a
united and socially capitalized past.[15]

Thus, given the centrality of civic and even national unity to Putnam's
theory, let us consider the challenges posed by such a transcendent unity
when seen from the perspective of both a classical liberal theory of individual rights and a multicultural theory of group recognition and respect
for diversity.

overly committed to the view of civil society as a transmission belt for dominant values. Though all give ritual or rhetorical affirmation to the importance of diversity and
the independence of associations, this was often qualified by a larger commitment to
the transmission belt model' (p. 208). As discussed in chapter 4, this valorization of the
middle (through a nostalgic appeal to the solidarity of the past) is a profound concern
for cultural minorities. Although it is beyond the scope of this analysis to discuss, this
neo-republican vision of an American nation that needs to 'come together' again can be
found in a wide and influential range of commentaries by some of the leading political
commentators in America today. See, for example, Rorty (1999), Schlesinger (1998),
Miller (1998) and Gitlin (1995). Thus, this vision of a 'coming together' goes beyond
social capital theory and is, in part, the result of a backlash against the cultural 'warfare'
in America in recent years.

[15] See Arneil (2005) for a more fully developed version of how social capital has become,
for New Labour in the United Kingdom, a vehicle by which to respond to 9/11 and
multiculturalism through a language of civic renewal and unity, including the search for
the meaning of 'Britishness'.

Civic unity and liberal justice Liberal justice regards the fundamental rights of an individual to hold values and beliefs different from others to be of paramount importance in a democratic community. Thus, the freedom to be an atheist or a communist, to be gay or lesbian, or to follow a minority religion, and the necessity of preserving and protecting these freedoms from state interference, or even the weight of community opinion to conform to a particular set of values, constitute a central imperative of liberal justice. We have seen in groups such as the Boy Scouts of America, as well as from studies on the levels of intolerance amongst members of the evangelical Church, that within leading civic institutions of American society the coalescing around a set of 'traditional bedrock values' is a threat to the civil rights of individuals who do not share the majority's viewpoints or lifestyle. Moreover, the rights to privacy and due process accorded by law in individuals' homes is similarly threatened by some of the links drawn by President Bush between national interest and community service in the wake of 9/11.

The theoretical link is manifest in concrete terms through the two domestic policy initiatives discussed in chapter 6. The general thrust of Citizen Corps, but more specifically programmes such as TIPS and Neighborhood Watch, raise profound concerns with respect to rights of privacy. The real problem with 'social capital' in this context is that the community becomes a vehicle by which state officials may acquire information about individuals without meeting the high standards of civil rights required by state actors. Put simply, neighbours and local service people could, in the original policy recommendations, watch and record a neighbour's or customer's actions without any reference to the legal requirements of police officers or federal officials. Civil libertarians were very concerned about this aspect of the *practice* of social capital in America. Neither the appeal to community service (as opposed to state intervention) nor the patriotic feelings that emerged from 9/11 should be used to mute debate on these important questions of liberal justice and civil rights. Finally, the proposed 'charitable choice' provisions of the original White House faith-based community initiatives, which would have exempted religious organizations in the delivery of federally funded social services from civil rights legislation, are equally threatening to the religious freedom of individuals from minority religions. While neither TIPS nor the faith-based initiatives came to full fruition with the clauses granting exemption from civil rights legislation, the latter remains an active file amongst the domestic policy initiatives of the Bush administration.[16]

---

[16] In September 2003 Bush called on Congress to support his faith-based initiatives in a speech in Houston. 'I say that because I know first-hand what it takes to quit

A second key point is that liberal justice takes a specific view with respect to the role of the state and the courts, based on a fundamental assumption about human nature: that there will always be conflicting, and in some cases incommensurable, views of the 'good'. 'Coming together', therefore, will only go so far in human affairs. What is ultimately required, liberals argue, is to arrange institutions in order to absorb and manage conflict, however deeply felt, allow it to be expressed through debate and dialogue, and, as far as it is possible, create compromises in order to prevent conflict from deteriorating into violence. On certain issues, however, it must also be recognized that no amount of dialogue will reach a compromise. In these cases, the court or legislative body or political executive must make a decision. Political debate, as was discussed in chapter 5, has over the last thirty years been pushed increasingly towards exactly these kinds of issues, involving incommensurable differences on cultural issues. For example, the entry of women into the political arena brought a demand for legislative changes with respect to abortion, but only through the power of the courts to change the criminal status of such activity. Similarly, gay and lesbian activists have brought the issue of homosexuality into the public sphere in their demands for equal status; and disability activists have challenged existing norms around disability in the form of the Americans with Disabilities Act. Bringing these divisive issues into the public arena introduces incommensurable views. Ultimately, the rights of these individual Americans were secured *only* through the power of Congress or the courts to overcome such deep divisions, and not without a profound cost to the unity of the community. Justice, in essence, is achieved only through diversity and division.

To the extent that social capital seeks to avoid such conflict and reify a 'silent middle' against the seemingly cantankerous cultural margins represented by either feminism or multiculturalism in various guises, it threatens hard-fought-for victories by both women and cultural minorities. Equally importantly, if liberal justice is to be served then the notion that American communities may somehow overcome their differences – for example, in relationship to abortion – is sheer folly. Liberal justice would suggest that it is better to deal with such highly divisive issues through such transparent fora as courts and legislative bodies, which may, on occasion, rule with the minority against a majority middle class. Recent

drinking . . . It takes something other than a textbook or a manual to change a person's heart. Our society must not fear the use of faith to solve life's problems. Congress must not block these important initiatives. Congress needs to hear the call' (Lozano, 2003). Since Bush's re-election Jim Tovey, director of the White House office on Faith-Based Initiatives, has suggested that Bush may expand the use of executive order to push this agenda forward.

decisions by the Supreme Court to overturn, for example, sodomy laws in Texas and affirm, with qualifications, the principle of affirmative action in higher education are examples of where, in the interests of liberal justice, the court may go against the majority to rule in favour of the rights of a minority group.[17] Left in the hands of the community, divisions are either marginalized or (as was shown with respect to the Church's handling of same-sex unions) ignored altogether, and hard decisions are either not taken or deferred in the interest of consensus and 'unity'. Justice delayed, it has been said, is justice denied.

Civic unity and multicultural justice   The civic unity thesis poses a different, but related, set of obstacles to the realization of the principles of multicultural justice. Where the liberal view of justice is concerned with protecting the individual's rights to liberty against the majority, the multicultural perspective is concerned with protecting and preserving minority cultural differences against the homogenizing power of a dominant set of group norms (Taylor, 1994; Kymlicka, 1995). Thus, multicultural justice seeks to create the conditions for historically subordinated groups not only to exist, as individuals, but to flourish, as groups, free from the forces of exclusion, assimilation or eradication. For communitarian Charles Taylor, the fundamental problem is that of 'misrecognition', defined as a failure by the dominant community to recognize cultural differences because of the overarching need in liberal theory to view everybody as the 'same'. Even liberal theorists such as Amy Gutmann acknowledge the need to recognize cultural group difference within democratic states such as the United States.

Recognizing and treating members of some groups as equals now seems to require public institutions to acknowledge rather than ignore cultural particularities, at least for those people whose self-understanding depends on the vitality of their culture. This requirement of political recognition of cultural particularity – extended to all individuals – is compatible with a form of universalism that counts the culture and cultural context valued by individuals as among their basic interests. (Gutmann, 1994, p. 5)

While the liberal challenge to civic unity has been heard in the United States (albeit in a muted way since 9/11), the question of multicultural justice has not received the same attention. To the extent that the twentieth century may be regarded as one in which different groups of people successfully fought to be recognized as such in American society, the idea

---

[17] It is also possible, of course, from a liberal perspective, that such decisions (for example, with respect to abortion) may be reversed over time. This will depend, inevitably, on the nature of future appointments to the US Supreme Court.

that this trend should, in any way, be 'reversed' is highly problematic. Yet the 'pulling together' of community around a shared set of norms raises questions with respect to the collective integrity of religious or cultural minorities; the dangers, in Charles Taylor's words, of misrecognition or assimilation.

The underlying appeal in social capital theory to a 'missing middle' in American social and political life is threatening not only to individual rights, as described above, but to the recognition of cultural minorities as groups with, in some cases, the need to protect their culture from assimilation. Thus, where the liberal justice argument makes the case that gay and lesbian Americans must be free as individuals from any kind of discrimination in employment, housing, schooling or the delivery of social services, the multicultural argument for justice would go beyond individual rights to the public need for recognition as a group. Some specific examples of groups who wish to retain a cultural identity separate from a dominant one, as described in the preceding chapters, include the Asian-American Church, which wishes to retain a cultural identity separate from the rest of the mainline Churches; the queer community, many of whom do not simply want to be included in the existing norms of a 'heteronormative' society but want to preserve a different identity as 'queer Americans'; the Deaf community, who wish to resist the assimilation within a dominant 'oralist' society; Native Americans, who wish to retain their unique cultures as well as live in accordance with treaties signed by European powers; and, in Canada, many people in Quebec who wish to preserve their French-language culture.

It turns out that multicultural justice (which includes the public recognition of difference and group rights) is even more difficult to reconcile with the 'transmission belt of shared norms' view of civic society than liberal justice (understood as individual freedoms and the right to non-discrimination). Thus, the call for the reassertion of unity and the middle class in America undermines the important (albeit divisive) fight for recognition, and tends to push American society towards cultural homogenization around majority shared norms at the centre. Justice is only achieved, as history has demonstrated, when the cultural margins of society make collective demands against the middle. When the reverse occurs, and the middle demands cohesion from the margins, the threat emerges of either a tyranny of the majority (for the liberal critics) or the coercion of the 'bell curve' through the power of 'norms' (for multicultural and postmodern critics).

The cultural justice arguments overlap with the liberal critique of the role of the American state in the 'coming together' of civil society. As demonstrated in the previous chapter, the American government has used 'social capital' and civic unity for its own particular political purposes, including justifying domestic policies against terrorism in the United States that implicitly target, without actually saying so, certain ethnic groups (hidden under the rubric of community 'security'). These arguments go beyond the liberal case for the civil rights of the individual to the recognition of the impact on specific cultural groups. To take the specific example of TIPS or Neighborhood Watch, the liberal concerns over every individual's right to privacy, while important, do not address the issue of the ethnic or cultural *group* that is being targeted by this policy, namely Arab and/or Muslim Americans. Thus, both the architects of the programme in the White House and its liberal critics are largely silent on this underlying assumption of 'civic service' in the name of community and the cultural threats it implies. Multicultural justice makes explicit the question of identity politics in such policy matters, and argues that the particular burdens that specific cultural groups carry must be brought to bear in the analysis of civic participation and trust.

Finally, and most importantly, the 'pulling apart' of community, from the perspective of multicultural justice, has a very different meaning from the one given by Putnam in his analysis. Although he is correct to suggest that there has been a generational change over the last thirty years in American communities, the nature of this change should not be seen as, fundamentally, a transition from service to *anomie* but, rather, from acceptance of the status quo to dissent. There has been a struggle to renegotiate the terms of community and its norms as the result of waves of protest (from feminists to African-American activists, from gays and lesbians to people with disabilities) as each particular community becomes cognizant of its own particular relationship to the historical forces of exclusion and assimilation. Thus, the 'pulling apart' of American society has resulted not so much from television or suburbia or technology or mobility (although these may be contributory factors to the decline in trust or participation) but from the irresistible force of liberal and multicultural justice, seeking human emancipation and cultural respect and integrity, respectively.

These gains have not been achieved without an enormous cost to social solidarity and cohesion and trust. As each group fought for its equal status, powerful forces countered its efforts. As the struggles have moved forward, both sides of the debate have experienced, and continue to experience, the divisiveness and mistrust engendered by conflicts involving deeply held principles. Those subordinated groups, who, in the heady days of the 1960s, had hoped for so much more, have felt betrayed subsequently by the lack of progress. It is not surprising that cultural minorities have high levels of distrust as their efforts either to be equal, or to be included or recognized by the majority, have not been realized as quickly as they had hoped. Conversely, white American males have felt their traditional position in society continually eroded by a combination of cultural and economic forces beyond their control. The promises made to them in 1950s America of a future as bread-winning heads of households have, in subsequent generations, been dashed as the rules of the economic, cultural and political games shifted beneath their feet. The result has been a similar sense of betrayal and disengagement, as they attempt to keep up with the breadth and the pace of change to their traditional role of male breadwinner, as well as the loss of public and private power.

Thus, the danger posed by the vision of civic unity implicit in Putnam's notion of *social* capital ultimately depends on the meaning one gives to the perceived 'pulling apart' and 'coming together' of American society, as well as to the 'collapse' and 'revival' of American community captured in the subtitle of *Bowling Alone*. I would argue that the 'pulling apart' of American community, seen by Putnam as a problem to be solved, should, rather, be viewed as a painful but ultimately positive process that has served the interests of both liberal and multicultural justice; it should be continued, rather than foreclosed, as Americans look to the future. It is premature to talk about social solidarity and unity within the community around an existing set of norms until power is more equitably distributed between all members of society, and cultural minorities are recognized and embraced in the public sphere as well as the private.

Conclusions

Important and influential as social capital has been to the theoretical shifts in both economic and political theory with which we began this book, they do not, in the end, provide the ultimate explanation for the powerful appeal of *Bowling Alone*. Its popularity ultimately lies in the appeal of the central narrative of an American community previously strong and united, but now wrenched apart, that might once again be pulled together, revived and redeemed through a renewed commitment to participation and shared civic values. This narrative, relying not just on the Christian story of a fall from grace followed by the promise of redemption but also by the Tocquevillean story of a 'nation of joiners', provides powerful succour to a generation that has experienced profound societal division and change. Putnam himself comments on the popular response to his theory of civic decline:

Though it proves nothing, I have to report a striking distinction between the reactions of academic audiences and of public audiences. Academics always want to know whether it's really true that we are disengaging. [. . .] They almost never have any comments on what could be done about it, if it were true. Public audiences almost never ask whether it is true, because it rings so true to their own experience. They are always deeply concerned about how to fix the problem. Their questions are tougher. (p. 509)

All that needs to be done, therefore, to put America on the path of civic redemption, is to *fix* the problem (rather than analyse any further what the problem might be), and the solution lies in the hands of the citizens themselves. Such an appeal provides an important balm at a time of such insecurity and flux.

The discrepancy between the enthusiastic endorsement, by citizens and state actors in the United States, of the thesis of 'decline' and academic scepticism about the nature of the problem should not reassure social capital theorists but, instead, give them pause for thought. While the popular sense of 'pulling apart' is an important and legitimate reaction to all the many changes that occurred in America during the last half of the twentieth century, it is the job of academics, and indeed political and community leaders, not simply to tap into this welling-up of a charged response to major social changes with familiar and comforting narratives but, rather, to subject such nostalgic feelings to a careful and explicitly normative scrutiny as to what kind of community it is that Americans are hoping, in their own eyes, to (re)build. Is it possible to reconcile the emotional needs of a 'coming together' around old models of community, and the emphasis on civic unity and shared norms that accompanies it, with the demands of cultural diversity, equity and justice that lie at the heart of this critical analysis? In this context, academics (and I count myself amongst this number), with all due respect, *are* asking the *tough* questions: not simply how we 'fix' the problem, but what *is* the problem we are attempting to fix?

In the previous pages I have sought to challenge the idea that 'community' in America over the course of the twentieth century is a single narrative of decline that should be considered beyond debate, so that we can now move on to the 'tougher question' of how to 'fix the problem' in a narrow, technical sense. Putnam's analysis, appealing as it might intuitively be to a large number of Americans, simply does not apply to all members of American society equally. Thus, from the perspective of women and cultural minorities, the community over the last forty years has not so much collapsed as changed; and these changes have largely been the result of demands for justice. Thus, I would argue that what is really needed is *not* a technical discussion of how to 'fix' the problem but a continuing conversation about what the nature of the problem *is*, including a recognition of how the answer to this question might differ depending on whether you are at the centre or the margins of community life. Justice in diverse communities is my central concern here; and, if one takes seriously the community not as a means to other ends, as social capital theory suggests, but as an end in itself, justice requires that people should feel not only that they belong (by addressing the problems of exclusion or segregation) but that they can flourish (by addressing the liberal and multicultural threats to both the individual and the group, respectively). It goes without saying that these principles of justice will necessarily lead to conflicts between different kinds of demands. It is the role of the democratic state (with the participation of its citizens) and the courts (based on the rule of law) to resolve such conflicts.

Thus, the American community of the past, present and future, like the modern concepts of citizen and state, may continue, if we are not cognizant of its diversity and historical evolution, to be constructed along gendered and cultural lines wherein certain groups either do not belong or cannot flourish. While social capital theory assumes that the goal is to increase the *number* of connections, in order to create trust, mutual reciprocity and social solidarity, my argument is that it is not just the number of connections but their *nature* that must be addressed, both in the past and the present. The challenge posed by this book, therefore, is evaluating the extent to which, in the future, diverse communities and the associations that constitute them can meet the ethical demands of justice and diversity. To this end, the past and the present have indeed provided us with some lessons, as Putnam suggests – but different from the ones that he proposes. Communities that embrace civic unity have always engaged in exclusionary, assimilationist 'connections', and even eradication, in the service of a particular kind of unified American vision: the extent to which social capital embraces such a principle of transcendent unity as a centrepiece of community will, necessarily, raise these same questions in the future. Past legacies were disrupted over the course of the twentieth century by a positive 'pulling apart' of this traditional vision of civic space and its existing shared norms. Ultimately, and most crucially, therefore, we must be careful not to undo in the future, in the name of community building, what has been achieved in the past and present in the name of justice. As we look to the future, we must ensure that we build not simply socially *connected* communities but *just* ones.

References

Abramson, Paul. 1990. 'The decline of over-time comparability in National Election Survey studies', *Public Opinion Quarterly* 54(2): 177–90.

ACLU. 2002. *ACLU Says Bush Administration should not Allow Operation TIPS to Become an End Run around the Constitution*, press release, American Civil Liberties Union, New York, 15 July; available at www.aclu.org/news/2002/n071502a.html; accessed 22 July 2002.

Adair, Ian. 2002. 'Membership report', *The Word: Triathlon BC Newsletter* 3: 1.

Adams, David Wallace. 1997. *Education for Extinction: American Indians and the Boarding School Experience (1875–1928)*, Lawrence: University Press of Kansas.

Addams, Jane. 1919. 'Americanization', *Publications of the American Sociological Society* 14: 206–14.

Aldridge, Stephen, David Halpern and Sarah Fitzpatrick. 2002. *Social Capital: A Discussion Paper*, London: Cabinet Office, Performance and Innovation Unit; available at www.strategy.gov.uk/downloads/seminars/social_capital/socialcapital.pdf.

Alesina, Alberto, and Eliana Ferrara. 2002. 'Who trusts others?', *Journal of Public Economics* 85: 207–34.

Alfred, Taiaiake. 1999. *Peace, Power and Righteousness: An Indigenous Manifesto*, Oxford: Oxford University Press.

Almond, Gabriel A., and Sidney Verba. 1963. *The Civic Culture*, Princeton, NJ: Princeton University Press.

Altman, Dennis. 2001. 'Case to the contrary', *Gay and Lesbian Review* 8(2): 3–4.

American Jewish Committee. 2002. *AJC Welcomes Federal Court Decision Striking down Wisconsin Faith-Based Programs*, press release, American Jewish Committee, New York, 10 January: available at www.ajc.org.

Arneil, Barbara. 1999. *Politics and Feminism*, Oxford: Blackwell.

    2005. *The Meaning and Utility of Social Capital in Liberal Democratic Politics*, plenary paper presented at the conference 'Whither Social Capital? Past, Present and Future', London South Bank University, 6–7 April.

Arrow, Kenneth. 2000. 'Observations on social capital', in Partha Dasgupta and Ismail Serageldin (eds.), *Social Capital: A Multifaceted Perspective*, Washington, DC: International Bank for Reconstruction and Development, World Bank, 3–5.

Atlanta Journal and Constitution. 2002. 'Bush subverts "heart and soul" of Constitution', *Atlanta Journal and Constitution* 27 December: 16A.

Baer, Douglas, James Curtis and Edward Grabb. 2001. 'Has voluntary association activity declined? Cross-national analyses for fifteen countries', *Canadian Review of Sociology and Anthropology* 38(3): 249–75.

Barman, Jean. 1995. 'Schooled for inequality: the education of British Columbia aboriginal children', in Jean Barman, Neil Sutherland and J. Donald Wilson (eds.), *Children, Teachers, and Schools in the History of British Columbia*, Calgary: Detselig, 389–409.

Barnes, S. H., and M. Kaase. 1979. *Political Action: Mass Participation in Five Western Democracies*, Beverly Hills: Sage Publications.

Baron, Stephen, John Field and Tom Schuller (eds.). 2000. *Social Capital: Critical Perspectives*, Oxford: Oxford University Press.

Barrett, James R. 1992. 'Americanization from the bottom up: immigration and the remaking of the working class in the United States, 1880–1930', *Journal of American History* 79(3), Discovering America: a special issue: 996–1020.

Bashevkin, Sylvia. 2002. *Welfare Hot Buttons: Women, Work, and Social Policy Reform*, Pittsburgh: University of Pittsburgh Press.

Bellah, Robert. 1985. *Habits of the Heart: Individualism and Commitment in American Life*, Berkeley: University of California Press.

Belsky, Jay, and David Eggebeen. 1991. 'Early and extensive maternal employment and young children's socioemotional development', *Journal of Marriage and the Family* 54: 1083–110.

Bennett, Lance. 1998. 'The uncivic culture: communication, identity and the rise of lifestyle politics: 1998 Ithiel de Sola Pool Lecture', *PS: Political Science and Politics* 31(4): 740–61.

Berkowitz, Bill. 2001. 'Girl Scouts on the firing line', *Lesbian News* 27(4): 52–4.

Blair, Tony. 2002. 'New Labour and community', *Renewal* 10(2): 9–14.

Bluestone, B., and S. Rose. 1997. 'Overworked and underemployed: unraveling an economic engine', *The American Prospect Online 31*, www.prospect.org/archives/31/31bluefs.html.

Blunkett, David. 2004. *New Challenges for Race Equality and Community Cohesion in the Twenty-First Century*, speech given to the Institute of Public Policy Research, London, 7 July.

Boix, C., and D. Posner. 1998. 'Social capital: explaining its origins and effects on government performance', *British Journal of Political Science* 29(3): 686–93.

Bolton, Charles, and Cal Ledbetter. 1983. 'Compulsory Bible reading in Arkansas and the culture of Southern fundamentalism', *Social Science Quarterly* 64: 670–6.

Bourdieu, Pierre. 1973. 'Cultural reproduction and social reproduction', in R. Brown (ed.), *Knowledge, Education and Social Change*, London: Tavistock, 71–112.

    1984. *Distinction: A Social Critique of the Judgment of Taste*, Cambridge, MA: Harvard University Press.

    1986. 'The forms of capital', in John G. Richardson (ed.), *Handbook of Theory and Research for the Sociology of Education*, Slough: Greenwood Press, 241–58.

Bradley, Martin, Norman Green, Dale Jones, Mac Lynn and Lou McNeil. 1992. *Churches and Church Membership in the United States 1990*, Atlanta: Glenmary Research Center.

Brady, Henry E., Robert Putnam, Andrea L. Campbell, Laurel Elms, Steven Yonish and Dorie Apollonio. 2000. *Roper Social and Political Trends Data (1973–1994) Codebook*, Roper Center for Public Opinion Research, University of Connecticut, Storrs.

Brehm, John, and Wendy Rahn. 1995. 'An audit of the deficit in social capital', unpublished manuscript, Duke University, Durham, NC.

Brosterman, Norman. 1997. *Inventing Kindergarten*, New York: Harry Abrams.

Brotherton, Phaedra. 2002. 'Making AAUW more inclusive', *Black Issues in Higher Education* 19(3): 36–7.

Brown, Gordon. 2004. Speech by the Chancellor of the Exchequer at the British Council Annual Lecture, available at www.hm-treasury.gov.uk/newsroom_and_speeches/press/2004/press_63_04.cfm.

Brown, Matthew Hay. 2001. 'Sikhs hurt in fallout of hate', *Hartford Courant* 17 September: A9.

Brown, Wendy. 2004. '"The most we can hope for . . .": human rights and the politics of fatalism', *South Atlantic Quarterly* 103(2): 451–64.

Burgess, Charles. 2001. 'Scouts embroiled in culture war', *San Francisco Chronicle* 13 August: A2.

Burns, Nancy, Kay Scholzman and Sidney Verba. 2001. *The Private Roots of Public Action: Gender, Equality and Political Participation* Cambridge, MA: Harvard University Press.

Butler, Jennifer, and Donna Lopiano. 2003. *The Women's Sports Foundation Report: Title IX and Race in Intercollegiate Sport*, East Meadow, NY: Women's Sports Foundation.

Butler, Judith. 1990. *Gender Trouble: Feminism and the Subversion of Identity*, New York: Routledge.

Button, James W., Barbara A. Rienzo and Kenneth D. Wald. 1997. *Private Lives, Public Conflicts: Battles over Gay Rights in American Communities*, Washington, DC: Congressional Quarterly Books.

Cappella, Joseph N., and Kathleen Hall Jamieson. 1997. *Spiral of Cynicism: The Press and the Public Good*, New York: Oxford University Press.

CBS. 2003. *60 Minutes*, segment on Hadassah Medical Centre, www.cbsnews.com/stories/2003/10/31/60minutes/main581163.shtml; accessed December 2003.

Chambers, Simone, and Jeffrey Kopstein. 2001. 'Bad civil society', *Political Theory* 29(6): 837–65.

Chappell, Marisa. 2002. 'Rethinking women's politics in the 1970s: the League of Women Voters and the National Organization for Women confront poverty', *Journal of Women's History* 13(4): 155–79.

Chin, Kip L. 1994. 'ABWA ranks high among 400 businesswomen's networks', *Women in Business* 46(4): 6.

Christian Century, The, 1999. 'Anglican diocese faces bankruptcy', *The Christian Century* 116(27): 960.

Christian Science Monitor. 2001. 'The *Monitor*'s view', *Christian Science Monitor* 93(132): 8.

Clemens, Elisabeth. 1999. 'Organizational repertories and institutional change: women's groups and the transformation of American politics, 1890–1920', in Theda Skocpol and Morris P. Fiorina (eds.), *Civic Engagement in American Democracy*, Washington, DC: Brookings Institution, 81–110.

Cohen, Jean. 1999. 'Trust, voluntary association and workable democracy: the contemporary American discourse on civil society', in Mark Warren (ed.), *Democracy and Trust*, Cambridge: Cambridge University Press, 208–48.

Cohen, Jean, and Andrew Arato. 1992. *Civil Society and Political Theory*, Cambridge, MA: MIT Press.

Coleman, James. 1988. 'Social capital in the creation of human capital', *American Journal of Sociology* 94 (Supplement): S95–S120.

Costa, Dora L., and Matthew Kahn. 2003. 'Civic engagement and community heterogeneity: an economist's perspective', *Perspectives on Politics* 1(1): 103–11; available at web.mit.edu/costa/www/costa.kahn.1.4pdf.pdf.

Crawford, Susan, and Peggy Levitt. 1999. 'Social change and civic engagement: the case of the PTA', in Theda Skocpol and Morris P. Fiorina (eds.), *Civic Engagement in American Democracy*, Washington, DC: Brookings Institution, 249–96.

Crocker, Ruth Hutchinson. 1992. *Social Work and Social Order: The Settlement Movement in Two Industrial Cities, 1889–1930*, Urbana: University of Illinois Press.

Culver, Virginia. 2001. 'Methodist court bars openly gay ministers', *Denver Post* 6 November: A11.

Curran, Barbara A. 1995. *Women in the Law: A Look at the Numbers*, Chicago: Commission on Women in the Profession, American Bar Association.

Danziger, Sheldon, and Daniel H. Weinberg. 1994. 'The historical record', in Sheldon Danzinger, Gary D. Sandefur and Daniel H. Weinberg (eds.), *Confronting Poverty: Prescriptions for Change*, Cambridge, MA: Harvard University Press, 18–50.

Darcy, R., Susan Welch and Janet Clark. 1994. *Women, Elections and Representation*, 2nd edn., Lincoln: University of Nebraska Press.

Davis, Allen F. 1967. *Spearheads for Reform: The Social Settlements and the Progressive Movement, 1890–1914*, New York: Oxford University Press.

Davis, Elizabeth. 1933. *Lifting as They Climb*, Washington, DC: National Association of Colored Women.

Davis, Lennard. 1995. *Enforcing Normalcy: Disability, Deafness and the Body*, New York: Verso.

1997. *Disability Studies Reader*, New York: Routledge.

Day, R. L. E. 2000. *Multiculturalism and the History of Canadian Diversity*, Toronto: University of Toronto Press.

Delacourt, Susan. 2001. 'More ethnic diversity means less trust: expert', *National Post* 6 December: A2.

Dewey, John. 1915. 'Splitting up the school system', *New Republic* 2: 283–4.

Diner, Steven. 1998. *A Very Different Age: Americans of the Progressive Era*, New York: Hill and Wang.

Dubé, Yves, J. E. Howes and D. L. McQueen. 1957. *Housing and Social Capital*, study prepared for Royal Commission on Canada's Economic Prospects, Hull: Queen's Printer.

Dyck, N. 1997. *Differing Visions: Administering Indian Residential Schooling in Prince Albert, 1867–1967*, Black Point, NS: Fernwood Publishing.

Easton, David. 2002. 'The future of the post-behavioral phase in political science', in Kristen Monroe (ed.), *Contemporary Empirical Political Theory*, Berkeley: University of California Press, 13–46.

Eberly, Don (ed.). 2000. *The Essential Civil Society Reader*, Oxford: Rowman and Littlefield.

Eckstrom, Kevin. 2002. 'Ecumenism: Catholics, Evangelical and mainline Protestants look to form broad Christian group', *Los Angeles Times*, Pt 2, 21.

Encyclopedia of Associations. 2002. *Encyclopedia of Associations*, 38th edn., Mason, OM: Thomson Custom Publishing.

Etzioni, Amitai. 1995. *The Spirit of Community*, London: Fontana.
   2000. 'Communitarianism and the moral dimension', in Don Eberly (ed.), *The Essential Civil Society Reader*, Oxford: Rowman and Littlefield, 123–39.
   2001. 'Survey article: on social and moral revival', *Journal of Political Philosophy* 9(3): 356–71.

Everitt, Joanna. 2006. 'Gender-role orientations and the conversion of social capital into political engagement', in Brenda O'Neill and Elisabeth Gidengil (eds.), *Gender and Social Capital*, New York: Routledge, chap. 11.

Faludi, Susan. 1999. *Stiffed: The Betrayal of the American Man*, New York: W. Morrow and Co.

Ferber, Marianne, and Brigid O'Farrell (eds.). 1991. *Work and Family: Policies for a Changing Workforce*, Washington, DC: National Academy.

Fine, Ben, and Francis Green. 2000. 'Economics, social capital and the colonization of the social sciences', in Stephen Baron, John Field and Tom Schuller (eds.), *Social Capital: Critical Perspectives*, Oxford: Oxford University Press, 78–93.

Fiorina, Morris P. 1999. 'Extreme voices: a dark side of civic engagement', in Theda Skocpol and Morris P. Fiorina (eds.), *Civic Engagement in American Democracy*, Washington, DC: Brookings Institution, 395–425.

Fleischer, Doris, and Frieda Zames. 2001. *The Disability Rights Movement: From Charity to Confrontation*, Philadelphia: Temple University Press.

Foot, Richard. 1999. 'United church facing major cuts to pay damages', *National Post* 6 November: A12.

Foucault, Michel. 1980. *Power/Knowledge – Selected Interviews and Other Writings 1972–1977*, Colin Gordeon (ed.), Brighton: Harvester Press.

France, David. 2001. 'Scouts divided', *Newsweek* 138(6): 44.

Franzen, Ernst-Ulrich. 2002. 'Keeping the faith pays off', *Milwaukee Journal Sentinel* 11 February: 12A.

Fraser, Nancy. 1994. 'After the family wage: gender equity and the welfare state', *Political Theory* 22(4): 591–618.
   1998. 'From redistribution to recognition? Dilemmas of justice in a "postsocialist" age', in Anne Phillips (ed.), *Feminism and Politics*, New York: Oxford University Press, 430–60.

Fukuyama, Francis. 1999. *The Great Disruption: Human Nature and the Reconstitution of Social Order*, New York: Free Press.

2001. 'Social capital, civil society, and development', *Third World Quarterly* 22(1): 7–20.

Gambetta, Diego. 1988. *Trust: Making and Breaking Cooperative Relations*, Oxford: Blackwell.

Gerbner, George, L. Gross, M. Morgan and N. Signorielli. 1994. 'Growing up with television: the cultivation perspective', in *Media Effects: Advances in Theory and Research*, Hillsdale, NJ: Lawrence Erlbaum, 17–41.

Gerson, Louis. 1976. 'Ethnics in American politics', *Journal of Politics* 38(3), 200 years of the Republic in retrospect: a special bicentennial issue: 336–46.

Gerstenzang, James. 2002a. 'Bush blesses charity plan', *Los Angeles Times* 8 February: A16.

2002b. 'Bush circumventing Congress on domestic policy', *Los Angeles Times* 15 December, part I: 42.

Gething, Judith. 1997. 'Christianity and coverture: impact on the legal status of women in Hawaii, 1820–1920', *Hawaiian Journal of History* 11: 188–220.

Gibson, James L. 1989. 'The structure of attitudinal tolerance in the United States', *British Journal of Political Science* 19(4): 562–70.

Giddens, Anthony. 2000. *The Third Way and its Critics*, Oxford: Polity Press.

Giddings, Paula. 1984. *When and Where I Enter: The Impact of Black Women on Race and Sex in America*, New York: William Morrow and Co.

Girl Scouts. 1999. *What Does Strong Mean?*, Annual Report 1999, New York: Girl Scouts of the USA; available at www.girlscouts.org.

2000. *Today's Girls: Tomorrow's Leaders*, Annual Report 2000, New York: Girl Scouts of the USA; available at www.girlscouts.org.

2001. 'News release', 11 January, www.girlscouts.org; accessed 22 June 2002.

2002. 'News release', 31 January, www.girlscouts.org; accessed 22 June 2002.

2003. *Annual Report 2003*. New York: Girl Scouts of the USA; available at www.girlscouts.org.

Gitlin, Todd. 1995. *The Twilight of Common Dreams: Why America is Wracked by Culture Wars*, New York: Henry Holt and Co.

Gordon, Linda. 1988. *Heroes of Their Own Lives: The Politics and History of Family Violence – Boston, 1880–1960*, New York: Viking.

1991. 'Black and white visions of welfare: women's welfare activism, 1890–1945', *Journal of American History* 78(2): 559–90.

Grant, Agnes. 1996. *No End of Grief: Indian Residential Schools in Canada*, Winnipeg: Pemmican Publications.

Green, Andy, and John Preston. 2001. 'Education and social cohesion: reentering the debate', *Peabody Journal of Education* 76(3/4): 247–85.

Green, John C. 2000. 'Antigay: varieties of opposition to gay rights', in Craig Rimmerman, Kenneth Wald and Clyde Wilcox (eds.), *The Politics of Gay Rights*, Chicago: University of Chicago Press, 121–38.

Grimshaw, Patricia. 1989. *Paths of Duty: American Missionary Wives in Nineteenth-Century Hawaii*, Honolulu: University of Hawai'i Press.

2000. 'Settler anxieties, indigenous peoples, and women's suffrage in the colonies of Australia, New Zealand and Hawaii, 1888 to 1902', *Pacific Historical Review* 69(4): 553–5.

Guth, James L., Ted Jelen, Lyman Kellstedt, Corwin Smidt and Kenneth Wald. 1988. 'The politics of religion in America: issues for investigation', *American Politics Quarterly* 16(3): 357–97.

Gutmann, Amy. 1994. 'Introduction', in Amy Gutmann (ed.), *Multiculturalism: Examining the Politics of Recognition*, Princeton, NJ: Princeton University Press, 3–24.

Hacking, Ian. 2000. *The Social Construction of What?*, Cambridge, MA: Harvard University Press.

Hadassah. 2001. *Hadassah Expresses Concern about Statements Related to Faith-Based Funding*, press release, Hadassah, New York, 25 May; available at www.hadassah.org/issues/faith.htm; accessed 4 July 2002.

Hall, Peter A. 1999. 'Social capital in Britain', *British Journal of Political Science* 28: 417–61.

   2002. 'The role of government and the distribution of social capital', in Robert D. Putnam (ed.), *Democracies in Flux: The Evolution of Social Capital in Contemporary Society*, Oxford: Oxford University Press, 21–58.

Hardin, Russell. 2002. *Trust and Trustworthiness*, New York: Russell Sage Foundation.

Harley, Sharon. 1990. 'For the good of family and race: gender, work and domestic roles in the black community, 1880–1930', *Signs*, 15 (Winter): 336–49.

Harper, Rosalyn. 2002. *The Measurement of Social Capital in the United Kingdom*, paper presented at the ONS/OECD conference 'The Measurement of Social Capital', Office for National Statistics. London, 25–7 September; available at www.oecd.org/documents/24/0,2340,en_2649_34543_2380248_1_1_1_1,00.html.

Harris, Cole. 1991. 'Power, modernity, and historical geography', *Annals of the Association of American Geographers* 81(4), 671–83.

Hart, Vivien. 1978. *Distrust and Democracy: Political Distrust in Britain and America*, Cambridge: Cambridge University Press.

Harvey, Bob. 1999. 'Churches fear financial ruin from lawsuits: alleged abuse at native schools spawns millions in claims', *Ottawa Citizen* 1 April: 9.

Haughey, Nuala. 2001. 'Living in bin Laden's shadow', *Irish Times* 30 October: 11.

Hawes, Kay. 1999. 'Women's sports seeking fast track to championship status', *NCAA News*, 15 February; available at www.ncaa.org/news/1999/19990215/active/3604n02.html.

Helliwell, John. 2003. *Immigration and Social Capital: Issue Paper*, issue paper presented at the international conference 'The Opportunity and Challenge of Diversity: A Role for Social Capital?', Montreal, 23–5 November.

Helliwell, John, and Robert D. Putnam. 1999. *Education and Social Capital*, Working Paper no. 7121, National Bureau of Economic Research, Cambridge, MA.

Herman, Didi. 2000. 'The gay agenda is the Devil's agenda: the Christian right's vision and the role of the state', in Craig Rimmerman, Kenneth Wald and Clyde Wilcox (eds.), *The Politics of Gay Rights*, Chicago: University of Chicago Press, 139–60.

Higham, John. 1971. *Strangers in the Land: Patterns of American Nativism, 1860–1925*, New York: Atheneum.

Hilliard, Robert L., Michael C. Keith and Donald Fishman. 1999. *Waves of Rancor: Tuning in the Radical Right (Media, Communication, and Culture in America)*, Armonk, NY: M. E. Sharpe.

Himmelweit, H. T., A. N. Oppenheim and P. Vince. 1958. *Television and the Child: An Empirical Study of the Effect of Television on the Young*, Oxford: Oxford University Press.

Hing, Bill Ong. 1993. *Making and Remaking Asian America through Immigration Policy*, Stanford, CA: Stanford University Press.

Honig, Bonnie. 2001. *Democracy and the Foreigner*, Princeton, NJ: Princeton University Press.

Hooghe, Marc, 2002. *Is Reciprocity Sufficient? Trust and Reciprocity as Forms of Social Capital*, paper presented at the 98th annual meeting of the American Political Science Association, Boston, 29 August–1 September.

Howland, Courtney, and Thomas Buergenthal. 2001. *Religious Fundamentalisms and the Human Rights of Women*, New York: Macmillan.

Huff, Delores J. 1997. *To Live Heroically: Institutional Racism and American Indian Education*, Albany, NY: SUNY Press.

Hunter, James Davison. 1991. *Culture Wars: The Struggle to Define America*, New York: Basic Books.

1994. *Before the Shooting Begins: Searching for Democracy in America's Culture War*, New York: Free Press.

Huntington, Ellsworth. 1935. *Tomorrow's Children: The Goal of Eugenics*, New York: John Wiley.

Inglehart, Ronald. 1990. *Culture Shift in Advanced Industrial Society*, Princeton, NJ: Princeton University Press.

1997. *Modernization, Postmodernization: Cultural, Economic, and Political Change in 43 Societies*, Princeton, NJ: Princeton University Press.

1999. 'Trust, well-being and social capital', in Mark Warren (ed.), *Democracy and Trust*, Cambridge: Cambridge University Press, 88–120.

Jelen, Ted. 1982. 'Sources of political intolerance: the case of the American South', in Laurence Moreland, Tod Baker and Robert Steed (eds.), *Contemporary Southern Political Attitudes and Behavior*, New York: Praeger, 73–91.

1993. 'The political consequences of religious group attitudes', *Journal of Politics* 55(1): 178–90.

Jenkins, Phillip. 2002. *The Next Christendom: The Coming of Global Christianity*, Oxford: Oxford University Press.

Jeung, Russell. 2002. 'Asian American pan-ethnic formation and congregational culture', in Pyong Gap Min and Jung Ha Kim (eds.), *Religions in Asian America: Building Faith Communities*, Walnut Creek, CA: AltaMira Press, 215–43.

Jonas, Michael. 2005. 'Sen. Clinton urges use of faith-based initiatives', *Boston Globe* 20 January; available at www.baston.com/news/local/articles/2005/01/20/sen_clinton_urges_use_of_faith_based_initiatives/; accessed January 2005.

Jones, James H. 1992. *Bad Blood: The Tuskagee Syphilis Experiment*, New York: Free Press.

Kaplan, Morris B. 1997. *Sexual Justice: Democratic Citizenship and the Politics of Desire*, London: Routledge.

Kemp, Kathy. 2001. 'The Survey says 81% of Birmingham area residents have connections churches', *Birmingham News* 1 March: A1.

Kershaw, Paul. 2005. *Carefair: Rethinking the Rights and Responsibilities of Citizenship*, Vancouver: University of British Columbia Press.

King, Desmond. 1999. *In the Name of Liberalism: Illiberal Social Policy in the United States and Britain*, Oxford: Oxford University Press.

2000. *Making Americans: Immigration, Race and the Origins of the Diverse Democracy*, Cambridge, MA: Harvard University Press.

2005. *The Liberty of Strangers: Making the American Nation*, Oxford: Oxford University Press.

Koven, Seth, and Sonya Michel. 1990. 'Womanly duties: maternalist politics and the origins of welfare states in France, Germany, Great Britain, and the US, 1880–1920', *American Historical Review* 95(4): 1076–108.

Kudlick, Catherine J. 2001. 'The outlook of *The problem* and the problem with the *Outlook*', in Paul Longmore and Lauri Umansky (eds.), *The New Disability History: American Perspectives*, New York: New York University Press, 187–213.

Kymlicka, Will. 1995. *Multicultural Citizenship*, Oxford: Oxford University Press.

2002. *Contemporary Political Philosophy*, 2nd ed., Oxford: Oxford University Press.

Ladd, Everett. 1996. 'The data just don't show erosion of America's "social capital"', *The Public Perspective* 7(4): 1–22.

1999. *The Ladd Report*, New York: Free Press.

Lane, Harlan. 1997. 'Constructions of Deafness', in Lennard J. Davis (ed.), *The Disability Studies Reader*, New York: Routledge, 153–71.

Lasch-Quinn, Elisabeth. 1993. *Black Neighbors: Race and the Limits of Reform in the American Settlement House Movement, 1890–1945*, Chapel Hill: University of North Carolina Press.

Leuchtenburg, William. 1952. 'Progressivism and imperialism: the Progressive movement and American foreign policy, 1898–1916', *Mississippi Valley Historical Review* 39(3): 483–504.

Levi, Margaret. 1996. 'Social and unsocial capital: a review essay of Robert Putnam's *Making Democracy Work*', *Politics and Society* 24(1): 45–55.

Lightman, David. 2001. 'Momentum Svilas for gay bill; a vote barring job discrimination against gays and lesbians is expected to send Bush a message on his faith-based initiatives', *Hartford Cousant* 1 August: A2.

Lijphart, Arend. 1997. 'Unequal participation: democracy's unresolved dilemma', *American Political Science Review* 91(1): 1–14.

Lissak, Rivka. 1983. 'Myth and reality: the pattern of relationship between the Hull House Circle and the "new immigrants" on Chicago's West Side: 1890–1919', *Journal of American Ethnic History* 2: 21–50.

1989. *Pluralism and Progressives: Hull House and the New Immigrants, 1890–1919*, Chicago: University of Chicago Press.

Longmore, Paul, and Lauri Umansky (eds.). 2001. *The New Disability History: American Perspectives*, New York: New York University Press.

Lopez, Kathryn Jean. 2000. 'The cookie crumbles', *National Review* 52(20): 30.

Lord, Mary. 1999. 'What next for the PTA?', *US News and World Report* 126(21): 62–5.

Los Angeles Times. 2002. 'Jewish group opposes plan for faith initiative', *Los Angeles Times* 23 Februry, part 2: 19.

Lowndes, Vivien. 2000. 'Women and social capital: a comment on Hall's "Social capital in Britain"', *British Journal of Political Science* 30: 533–40.

Lozano, Juan A. 2003. 'Bush praises Houston center for its faith-based work', *Associated Press Wire* 12 September.

Luker, Ralph E. 1977. 'The Social Gospel and the failure of racial reform, 1877–1898', *Church History* 46: 80–99.

    1984. 'Missions, institutional churches, and settlement houses: the black experience, 1885–1910', *Journal of Negro History* 69(3/4): 101–13.

MacBeth, Tannis. 1991. 'The impact of television: a longitudinal Canadian study', in Benjamin Singer (ed.), *Communication in Canadian Society*, Nokomis, FL: Nelson Publishing, 119–45.

MacBeth Williams, Tannis. 1986. *The Impact of Television: A Natural Experiment in Three Communities*, Orlando: Academic Press.

Macpherson, C. B. (ed.). 1968. 'Introduction', Thomas Hobbes, *Leviathan*, Harmondsworth: Penguin, 1–51.

Madigan, Erin. 2005. 'More states reach out to faith-based organizations', *stateline.org*, 12 January; available at www.stateline.org/stateline/?pa=story&sa=showStoryInfodid=423910.

Maloney, William A., Graham Smith and Gerry Stoker. 2000. 'Social capital and associational life', in Stephen Baron, John Field and Tom Schuller (eds.), *Social Capital: Critical Perspectives*, Oxford: Oxford University Press, 212–25.

Martin, William. 1996. *With God on Our Side: The Rise of the Religious Right in America*, New York: Broadway Books.

Marus, Robert. 2005. 'Faith-based initiatives plan will continue in Bush second term', *Texas Baptist Newsjournal*, 7 January; available at www.baptiststandard.com/postroke/index.php?module=htmlpages&func=display&pid=2829.

McClymer, John F. 1980. *War and Welfare: Social Engineering in America, 1890–1925*, Westport, CT: Greenwood Publishing.

    1982. 'The Americanization movement and the education of the foreign-born adult, 1914–1925', in Bernard J. Weiss (ed.), *American Education and the European Immigrant, 1840–1940*, Urbana: University of Illinois Press, 96–116.

Meckler, Laura. 2005. 'Bush takes battle over funding of "faith-based" groups to states', *Washington Post* 4 January: A13.

Mehler, Barry. 1987. 'Eliminating the inferior: American and Nazi sterilization programs', *Science for the People* November–December: 14–18.

Mehta, Uday Singh. 1990. 'Liberal strategies of exclusion', *Politics and Society* 18(4): 427–583.

1999. *Liberalism and Empire: A Study in Nineteenth-Century British Liberal Thought*, Chicago: University of Chicago Press.

Mercredi, Ovide, and Mary Ellen Turpel. 1993. *In the Rapids: Navigating the Future of First Nations*, Toronto: Viking/Penguin.

Miller, Diane Helene. 1998. *Freedom to Differ: The Shaping of the Gay and Lesbian Struggle for Civil Rights*, New York: New York University Press.

Miller, Warren. 1990. 'Response: continuity in NES studies', *Public Opinion Quarterly* 54(2): 191–4.

Mills, Charles. 1997. *The Racial Contract*, Ithaca, NY: Cornell University Press.

Min, Pyong Gap, and Jung Ha Kim. 2002. *Religions in Asian America: Building Faith Communities*, Walnut Creek, CA: AltaMira Press.

Mohanty, Chandra Talpade. 1988. 'Under Western eyes: feminist scholarship and colonial discourse', *Feminist Review* 30: 65–88.

Moose Magazine Online. 2002. 'Brothers, together we can make a difference', *Moose Magazine Online*, August–October, www.mooseintl.org/moosemagazine; accessed December 2003.

2003a. 'Sailing into the future', *Moose Magazine Online*, February–April, www.mooseintl.org/moosemagazine; accessed December 2003.

2003b. 'Fraternity's Women continue to give much and get an expanding role', *Moose Magazine Online*, August–October, www.mooseintl.org/moosemagazine; accessed December 2003.

2003c. 'Hard choices for the present – and a vision for the future', *Moose Magazine Online*, August–October, www.mooseintl.org/moosemagazine; accessed December 2003.

Morgan, David, and Kenneth Meier. 1980. 'Politics and morality: the effects of religion on referenda voting', *Social Science Quarterly* 61: 144–8.

Mosher, Michael A. 2002. 'Are civil societies the transmission belts of ethical tradition?', in Simone Chambers and Will Kymlicka (eds.), *Alternative Conceptions of Civil Society*, Princeton, NJ: Princeton University Press, 207–30.

Mullins, Mark R. 1987. 'The life cycle of ethnic Churches in sociological perspective', *Japanese Journal of Religious Studies* 14: 321–34.

NCAA. 1999. *Report of the NCAA Committee on Women's Athletics*, supplement no. 9, Indianapolis: National Collegiate Athletic Association; available at www.ncaa.org/databases/reports/1/20000/mc/20001-dl-mc-agendas09.htm.

2003a. *Participation: 1982–2002 Sponsorship and Participation Report*, Indianapolis: National Collegiate Athletic Association; available at www.ncaa.org.

2003b. *Student–Athlete Ethnicity Report 1999–2000 – 2002–2003*, Indianapolis: National Collegiate Athletic Association; available at www.ncaa.org/library/researchethnicityreport/2002–03/ethnicityReport.pdf.

Neuhaus, Richard. 1984. *The Naked Public Square*, Grand Rapids, MI: Eerdman's.

Neverdon-Morton, Cynthia. 1989. *Afro-American Women of the South and the Advancement of the Race 1895–1925*, Knoxville: University of Tennessee Press.

Norris, Pippa. 1996. 'Does television erode social capital? A reply to Putnam', *PS: Political Science and Politics* 29(3): 474–80.

2000. *A Virtuous Circle: Political Communications in Postindustrial Societies*, Cambridge: Cambridge University Press.

2002. *Democratic Phoenix: Reinventing Political Activism*, Cambridge: Cambridge University Press.

Norris, Pippa, and Ronald Inglehart. 2006. 'Gendering social capital: bowling in women's leagues?', in Brenda O'Neill and Elisabeth Gidengil (eds.), *Gender and Social Capital*, New York: Routledge, chap. 4.

Nunn, Clyde Z., Harry J.Crockett and J. Allen Williams Jr. 1978. *Tolerance for Nonconformity*, San Francisco: Jossey-Bass.

OECD. 2001. *The Well-Being of Nations: The Role of Human and Social Capital*, Paris: Centre for Educational Research and Education, Organisation for Economic Co-operation and Development.

Offe, Claus. 1999. 'How can we trust our fellow citizens?', in Mark Warren (ed.), *Democracy and Trust*, Cambridge: Cambridge University Press, 42–87.

O'Neill, Brenda. 2006. 'Canadian women's religious volunteerism: compassion, connections, and comparisons', in Brenda O'Neill and Elisabeth Gidengil (eds.), *Gender and Social Capital*, New York: Routledge, chap. 8.

Parcel, Toby, and Elizabeth Menaghan. 1994. 'Early parental work, family social capital and early childhood outcomes', *American Journal of Sociology* 99(4): 972–1009.

Pateman, Carole. 1988. *The Sexual Contract*, Oxford: Polity Press.

1989. *The Disorder of Women: Democracy, Feminism and Political Theory*, Stanford, CA: Stanford University Press.

Patterson, Orlando. 1999. 'Liberty against the democratic state: on the historical and contemporary source of American distrust', in Mark Warren (ed.), *Democracy and Trust*, Cambridge: Cambridge University Press, 151–207.

Patterson, Thomas. 1993. *Out of Order*, New York: Knopf.

Phelan, Shane. 2001. *Sexual Strangers: Gays, Lesbians, and Dilemmas of Citizenship*, Philadelphia: Temple University Press.

Phillips, Anne. 1995. *The Politics of Presence*, Oxford: Clarendon Press.

Portes, Alejandro. 1998. 'Social capital: its origins and applications in modern sociology', *Annual Review of Sociology* 24: 1–24.

Privy Council Office. 2003. Social Capital: Building on a Network-Based Analysis, draft discussion paper, Privy Council Office, Ottawa.

2004. *Expert Workshop on the Measurement of Social Capital for Public Policy*, PCO/OECD synthesis report, Privy Council Office, Ottawa.

Putnam, Robert D. 1993. 'The prosperous community', *The American Prospect* 4(13): 35–42.

1995a. 'Bowling alone: America's declining social capital', *Journal of Democracy* 6(1): 65–78.

1995b. 'Tuning in, tuning out: the strange disappearance of social capital in America', *PS: Political Science and Politics* 28(4): 664–83.

1996. *The Decline of Civil Society: How Come? So What?*, John L. Manion Lecture, Canadian Centre for Management Development, Ottawa, 22 February.

2000. *Bowling Alone: The Collapse and Revival of American Community*, New York: Touchstone.

2001. 'A better society in a time of war', *New York Times* 19 October: A19.

2002a. 'Bowling together', *The American Prospect* 13(3): 20–2.

(ed.). 2002b. *Democracies in Flux: The Evolution of Social Capital in Contemporary Society*, Oxford: Oxford University Press.

Putnam, Robert, and Lewis Feldstein. 2003. *Better Together*, New York: Simon and Schuster.

Putnam, Robert D., and Kristin A. Goss. 2002. 'Introduction', in Robert Putnam (ed.), *Democracies in Flux: The Evolution of Social Capital in Contemporary Society*, Oxford: Oxford University Press, 3–21.

Rahn, Wendy M., and John Transue. 1998. 'Social trust and value change: the decline of social capital in American youth, 1976–1995', *Political Psychology* 19: 545–65.

Rather, Dan. 2001. 'Truth of the battlefield', *Harvard International Review* 23(1), available at http://hir.harvard.edu/articles/1004/3/.

Rawls, John. 1971. *A Theory of Justice*, Cambridge, MA: Belknap Press of Harvard University.

Reich, Rob. 2002. *Bridging Liberalism and Multiculturalism in American Education*, Chicago: University of Chicago Press.

Reilly, Philip, 1991. *The Surgical Solution: A History of Involuntary Sterilization in the United States*, Baltimore: Johns Hopkins University Press.

Rice, Patricia. 2001. 'Sikhs in US fear repsisals because of turbans', *St. Louis Post Dispatch* 29 September: 16.

Rimmerman, Craig. 2002. *From Identity to Politics: The Lesbian and Gay Movements in the United States*, Philadelphia: Temple University Press.

Rimmerman, Craig, Kenneth D. Wald and Clyde Wilcox (eds.). 2000. *The Politics of Gay Rights*, Chicago: University of Chicago Press.

Rodgers-Melnick, Ann. 2002. 'Presbyterians affirm Jesus as savior, sidestep debate on homosexuality', *Pittsburgh Post-Gazette* 21 June: A12.

Rorty, Richard. 1999. *Achieving Our Country*, Cambridge, MA: Harvard University Press.

Ross, Elizabeth Dale. 1976. *The Kindergarten Crusade: The Establishment of Preschool Education in the United States*, Athens: Ohio University Press.

Ross, Rosetta. 2003. *Witnessing and Testifying: Black Women, Religion and Civil Rights*, Minneapolis: Fortress Press.

Royal Commission on Aboriginal Peoples. 1996. *Report of the Royal Commission on Aboriginal Peoples*, Vol. II, Government of Canada, Ottawa: Canada Communications Group Publishing.

Sanbonmatsu, John. 2001. 'Letters to the Editor', *New York Times* 25 October: A20.

Sandel, Michael. 1984. *Liberalism and Its Critics*, New York: New York University Press.

Sanders, Thomas H., and Robert D. Putnam. 2002. 'Walking the civic talk after September 11', *Christian Science Monitor* 19 February: 11; available at www.csmonitor.com/2002/0219/p11s02-coop.html.

Savage, Mike. 2005. *Voluntary Associations and Social Capital: Challenging Toc-quevillian Perspectives*, plenary paper presented at the conference 'Whither Social Capital? Past, Present and Future', London South Bank University, 6–7 April.

Schlesinger, Arthur. 1998. *The Disuniting of America: Reflections on a Multicultural Society*, New York: W. W. Norton.

Scott, Anne Firor. 1990. 'Most invisible of all: black women's voluntary associations', *Journal of Southern History* 56(1): 3–22.

SGMA. 1998. *Gaining Ground: A Progress Report on Women in Sports*, Washington, DC: Sporting Goods Manufacturers Association.

2000. *Gaining Ground: A Progress Report on Women in Sports*, Washington, DC: Sporting Goods Manufacturers Association.

Shapiro, Michael. 2001. *For Moral Ambiguity: National Culture and the Politics of the Family*, Minneapolis: University of Minnesota Press.

Skinner, Quentin, Partha Dasgupta, Raymond Geuss, Melissa Lane, Peter Laslett, Onora O'Neill, W. G. Runciman and Andrew Kuper. 2002. 'Political philosophy: the view from Cambridge', *Journal of Political Philosophy* 10(1): 1–19.

Skocpol, Theda. 1992. *Protecting Soldier and Mothers: The Politics of Social Provision in the United States: 1870s to 1920s*, Cambridge, MA: Belknap Press of Harvard University.

1996. 'Unsolved mysteries: the Tocqueville files – unravelling from above', *The American Prospect* 7(25); available at www.prospect.org/print/V7/25/25-cnt2.html.

1999. 'Recent transformations of civic life', in Theda Skocpol and Morris P. Fiorina (eds.), *Civic Engagement in American Democracy*, Washington, DC: Brookings Institution, 461–509.

2000. *The Missing Middle: Working Families and the Future of American Social Policy*, New York: W. W. Norton.

2002. 'From membership to advocacy', in Robert D. Putnam (ed.), *Democracies in Flux: The Evolution of Social Capital in Contemporary Society*, Oxford: Oxford University Press, 103–36.

2004. 'Voice and inequality: the transformation of American civic democracy', *Perspectives on Politics* 2(1): 3–20.

Skocpol, Theda, and Morris P. Fiorina. 1999. 'Making sense of the civic engagement debate', in Theda Skocpol and Morris P. Fiorina (eds.), *Civic Engagement in American Democracy*, Washington, DC: Brookings Institution, 1–23.

Smith, Rogers. 1993. 'Beyond Tocqueville, Myrdal, and Hartz: the multiple traditions in America', *American Political Science Review* 87(3): 549–66.

Snyder, Agnes. 1972. *Dauntless Women in Childhood Education*, Olney, MD: Association for Childhood Education International.

Solow, Robert. 2000. 'Notes on social capital and economic performance', in Partha Dasgupta and Ismail Serageldin (eds.), *Social Capital: A Multifaceted Perspective*, Washington, DC: International Bank for Reconstruction and Development, World Bank, 6–10.

Stebner, Eleanor J. 1997. *The Women of Hull House*, Albany, NY: SUNY Press.

Steele, Andrew. 1998. *Mars Casts His Ballot: Men and the Gender Gap in Canadian Elections*, unpublished MA thesis, Department of Political Science, University of British Columbia, Vancouver.

Stephen, Andrew. 2001. 'Boy Scouts fail the tolerance test', *New Statesman* 130(4549): 16.

Stiker, Henri-Jacques. 1999. *A History of Disability*, trans. William Sayers, Ann Arbor: University of Michigan Press.

Stolle, Dietlind. 1998. 'Why do bowling and singing matter: characteristics, membership and generalized trust', *Political Psychology* 19: 497–525.

2001. 'Getting to trust', in Paul Dekker and Eric Uslaner (eds.), *Social Capital and Participation in Everyday Life*, London: Routledge, 118–33.

Straus, Brian. 2003. 'Women's pro soccer league forced to fold', *Washington Post* 16 September: AO1.

Sullivan, John L., James Pierson and George Marcus. 1982. *Political Tolerance and American Democracy*, Chicago: University of Chicago Press.

Sullivan, Tim. 2000. 'PTO vs. PTA', *PTOtoday*, 2(1): 1–6; available at www.ptotoday.com/0800ptopta2.html.

Tannenbaum, Bernice. 2002. 'The Hadassah journey', *Hadassah Magazine* 83(6); available at www.hadassah.org/NEWS/magazine/Feb-02/feature1.htm.

Taylor, Catharine P. 2002. 'Girl Scouts extend multicultural reach', *Advertising Age* 73(3): 18–20.

Taylor, Charles. 1994. 'The politics of recognition', in Amy Gutmann (ed.), *Multiculturalism: Examining the Politics of Recognition*, Princeton, NJ: Princeton University Press, 25–73.

Texas Freedom Network. 2002. *The Texas Faith-Based Initiatives at Five Years: Warning Signs as President Bush Expands Texas-style Program to National Level*, Education Fund, Texas Freedom Network, Austin, 10 October; available at www.tfn.org/issues/charitablechoice/report02.html; accessed 6 June 2003.

Tully, James. 1995. *Strange Multiplicity: Constitutionalism in an Age of Diversity*, Cambridge: Cambridge University Press.

Turner, Richard Brent. 1997. *Islam in the African-American Experience*, Bloomington: University of Indiana Press.

Twain, Mark, and Charles Dudley Warner. 1873. *The Gilded Age: A Tale of Today*, in Mark Twain, *The Gilded Age and Later Novels*, 2002, New York: Library of America.

Tyre, Peg. 2001. 'Where the girls are', *Newsweek* 138(6): 51–2.

United States Senate. 2002. *An Act to Establish the Department of Homeland Security and for Other Purposes*, H.R. 5005, Washington, DC: Congressional Printing Service.

USA Freedom Corps. 2002. *Handbook of the USA Freedom Corps*, Washington, DC: Congressional Printing Service.

Uslaner, Eric. 1999. 'Democracy and social capital', in Mark Warren (ed.), *Democracy and Trust*, Cambridge: Cambridge University Press, 121–50.

2002. *The Moral Foundations of Trust*, Cambridge: Cambridge University Press.

Wald, Kenneth. 1997. *Religion and Politics in the United States*, 3rd edn., Washington, DC: Congressional Quarterly Press.

Wald, Kenneth, Dennis Owen and Samuel S. Hill Jr. 1990. 'Political cohesion in Churches', *Journal of Politics* 52(1): 197–216.

Waring, Marilyn. 1988. *If Women Counted: A New Feminist Economics*, San Francisco: Harper and Row.

1999. *Counting for Nothing: What Men Value and What Women are Worth*, 2nd edn., Toronto: University of Toronto Press.

Warren, Mark (ed.). 1999. *Democracy and Trust*, Cambridge: Cambridge University Press.

Washington Post. 2002a. 'What is operation TIPS?', *Washington Post* 14 July: B06.

2002b. 'Faith-based by fiat', *Washington Post* 13 December: A44.

2003. 'Faith-based battle', *Washington Post* 12 May: A18.

Weitz, Laurie. 2002. 'The Hadassah promise', *Hadassah Magazine* 83(6); available at www.hadassah.org/NEWS/magazine/Feb-02/feature1.htm.

Westheider, James E. 1997. *Fighting on Two Fronts: African-Americans and the Vietnam War*, New York: New York University Press.

Wilcox, Clyde, and Ted Jelen. 1990. 'Evangelicals and political tolerance', *American Political Quarterly* 18(1): 25–46.

Williams, Melissa. 2002. *Sharing the River: Aboriginal Representation in Canadian Political Institutions*, paper presented at the Canadian Political Science Association annual conference, Toronto, 5–9 June.

Wolfe, Alan. 1998. *One Nation After All*, New York: Viking.

Wolin, Sheldon. 1960. *Politics and Vision: Continuity and Innovation in Western Political Thought*, Boston: Little Brown.

Wong, Kwok-fu Sam. 2005. *Putting 'Men' back into Social Capital Theory*, paper presented at the conference 'Whither Social Capital? Past, Present and Future', London South Bank University, 6–7 April.

Wuthnow, Robert. 1988. *The Restructuring of American Religion: Society and Faith since World War II*, Princeton, NJ: Princeton University Press.

1998. *After Heaven: Spirituality in America Since the 1950s*, Berkeley: University of California Press.

1999. 'Mobilizing civic engagement: the changing impact of religious involvement', in Theda Skocpol and Morris P. Fiorina (eds.), *Civic Engagement in American Democracy*, Washington, DC: Brookings Institution, chap. 9.

2002a. 'Bridging the privileged and the marginalized?', in Robert Putnam (ed.), *Democracies in Flux: The Evolution of Social Capital in Contemporary Society*, Oxford: Oxford University Press, 59–102.

2002b. *Loose Connections: Joining Together in America's Fragmented Communities*, Cambridge, MA: Harvard University Press.

Yang, Fenggang. 2002. 'Religious diversity among the Chinese in America', in Pyong Gap Min and Jung Ha Kim (eds.), *Religions in Asian America: Building Faith Communities*, Walnut Creek, CA: AltaMira Press, 71–98.

Young, Cathy. 2001. 'The dark side of a war-inspired civic virtue', *Boston Globe*, 1 November, A23.

Young, Iris Marion. 1990. *Justice and Politics of Difference*, Princeton, NJ: Princeton University Press.

Young, Jonathan. 1997. *Equality of Opportunity: The Making of the Americans with Disabilities Act*, Washington, DC: National Council on Disability; available at www.ncd.gov.

Index